{NLRC}   Mb/971bb3
BF 38 F73
C. 1
FRIEDMAN, MAURICE S.
CONTEMPORARY PSYCHOLOGY :

DATE DUE			
DEC 1 0 1985	DEC 2 8 1990		
APR 1 4 1986	JAN 8 1991		
JUN 3 0 1986	DEC 2 3 1991		
FEB 2 4 1987	NOV 2 1 1992		
FEB 2 4 1987			
MAR 3 0 1987			
DEC 1 3 1987			
DEC 2 0 1987			
APR 1 4 1988			
DEC 7 1990			

JUL 2 6 1985

JUL 2 6 196

Contemporary psychology

BF
38
F73

Contemporary Psychology

Revealing and Obscuring the Human

by Maurice Friedman

Duquesne University Press
Pittsburgh

Copyright © 1984 by Duquesne University Press

All rights reserved. No part of this book may be used or repro-
duced in any manner whatsoever without written permission except in the case of brief quotations for use in critical articles and
reviews.

Published by:
Duquesne University Press
600 Forbes Ave.
Pittsburgh, PA 15282

PRINTED IN THE UNITED STATES OF AMERICA

Library of Congress Cataloging in Publication Data

Friedman, Maurice S.
Contemporary psychology.

Includes bibliographical references and index.
1. Psychology—Philosophy.   2. Personality.
3. Psychotherapy—Philosophy.   4. Psychology and literature.   5. Philosophical antropology.   I. Title.
BF38.F73 1984   150   84-1643
ISBN 0-8207-0166-1
ISBN 0-8207-0168-8 (pbk.)

*For Aleene, who has helped
reveal the human*

CONTENTS

Preface   ix

PART ONE—INTRODUCTION   1

1/   "Maurice Friedman's Philosophy of the Human
     Image: The Foundation for His Critique of
     Contemporary Psychology" *by Richard Stanton*   3

2/   Philosophical Anthropology and the Image of the
     Human   11

3/   A Dialogical View of the Person   23

PART TWO—THE "THREE FORCES" OF
CONTEMPORARY PSYCHOLOGY: A CRITIQUE   27

4/   Scientism: B. F. Skinner   29

5/   Psychologism: Sigmund Freud and Carl G. Jung   39

6/   Aiming at the Self: The Paradox of Humanist
     Psychology and the Human Potential Movement   57

PART THREE—OBSCURING AND REVEALING
THE HUMAN IMAGE IN EXISTENTIAL PSYCHOLOGY
AND FAMILY PSYCHIATRY   77

7/   Existential Psychotherapy: Rollo May   79

8/   Phenomenology and Existential Analysis: Sartre, von Weizsäcker, Boss, and Binswanger   87

9/   The Politics of Dialogue: Ronald Laing   107

10/   The Family's Role in Hiding the Human Image: Pseudomutuality (Wynne) and Parentification (Boszormenyi-Nagy)   117

PART FOUR—THE HUMAN IMAGE AS THE HIDDEN GROUND OF PSYCHOLOGY AND LITERATURE   131

11/   Psychology and Literature   133

12/   Our Age of Anxiety   136

13/   Personal Freedom and Psychological Compulsion   145

14/   Fathers and Sons: The Divided Self   157

15/   The Crisis of Motives and the Problematic of Guilt   164

16/   Sex and Love   176

17/   Shame, Guilt, and Existential Trust   192

PART FIVE—CONCLUSION   205

18/   Psychology and the Hidden Human Image   207

Index   219

Preface

Contemporary Psychology: Revealing and Obscuring the Human is the first of three books that relate to one another without being dependent upon one another. The second is *Dialogical Perspectives in Psychotherapy.* The third is *The Confirmation of Otherness: In Family, Community, and Society,* published by the Pilgrim Press, New York, in 1983. By "contemporary psychology" I do not mean a survey or overview of all the important trends in contemporary psychology. What I do mean is an examination of a number of the central positions in modern psychology, an examination designed to evaluate them from the standpoint of the image of the human that is implicit in them. I certainly do not do justice to Freud in the half chapter devoted to him, and I have included nothing of the many important theorists that directly and indirectly derive from Freud. Instead I treat Freud and Jung together in one chapter, Skinner in another, and humanistic psychologists such as Carl Rogers and Erich Fromm only in passing and subsumed under a general approach. The historical section of *Dialogical Psychotherapies,* in contrast, contains separate chapters on the object relations school of Freudians (Fairbairn, Guntrip, and Kohut), the interpersonal school (Sullivan, Fromm, and Fromm-Reichmann), plus a chapter each on Rogers, Gestalt Therapy, "existentialists of dialogue," and Jung and the Jungians; and both books have chapters on family psychiatry. In *Contemporary Psychology,* however, the range is broader, not only through the presence of Skinner, but also through the addition of a whole section on the image of the human in psychology and literature. This section includes literary interpretations of the conclusions that I have reached concerning anxiety, the divided self, motivation, guilt, shame, sex and love, and existential trust.

My task is not only one of presentation but also of evaluation— evaluation, first and foremost, from the standpoint of the extent to which a given psychology reveals or obscures the hidden human image and, second and only in certain cases, from the standpoint of my own dialogical view of the person, which I set forth briefly in Chapter 3.

I am grateful to my friend and former student Dr. Richard Stanton for writing the Introduction (Chapter 1) to this book based on his doctoral dissertation, "Dialogue in Psychotherapy: Martin Buber, Maurice Friedman and Therapists of Dialogue." I am also indebted to my friend Rollo May and to my friend and former student Professor Richard Hycner for helpful critical comments and suggestions.

Richard Hycner warned my that my chapters on B. F. Skinner and Carl G. Jung in the second part of this book were so critical that they might discourage a Skinnerian or a Jungian from reading any further. I hope that this will not be the case. The aim of my critique of the three forces of contemporary psychology is not to discount their contributions, which are enormous, but to criticize the "isms" that are interwoven in them—"scientism" in the Second Force, "psychologism" in the First, and "potentialism" in the Third. There is a difference, however, in my feeling about their contributions to our understanding of the image of the human. Both Freud and Jung, in my opinion, have made invaluable, although partial, contributions to this understanding, whereas Skinner, for all of his great scientific and practical contributions, has helped to obscure the human image further in his book *Beyond Freedom and Dignity*. Although my chapter on Jung in *To Deny Our Nothingness* is also critical, if a great deal fuller than my presentation of his thought in *Contemporary Psychology: Revealing and Obscuring the Human*, the reader will find a sympathetic appreciation of Jung in my Preface to the third edition of my book *To Deny Our Nothingness: Contemporary Images of Man* (University of Chicago Press, Phoenix Books, 1978) and in the chapter entitled "Jungian: Carl Jung and Hans Trüb" in *Dialogical Perspectives in Pschotherapy* (1984 or 1985).

I wish to thank the readers of the Duquesne University Press for taking their time to put this book into the context of my total work and for their helpful and constructive suggestions, many of which I have followed.

MAURICE FRIEDMAN
Solana Beach, California
July 1983

PART ONE

Introduction

Chapter 1

Maurice Friedman's Philosophy of the Human Image

The Foundation for His Critique of Contemporary Psychology

by Richard Stanton

T HE paradoxical way in which persons both are unique *and* fully participate in each other's lives is an aspect of human existence that is central to psychology. Nowhere is this better exemplified than in the many works of Maurice Friedman. From his dialogic vantage, shared with Martin Buber, Friedman has elucidated the place of the human image in intrapersonal, interpersonal, and community events since the publication of his first major work in 1955. In a chapter of this book, Friedman points out that "we do not actually exist divided into 'inner' and 'outer' except for certain useful purposes. In reality we are in every moment in streaming interaction with everybody and everything." Yet psychology, in efforts to make sense out of multifarious experience, too often raises up one or another of its insights from useful purpose to distortion; from the level of a valid and specific contribution to knowledge to the level of a general theory which in its overreaching misguides us. Friedman's streaming interaction is meant to be understood as dialogical in nature: "We address others not by conscious mind or will but by what we are," he writes in a later essay. "We address them with more than we know, and they respond—if they really respond—with more than they know. Address and response can never be identified merely with conscious intent or even with 'intentionality'."

Friedman maintains that psychologists have as substrata to their views—whether conscious and articulated or not—beliefs, images of justice, social organization, epistemology, and related concerns. I believe that this empahasis has been one of Friedman's major contributions over the years, reminding us of this fact of professional and personal life (which is all too concealed by the psychologist's mantle). Importantly, this message is most often delivered by Friedman in a common language; that is, his critiques do not reach the field as if from "outside," as is often the case when one who is not identified as a psychologist speaks or writes of such matters. Indeed, the "inside" criticisms, from psychologists who are in fact specialized practitioners, more frequently sound as if they come from somewhere "outside" because of their faithfulness to the jargon of their specialty and the narrowness of their scopes. Hence, his broad contextural approach and his style of writing commend themselves, in my opinion, to both the psychologist and the interested reader of diverse background.

It was observed by Rollo May in 1961 that " 'the critical battles between approaches to psychology and psychoanalysis in our culture in the next decades, as always, will be on the battleground of the image of man. That is to say, the conception of man which underlies the empirical research.' "

In Chapter 2, Friedman communicates his own underlying philosophical anthropology. In Part Two Friedman critiques the "three forces" of contemporary psychology (pragmatic empiricism, psychoanalysis, and human potentialism), joining the battle over the human image by arguing compellingly with all three vantages. In these pieces, Friedman has used as raw materials a number of sections from several of his earlier books. Three books form a prior trilogy in their own right: *Problematic Rebel* (1963 and 1970), *To Deny Our Nothingness* (1967), and *The Hidden Human Image* (1974). Each in turn, to an increasing extent, addressed psychology and the human image. Some materials from that triad have been subsumed under the organic whole of the present undertaking. The three following statements are taken from the middle book, *To Deny Our Nothingness*. They are included here, not only because they illustrate best for me what Friedman *means* by the human image, but also because they contain the seeds of his affirmations of and arguments with psychology:

Man comes to awareness of himself as a self not just through his differences from others but in dialogue with other selves—in their response to him and in the way they call him into being. Because man lives as a separate self, yet in relation to other persons and to society, present, past, and to come, he needs an image of man to aid him in finding a meaningful way of life, in choosing between conflicting sets of values, in realizing his own unique potentialities. Our human existence itself is at once tradition and unexplored future, acceptance and rebellion. The image of man is an embodiment of an attitude and a response. Whether it is an image shared by only one man or by a society as a whole, the individual stands in a unique personal relation to it. His image of man is not some objective, universal Saint Francis, but the Saint Francis who emerges from his own meeting with this historical and legendary figure.

The image of man does not mean some fully formed, conscious model of what one should become. . . . For each one of us, it is made up of many images and half-formed images, and it is itself constantly changing and evolving. It proceeds and develops through every type of personal encounter we have: a friend stands by us in a crisis; a poet speaks to us through his poems; a great historical figure affects us through the impact he had on those among whom he lived; the characters of novels and plays seize our imagination and enter into our lives through a dialogue we carry on with them in the wordless depths of our being.[1]

World views are impossible to maintain, if one truly inhabits the modern world. The assurance formerly given by "having" a smooth, continuous knowledge of the world is not possible for us as it may have been for our ancestors. Participatory knowledge (whether in the philosophies of physical and life sciences or in the "human science" which psychology might/ought to be according to Amedeo Giorgi) is widely seen as having greater proximity to reality than does objective knowledge. In each of his books, Friedman has employed his own typologies (starting with the Modern Promethean, the Modern Exile, and the Modern Job of *Problematic Rebel*) by way of analyzing contemporary images and concepts. Concepts are called into question for their relative lack of fluidity and are contrasted with the preferable *image of the human.*

1. Maurice Friedman, *To Deny Our Nothingness: Contemporary Images of Man,* 3rd rev. ed. with new Preface and Appendix (Chicago: University of Chicago Press Phoenix Books [paperback], 1978), pp. 18 f.

Friedman is grounded not in the Husserl line of phenomenology, but in the Dilthey line; and Friedman has stretched this line to a greater appreciation of the unique—a unique which transcends all typologies. Friedman maintains that one has to have a relationship to a thing first—that is, in its uniqueness—before one can deal with it typologically. Hence, his attitude toward the dialectic in psychotherapy, the relationship of practice and theory, *begins* with the unique. For Friedman, one begins with the unique, and then the theory may help you, in the "musical, artistic" way of which Buber speaks. Friedman sees that one must know how and when one's theory or school or other cases one has dealt with apply in this particular case. The therapist must get a relationship to the uniqueness of *this* person in *this* situation at *this* time, including his or her self as part of the uniqueness. Then one may have the sense of how to apply it.

The themes of *Problematic Rebel* are ultimately those of psychology: our exile from the worlds of religious certainty with the passing of our ability to dwell in an "unchanging" universe is the felt discontinuity at the origin of the modern search for meaning. Brought into dialogue with that underlying note are issues of freedom, compulsion, and guilt (real and neurotic), our inner divisions, and the unconscious. We are both free and not free at once, like Dostoievsky's Underground Man. Friedman finds that "the self experiences the vertigo of being a free and directing consciousness, on the one hand, and an 'eddy in the social current'— to use George Herbert Mead's phrase—on the other." These concerns are largely dealt with, in Buber's words about *Problematic Rebel,* in "the narrative literature of two generations—that of Melville and Dostoievsky and that of Kafka and Camus."

If the themes of *Problematic Rebel* are the often more implicit than explicit grounds of contemporary psychology, with *To Deny Our Nothingness* Friedman raises the "three forces" fully into view for critique and partial affirmation. There he examines as the Modern Gostic, Psychological Man, and the Modern Pragmatist the interactions of psychology with the human image. Part Two of this book is integrally rooted in those essays which gave a psychological core to the considerations of *To Deny Our Nothingness.*

To Deny Our Nothingness is employed both in the United States and in Europe as a text in courses offered under the auspices of psychology, literature, philosophy, and religion departments to my certain knowledge; and I would imagine that somewhere it is in use in anthropology courses as well. Leslie Farber[2] wrote of the book (before its success):

> Despite their historical kinship, philosophy and psychoanalysis have been no more than perfunctory neighbors, their occasional efforts at talks together being too guarded and self-serving to be illuminating. But the renowned philosopher, Maurice Friedman, is the rare exception. Insisting that abstractions from either discipline be firmly grounded in lived experience, he has, with no sacrifice in scholarship, developed in *To Deny Our Nothingness* a way of understanding the vicissitudes of modern character that will offer a whole other dimension to psychology, psychoanalysis and psychiatry. I regard this work as one of the most significant contributions to my field in many years.

To Deny Our Nothingness is an exceptional corrective or balancing piece, which ought to be read in seminar by any would-be clinician or researcher or teaching psychologist before he or she is unleashed upon the world. To borrow a term from community psychology, a reading of *To Deny Our Nothingness* could well serve to remind "change agents" of the cultural, intellectual, and existential diversity surrounding whatever "school" or modality of treatment or approach they may have attached themselves to. I think of it as a route back from the narrowness which is, perhaps necessarily, inflicted upon graduate students during the course of their formal educations. Of course, the book would serve established professionals in a similar fashion, providing they will hesitate long enough in their ride on the professional merry-go-round to read it.

There is a theme in Friedman's works which sounds repeatedly and which concerns the double-edged nature of the present era's major conceptual artifact: the psyche. This issue is a fundamental one; it is also, I believe, the most difficult part of Friedman's work for psychotherapists especially to take in—to truly understand. Yet, on its face, it is quite simple: Friedman rightly asserts that our culture's most central organizing principle, the

2. Leslie Farber, trained by Harry Stack Sullivan, was for some time the chair of the faculty of the Washington School of Psychiatry, was for years president of the Association of Existential Psychology and Psychiatry, and was the author of two important books on the meeting between psychiatry and philosophy.

"psyche," is immensely overused and frequently absolutized. In a way, much of Friedman's writing is that of a friendly critic of psychology; one who points out the abuse of an immensely powerful resource, a resource which ought not to be abandoned but whose use must be reformed. Friedman directly addresses the issue of the "limits of the psyche as *the* touchstone of reality" in two places; *Touchstones of Reality* and in an essay which more than a decade ago appeared as the core of an issue on *Quaker Religious Thought*. I feel that much of what Friedman notes as the obscuring of the human image takes place because of just such overreaching by psychology. The following quotation is taken from his *Quaker Religious Thought* essay and rather concisely lays out the issue:

> "Psyche" here is used in the most general sense possible—mind and soul, conscious and unconscious, thought, feeling, intuition, and sensation. Today the psychological in the sense of objective analysis and the psychic in the sense of subjective experience are confusedly intermingled. Yet this confused intermingling has taken shape in the popular mind not only as a single phenomenon but at *the* modern touchstone of reality in the way theology was for the Middle Ages, physics for the Newtonian age and the age of Enlightenment, and evolution for the mid-nineteenth to mid-twentieth centuries. Such "touchstones of reality" become both obstacle to and substitute for any immediacy or apprehension or reapprehension of the reality known in mutual contact. The limits of the psyche as touchstone of reality is a problem for this very reason—since for those who take the psyche or the psychological on faith as ultimate reality, the question of touchstones of reality in the more immediate and concrete sense in which they derive from concrete encounters or events can hardly arise.[3]

Distortions arise out of the psychologizing of reality: perhaps the most noteworthy one emerges when we start to think of experience as something happening inside of ourselves rather than as

3. Maurice Friedman, "Religion and Psychology: The Limits of the Psyche as Touchstone of Reality" with Comments by Elined P. Kotschnig, Joseph Havens, J. Calvin Keene, and Christine Downing and Replies by Maurice Friedman, *Quaker Religious Thought*, Vol. XII, No. 1 (Winter 1970), pp. 2–48.

See also Maurice Friedman, *Touchstones of Reality: Existential Trust and the Community of Peace* (New York: Dutton, 1972; Dutton Books [paperback], 1974), Chapter 13—"Psychology and Religion: The Limits of the Psyche as Touchstone of Reality," pp. 247—258.

something happening between us and the world. Naturally, things do happen within us, but the psyche is not "existence itself." Contrary to some teachings, neither consciousness nor the unconscious, nor some combination of these is the sum totality of reality. An adequately critical approach to a psychology ought to include the question in Friedman's work of "When and where does it go too far?" In the text of *Contemporary Psychology: Revealing and Obscuring the Human,* the reader will encounter this issue, sometimes in sharp focus and sometimes as an undertone to an argument. It is a corrective consideration which Friedman brings to bear upon both the older analytical approaches and the current movements. The overinflated concept of the psyche (whether manifest as explanatory tool or as lifeline) knows no single school as its home.

I earlier quoted Rollo May to the effect that "the critical battles between approaches to psychology and psychoanalysis in our culture in the next decades, as always, will be on the battleground of the image of man," or "human image." Maurice Friedman sees the human image as being no one thing, no set of constructs or conception, but as an image which unfolds in response to each new situation and its demands, as a dialogic human image. Such an idea is antagonistic to finalized conception, against the notion (as you will see in the following chapter) of a "fixed" human nature, somehow outside of history. It acknowledges simultaneously the significance of the unique and of the historical aspects of psychological reality in each situation, thus rejecting both absolute determination and total freedom. This is indeed a middle way. As such, it is an enormously important reminder to psychological thought.

Martin Buber wrote, in 1929, that "if there is nothing else that can so hide the face of our fellow man as morality can, religion can hide from us as nothing else can the face of God." He was referring in that essay to the misplaced reliance on "principle" and dogma as they are used as substitutes for dialogue in the "unforseeable moment." In our day it is more often psychology with which we obscure the faces of our fellow men, women, and God. We do not enable meeting through our abstract knowledge of the human psyche; but, curiously, we seem to distract ourselves, untracking a potential dialogue before the meeting can take place.

We are frequently seduced by our belief in the power and efficacy of our would-be tools.

I am honored and deeply pleased to be able to introduce this book to you. Maurice Friedman has organized in these pages a coherent vision which knowledgeably cuts across the many (and often moot) boundaries of psychology. Such apperception deserves your careful attention.

To me it is abundantly clear that people need restoration of dialogue at home, at work, and in their neighborhoods. This certainty has grown both through my association in the last dozen years with Maurice Friedman and his works and through my own work as a psychotherapist and occasional teacher. Some persons may need extended interpersonal help, therapy of a time-honored structure. Others, because of their own family history, need someone who will tease out that history on an extended basis and will seek to involve the whole family in the healing process. Still others require community interventions on a social level. But, wherever psychology attempts to meet human need, the human image may be called into question.

Chapter 2

Philosophical Anthropology and the Image of the Human

Contemporary Philosophy and Psychology: "Human Nature" Reconsidered

I F the divergent schools of contemporary philosophy are united in little else, they do at least join in rejecting the notion that Man has some fixed, identifiable, universal essence. We look to contemporary philosophy, therefore, not so much for new definitions of human nature as for a new critical awareness of the issues that surround this term. This critical awareness is of particular significance for psychology and psychoanalytic theory, since both have often taken over quite uncritically many of the formulations of classical philosophy.

One of the classic problems of "human nature" is that of "free will" versus "determinism." Transposed into the realm of psychology, it becomes the much more fruitful problem of personal freedom and psychological compulsion. The reality of unconscious compulsion makes it impossible to assert the existence of full, conscious freedom. But it is equally impossible to reduce Man to a purely deterministic system. Human existence—in the well person as in the ill—is a complex intermixture of personal freedom and psychological compulsion, a paradoxical phenomenon that can be understood only from within. As I have written in *Problematic Rebel:*

> The problem of the relation of personal freedom to psychological compulsion cannot be solved by the attempt to reduce man to a bundle of instinctual drives, unconscious complexes, the need for

security or any other single factor. . .Motivation is inextricably
bound up with the wholeness of the person, with his direction of
movement, with his struggles to authenticate himself. . .No general theory of psychogenesis and no general knowledge of a person
will tell us in advance what will be his actual mixture of spontaneity and compulsion in any particular situation.[1]

Another problem of human nature that psychoanalytic theory
has inherited from classical philosophy is that of mind-body dualism. At first glance, most psychoanalysis would seem to be a denial of this dualism. In fact, however, the problem has only been
transposed into the complex interrelationship between biological
instinct and consciousness or, on a subtler plane, between the
pleasure principle and the reality principle. Even the division between the conscious and the unconscious which is so central to
psychoanalysis is in a certain sense a variant of the Cartesian
mind-body dualism. Freud's "censor," Sartre points out, is in
"bad faith" with itself; for it must know what it censors and then
pretend not to know it. Thus, Freud's psychoanalysis introduces
into subjectivity the deepest structure of intersubjectivity. It
leaves a dualism between the unconscious and consciousness, a
dualism which is bridged only by an autonomous consciousness
which knows the drive to be repressed precisely *in order not to be*
conscious of it.

A still more significant criticism of the psychoanalytic theory of
the unconscious was hinted at in the Martin Buber's seminars on
the unconscious given in 1957 for the Washington (D.C.) School
of Psychiatry. According to Buber, Freud and the whole psychoanalytic world have tended to assume that the unconscious is a
sort of psychic deep freeze which contains ideas capable of being
repressed and capable of being brought to consciousness through
transference to the therapist or through encounter with the
"shadow." This assumption overlooks the fact that if the unconscious is really conscious, we may know its effects but can never
know it or its contents except as they are shaped and elaborated
by the conscious. Buber suggests that the unconscious is the
ground of personal wholeness before its elaboration into the phys-

1. Maurice Friedman, *Problematic Rebel: Melville, Dostoievsky, Kafka, Camus,* 2nd
radically rev. and enl. ed. (Chicago: University of Chicago Press [hardback],
Phoenix Books [paperback], 1970), pp. 470, 472.

ical and the psychic. Freud, he holds, and after him Jung, have made the simple logical error of assuming that the unconscious is psychic since they wished to deny that it is physical. They did not, Buber holds, see this third alternative and with it the possibility of bursting the bounds of psychologism by recognizing that the division of inner and outer that applies to the psyche and the physical need not apply to the unconscious. Here, in contrast, there might be direct meeting and direct communication (as in a handshake) between one unconscious and another.[2]

Philosophical Anthropology

The basis for Buber's approach to the unconscious is his philosophical anthropology, according to which what gives Man a world and an existence as a self over against other selves is the ability, unique to Man, of executing two primary ontological movements—that of distancing and that of entering into relation. If, as Buber holds, only these constitute Man as Man, then the attempt of some psychological and psychoanalytical theories to deal with Man in fundamentally biological terms, as if he were continuous with all other animals except for the modifications forced by civilization, is fundamentally in error. In error, too, is the individualism of the isolated consciousness which both Freud and Jung inherited from Descartes. Starting with "I think, therefore I am," Descartes was left with the insoluble problem of the knowledge of other minds. Edmund Husserl's phenomenology, Heidegger's ontology, and Sartre's existentialism have all transposed this problem by seeing the self as only existing in its transcendence toward a field of consciousness, or a world. The classic subject-object relation of knower and known is replaced here by the self and its world.

Immanuel Kant was the first philosopher explicitly to stake out philosophical anthropology as a branch of philosophy. Not only is the question, "What is man?" a part of the question, "What can I know?" but it is a very special part of this question, with prob-

2. Martin Buber, *A Believing Humanism: Gleanings*, trans. with an Introduction and Explanatory Comments by Maurice Friedman (New York: Simon & Schuster Paperbacks, 1969); "The Unconscious," notes taken by Maurice Friedman, pp. 153–173.

lems unique to itself. At the same time, as the view of Man the knower changed, the view of what Man is inevitably changed with it. Kant's great successor, Friedrich Hegel, removed Kant's dualism of the noumenal and the phenomenal into the concrete universal of the world-historical spirit. Among some of the radical neo-Hegelians, the continued cultivation of the philosophical soil they inherited was coupled with a rebellion against the idealist subject in favor of the whole human person (Kierkegaard and Nietzsche), against the historical spirit in favor of the concrete realities of social, economic, and political life (Feuerbach, Marx, and Nietzsche), against the isolated thinker in favor of the recognition of the origin of all thought and all philosophy in the dialogue of I and Thou (Feuerbach), or against metaphysics in favor of philosophical anthropology (Feuerbach and Nietzsche).[3]

An important advance in philosophical anthropology was the development of "phenomenology" by the German philosophers Wilhelm Dilthey and Edmund Husserl. Dilthey based his thought on the radical difference between the way of knowing proper to the "*Geisteswissenschaften*" (the human studies, such as philosophy, the social sciences, and psychology) and that proper to "*Naturwissenschaften*" (the natural sciences). In the former, the knowers cannot be merely detached scientific observers but must also participate themselves; for it is through their participation that they discover both the typical and the unique in the aspects of human life that they are studying. At the same time they must suspend the foregone conclusions and the search for causality that mark the natural scientist in favor of an open attempt to discover what offers itself. Only through this open understanding (*das Verstehen*) can one value the unique that reveals itself in every human phenomenon.

Husserl elaborated phenomenology into a full-fledged systematic philosophy. He went decisively beyond Descartes' *cogito* in his recognition that one cannot divorce the "I think" from what is thought, consciousness from intentionality. By the method of "parenthesizing," or phenomenological reduction, Husserl replaced the detached subject and independent object of older philosophy by a field of knowing in which the phenomena are accepted as

3. Cf. Karl Löwith, *From Hegal to Nietzsche: The Revolution in Nineteenth Century Thought*, trans. David E. Greene (New York: Holt, Rinehart & Winston, 1964).

pure phenomena without questioning their independent existence. From this he also obtained a "transcendental ego" which,
as the subject of knowing, transcended all contents of knowing,
including the psychophysical me. The exploration of the field of
transcendental experience thus becomes equivalent to the phenomenological knowledge of the world.

Husserl's existential successors either emphasized the direct experiential quality of his thought as opposed to the idealist, as did
Maurice Merleau-Ponty, or broke with the transcendental ego altogether while retaining the method of phenomenology, as did
Jean-Paul Sartre, or transformed phenomenology from a method
of knowledge into a "fundamental ontology," as did Martin
Heidegger. Both Sartre and Heidegger accept Husserl's motto
"To the things themselves" as an obstacle to scientism's attempt
to posit a substratum of independent but nonperceivable "matter" behind the phenomena. Only an existential analysis of the
existent will yield any knowledge of being. For Heidegger this
analysis is posited on his special use of *Dasein*—the person's "being there" in the world, thrown into a situation apart from which
neither subject nor consciousness has any meaning. Heidegger
and Sartre see the self as only existing in its transcendence toward
a field of consciousness or a world. To exist is to be there, in the
situation, and the situation includes, of course, the world of intersubjectivity in which we have to do with other persons. Yet
Heidegger and Sartre still basically see the ontological as essentially discovered in the self, with the relations to others as an "ontic" dimension of the existence of the self.

Martin Buber, who stems from Feuerbach and Dilthey rather
than from Husserl, sees the ontological as found in the *meeting* between person and person and between person and world, with the
realization of the self the indispensable accompaniment and corollary of the dialogue. Buber has sharpened the social theory of the
self to a distinction between direct, mutual interpersonal
relations—"I-Thou" or "the interhuman"—and indirect, nonmutual interpersonal relations—"I-It." The American social
psychologist and philosopher George Herbert Mead, the American psychiatrist Harry Stack Sullivan, and Erich Fromm all share
with Buber what Paul Pfuetze calls "the social self," but they
have not made the distinction Buber has made between direct and

indirect, mutual and nonmutual interpersonal relations. Nor is this distinction adequately grasped by Heidegger's *Mitsein* or Sartre's "world of intersubjectivity." Heidegger's "being-with" undoubtedly includes the I–Thou relationship in principle, but it gives very little attention to anything which could be recognized as such, and the ultimate relationship for him is explicitly with oneself. Sartre's intersubjectivity excludes free mutuality in principle in favor of a tormented interaction of subjectivity and objectivity in which one recognizes the other's freedom either as a threat and a limitation to one's own or as something to be possessed and dominated for a time through sexual love.

Buber's view of Man leads him to assert that the chasm between spirit and instincts is not an inherent structure of human nature, as Freud holds, but is a product of the sickness of Modern Man—the destruction of organic confidence and of organic community and the divorce between person and person.[4] It has also led Buber, and myself following him, to a more dialogical understanding of the task of the philosophical anthropologist than even Feuerbach and Dilthey. Philosophical anthropology goes beyond cultural anthropology in that it asks the question not just about human beings but about the human: about our wholeness and uniqueness, about what makes us human. As such, it necessarily transcends, even while making full use of, those sciences which deliberately deal with the human being only as a part and not as a whole—whether it be Economic Man, Political Man, Sociological Man, Psychological Man, or Biological Man. It can only touch on the problem of the human, however, insofar as it recognizes that the philosophical anthropologist himself or herself is a human being and as such is *as subject* and not just as object a part of what he or she seeks to know. One must share in and not merely observe the problematic of Modern Man. One must reject all attempts to reduce this problematic to any single motive or complex of motives or to comprehend the human simply on the analogy of biology or the behavior of animals. Only if as philosophical anthropologist one is a problem to oneself can one understand the human as a problem to itself.

4. Martin Buber, *Between Man and Man*, trans. Ronald Gregor Smith, with an Introduction by Maurice Friedman (New York: MacMillan Paperbacks, 1965), pp. 196 f.

Only if one knows from within one's own situation and in dialogue with the others with whom one has to do can one begin to approach that wholeness and uniqueness of the human which slips through the net of every concept of Man as object. To understand the human one must be a participant who only afterward against the distance from one's subject matter that will enable one to formulate the insights one has attained. Otherwise, one inevitably sees Man as a sum of parts some of which are labeled "objective" and hence oriented around the thing known, and some "subjective" and hence oriented around the knower.

Philosophical anthropology today begins on the far side of earlier notions of understanding the human in terms of a universal and timeless "human nature." It looks away from essences of the human in order to grasp human beings in their particularity and their complexity, their dynamic interrelatedness with others, and the interplay within them of possibility, freedom, and personal direction. Existentialism similarly replaces the concept of "human nature" by the concept of the "human condition." Man is without a predetermined essence because Man is free, but his freedom is a finite one, as Tillich points out. It must operate within the general human condition—the need to work one's existence as a self in relation to other selves and to the nonhuman world, the awareness of solitude, of possibility, and of death. These approaches represent radical changes in our view of Man and have far-reaching implications that have only begun to be spelled out. Yet the critical task of modern philosophy in relation to the concept of human nature cannot stop here.

The Image of the Human

If we wish to make a decisive break with the universal and essential "human nature" of earlier philosophy and attain a picture of the human in its uniqueness and wholeness, we must move from *concepts* about the human, no matter how profound, to the *image* of the human. It is this I have tried to do in my trilogy of books on the human image: *Problematic Rebel, To Deny Our Nothingness,* and *The Hidden Human Image.* The human image, as I use the term, is not only an image of what we are but also an image of authentic personal and social existence that helps us discover, in each age anew, what we may and can become, an image that helps us rediscover our humanity. "Image" in this context means not a static picture but a meaningful, personal direction, a response from within to what one meets in each new situation, standing one's ground and meeting the world with the attitude that is rooted in this ground. The human image embodies a way of responding. Because it is faithful response and not objective content that is central to the human image, each individual stands in a unique personal relation to his or her image of the human, even when it happens to be shared by a society as a whole. One becomes oneself in dialogue with other selves and in response to one's image, one's images of the human. Yet the more genuine the dialogue, the more unique the relationship and the more truly is the one who is becoming, becoming oneself. The fruit of such response is not that bolstering of the ego that comes from comparing oneself favorably with another or modeling oneself on an ideal, but the confirmation of one's unique personal existence, of the ground on which one stands.

The human image does not mean some fully formed, conscious model of what one should become—certainly not anything simply imposed on us by the culture or any mere conformity with society through identification with its goals. The paradox of the human image is that it is at once unique and universal, but universal only through the unique. For each one of us, the human image is made up of many images and half-formed images, and it is itself constantly changing and evolving. In contrast to any static ideal whatsoever, it always has to do only with the unique response to the concrete moment, a response which cannot be foreseen and cannot be repeated, objectified, or imitated.

The human image is our becoming in the truest sense of the word, that is, our becoming as a person and as a human being. In this becoming, what we call the "is" is not a static given. It is a dynamic, constantly changing material that is continually being shaped and given form not merely by inner and outer conditioning but by the directions that one takes as a person. Similarly, what we call the "ought" is not some abstract ideal but a constantly changing, flowing direction of movement that is at one and the same time a response to the present, a choice between possibilities in a given situation, and a line of advance into the future.

In *The Hidden Human Image* I pointed to the human image as the hidden ground underlying many disciplines that are usually seen as quite separate—philosophy, literature, religious studies, psychology, social sciences, intellectual and cultural history. I also pointed to the fact that the human image stands in continual need of being revealed—in each new situation—but, like a face or a myth, can never be fully revealed. It is like a river of eternity running beneath the depths of time. In addition, I pointed to the truly terrible way in which the human image has been obscured and all but eclipsed in our day by the Holocaust, atomic bombings, mass starvation, and a thousand gross and subtle ways in which we deny our common humanity and demonstrate "man's inhumanity to man." I pointed, too, to the tragic irony that much that in our day seeks to bring the human image out of its hiddenness only deepens its eclipse. All three of these meanings of the "hidden human image" will be our concern in this present book, but so, too, will be the paradox of our further obscuring the human image in our very attempts to reveal it!

Psychotherapy and the Human Image

An important aspect of my three books on the image of the human—*Problematic Rebel, To Deny Our Nothingness,* and *The Hidden Human Image*—has been exploring the meeting between the image of the human and psychotherapy. There is perhaps no field of more interest for the hidden human image than psychotherapy. On the one hand, "depth psychology," or "depth analysis," undertakes to reveal, to bring to the light of day, much that is hidden, including in the case of some persons their hidden humanity. On the other hand, psychotherapy in its various schools of theory and practice has contributed its share to the eclipse of Man, to the further hiding of the human image. This is in part because of the mechanistic approach that was taken toward science and even toward the human. Psychiatry in the nineteenth century was a specific matter of curing symptoms. It had little to do with the wholeness of the human. Psychoanalysis represented an important step in the direction of a concern for the whole person, but only a step. It arose under the aegis of "Science" and even, as we shall see, of scientism. In many branches of psychotherapy today, however, the movement is away from seeing it as an exact science toward seeing it as a humanistic task and a humanistic discipline.

Contemporary Man's image of himself and of authentic human existence meets psychotherapy at the precise point at which this image enters into the process of his becoming. There is a growing recognition today of the importance of philosophy and the human studies for the full understanding of the methods and goals of psychotherapy. When the Washington School of Psychiatry brought Martin Buber from Jerusalem in 1957 to give the fourth William Alanson White Memorial Lectures, the title of the series was "What Can Philosophical Anthropology Contribute to Psychiatry?" In his introduction to these lectures, Leslie H. Farber, the chair of the faculty of the Washington (D.C.) School of Psychiatry, pointed out that none of the sciences has asked the question about Man in his *wholeness* that is the concern of philosophical anthropology.

> The medical and biological sciences were asking, "What is man in his relation to nature—to natural history, the evolution of organisms, and the physical forces regulating his body?...And it was upon this natural basis that all the other sciences of man— anthropology, sociology, political science, and finally the new Freudian science of psychoanalysis—asked their question- ....None of the sciences were asking the *whole* question, What is man? Nor were they asking the unique question, Who am I, in my uniquely human existence?...These are not smaller or more personal questions; they are larger and more comprehensive than the ones which science has been asking. They include...man's personal being—my personal experience and knowledge of myself— as well as my philosophical and scientific knowledge of what "man is."[5]

Each school of psychotherapy has, with various degrees of clarity, its own image of the human. That image stands in fruitful dialectic with the therapeutic practice of the members of the school,

5. Leslie H. Farber, "Introduction" to Martin Buber, "The William Alanson White Memorial Lectures, Fourth Series," *Psychiatry,* Vol. XX, No. 2 (May 1957), pp. 95 f. Buber's lectures are included in Martin Buber, *The Knowledge of Man: A Philosophy of the Interhuman,* ed. with an Introductory Essay (Chapter 1) by Maurice Friedman (New York: Harper Torchbooks, 1966).

but it is not, for all that, a scientific product of that school. On the contrary, the far-reaching differences between the many schools of psychotherapy derive in part from the fact that implied in the positive goals they enunciate are different images of the human. Such central therapeutic terms as "health," "integration," "maturity," "creativity," and "self-realization" imply not only an image of the human but also usually essentially different ones for different schools and even different members of the same school. "The critical battles between approaches to psychology and psychoanalysis in our culture in the next decades, as always," writes Rollo May, "will be on the battleground of the image of man."[6]

Human nature is often taken by schools of psychotherapy to be itself the norm. The human being should live according to her "nature," according to her "real self," and the like. However, it is also a part of human nature to become ill. The very meaning of "health," therefore, implies some sense of what is authentic direction for the human being, for this particular person—in short, an image of the human. As Helen Merrell Lynd points out, the "real" or "spontaneous" self is not a given that need only be freed from its social encrustations. It is the product of a lifelong dialogue with our image of the human.

> Horney, Fromm, and even Sullivan at times, seem to assume that there is an already existent real or true or spontaneous self which can be evoked into active existence almost at will. There is a tacit assumption that somehow we know the dictates of the real self, and that we should live in terms of these rather than of a romanticized self-image or of the pseudo-self of others' expectations. But-
> ... such *a real self is something to be discovered and created, not a given, but a lifelong endeavor.*[7]

Especially helpful in Helen Merrell Lynd's *On Shame and the Search for Identity* are her clear insights into the implications of various personality theories for the image of the human which a particular psychology or psychoanalytic theory assumes, and her

6. Rollo May, "Some Comments on Existential Psychotherapy," an essay written for *The Worlds of Existentialism: A Critical Reader,* ed. with Introductions and a Conclusion by Maurice Friedman (Chicago: University of Chicago Press Phoenix Books, 1973), p. 447.

7. Helen Merrel Lynd, *On Shame and the Search for Identity* (New York: Harcourt Brace, Harbrace Books [paperback], 1969), p. 203; Italics added.

recognition that such images are matters of basic assumption even more than of scientific evidence and methodology.

> It does make a difference whether the individual is considered as eager, curious, and trusting until specific experience in a given society and historical period lead him to be anxious, cautious, and aggressive, or whether he is regarded as born with hostility, aggression, and fear which specific experiences may modify only to a limited degree in the direction of trust, sympathy, and interest.[8]

The possibility of mutual relations "between persons as an enlargement, not a contradiction, of individual freedom" is incompatible with personality theories "that see men primarily as need-satisfying objects or in terms of their particular status or role relations to oneself" quite as much as with those theories centered in "release of tension, return to quiescence, and self-preservation." "Much depends," she writes, "upon whether one believes that isolation and alienation are inevitable in man's fate or that openness of communication between persons, mutual discovery, and love are actual possibilities."

It is from the standpoint of its role in revealing and obscuring the hidden human image that we shall seek to evaluate contemporary psychology in the chapters that follow. Our understanding of this standpoint may be facilitated if we first look briefly at that dialogical view of the person that I have derived from my own forty-year dialogue with the thought of Martin Buber.

8. Lynd, *On Shame,* p. 142.

Chapter 3

A Dialogical View of the Person

" ALL real living is meeting." In the dialogical view we become persons in what Martin Buber calls the "I-Thou" relationship—the direct, reciprocal, present relation between the person and what comes to meet him or her as opposed to the indirect, nonmutual relation of "I-It." I-Thou is a dialogue in which the other is accepted in his or her unique otherness and not reduced to a content of my experience. I-It is a monologue, the subject-object relation of knowing and using that does not allow the other to exist as a whole and unique person but abstracts, reduces, and categorizes. In I-It, only a part of one's being—rational, emotional, intuitive, sensory—enters into the relation; in I-Thou, the whole being enters in.

In contrast to the free person stands the individual who is characterized by arbitrary self-will, or willfulness, who continually intervenes in order to use the outside world for his or her purposes. This does not mean that the free person acts only from within him or herself. On the contrary, it is only he or she who sees what is new and unique in each situation, whereas the unfree person sees only its resemblance to other things. But what comes to the free person from without is only the precondition for his or her acton; it does not determine its nature. The unfree person makes will to power a value in itself divorced from the will to enter into dialogue, with the inevitable result that he or she tends to use others as means to his or her ends. This is true even of the doctor and the psychotherapist who give others technical aid without entering into relationship with them. Help without mutuality is presumptuousness, writes Buber; it is an attempt to practice magic. "As soon as the helper is touched by the desire, in however subtle a form, to dominate or enjoy his patient, or to treat the latter's wish to be dominated or enjoyed by him as other than a wrong condition needing to be cured, the danger of falsification arises, beside which all quackery appears peripheral."

For the therapists the distinction between arbitrary and true will rests on a quite real and concrete experiencing of the client's side of the relationship. Only if they discover the "otherness" of clients will therapists discover their own real limits and what is needed to help the persons with whom they are working. They must see the position of the other in his or her concrete actuality yet not lose sight of their own. Only this will remove the danger that their will to heal will degenerate into arbitrariness.

Arbitrariness is a form of decisionlessness, of failure to make a decision with one's whole person. Decisionlessness makes a person divided and unfree, conditioned and acted upon. It is failure to direct one's inner power. Decision, in contrast, means transforming one's passion so that it enters with its whole power into the single deed. It is not a psychological event that takes place within the person but the turning of the whole being through which one enters once again into dialogue. Such decision means the transformation of the urges, of the "alien thoughts," of fantasy. We must not reject the abundance of this fantasy but transform it in our imaginative faculty and turn it into actuality. "We must convert the element that seeks to take possession of us into the substance of real life." The contradictions which distress us exist only that we may discover their intrinsic significance. There can be no wholeness "where down-trodden appetites lurk in the corners" or where the soul's highest forces watch the action, "pressed back and powerless, but shining in the protest of the spirit."

True decision can be made only with the whole being, and it is decision in turn that brings the person to wholeness. Yet this wholeness is never a goal in itself but only the indispensable base for going out to meet the Thou. Decision is made *with* the whole being, but it takes place *in* dialogue. The person who decides con-

tinually leaves the world of It for the world of dialogue in which I
and Thou freely confront each other in mutual effect, uncon-
nected with causality. It is in dialogue, therefore, that true decision takes place. Decision within dialogue is a corollary of
personal unification; for it means giving direction to one's passion.

This approach to will and decision is like psychoanalytic "sublimation" in that it makes creative use of basic energies rather
than suppressing them. But it differs from sublimation, as it is
conceived by Freud, in that this channeling of the urges takes
place as a by-product of the I–Thou relationship rather than as an
essentially individual event in which individuals use their relationship with other beings for their own self-realization. Freud's
sublimation takes place *within* the person, Buber's direction *between* person and person. In therapy itself, to Buber, it is will and
decision within dialogue that is decisive. Therapy should not pro-
ceed from the investigation of individual psychological complica-
tions but from the whole person; for it is only the understanding
of wholeness as wholeness that can lead to the real transformation
and healing of the person and of one's relations with one's fellow
men. None of the phenomena of the soul is to be placed in the
center of observation as if all the rest were derived from it. Persons ought not be treated as objects of investigation and encouraged to see themselves as "It's." They should be summoned to
set themselves to rights, to bring their inner being to unity so that
they may respond to the address of being that faces them.

In their dialogue with others and in their life with the community it is possible for persons to divert fear, anger, love, and sexual
desire from the casual to the essential by responding to what
comes to meet them, to what they become aware of as addressing
them and demanding from them an answer.

In order to be responsible, it is essential that we make use of
that "disciplined fantasy" that enables us to experience the other
person's side of the relationship. Only through a quite concrete
imagining of what the other is thinking, feeling, and willing can I
make the other present to myself in his or her wholeness, unity,
and uniqueness. This "imagining the real" is not "empathy," for
it does not mean giving up one's own standpoint in order to enter
that of the other. Rather it is a living partnership in which "I

MALASPINA COLLEGE LIBRARY

stand in a common situation with the other and expose myself vitally to his share in the situation as really his share." Without forfeiting anything of the felt reality of my own activity, I "at the same time live through the common event from the standpoint of the other." This "inclusion" of the other takes place most deeply and fully in marriage, the "exemplary bond" which, if it is real, leads to a "vital acknowledgement of many-faced otherness—even in the contradiction and conflict with it." In all human relations, in fact, the responsible quality of one's decision will be determined by the degree to which one really "sees the other" and makes the other present to one.

PART TWO

The "Three Forces" of
Contemporary Psychology:
A Critique

Chapter 4

Scientism: B. F. Skinner

T O the behaviorist, said the noted psychologist B. F. Skinner, "there is no difference between a man training for a race and a man racing for a train." Skinner wishes to understand the human being *purely from the outside* and in so doing to reject once and for all the openness of the humanistic approach in favor of the objective certainties of social engineers who will manipulate society according to a "scientific" plan:

> The point at which the scientific method will take superiority over the humanistic will be the point at which it gives man the techniques for the *manipulation* and *control* of human *behavior*....We are on the verge of a great change in *techniques of dealing with man* in every sphere, which *will result in a great change in our concept of man.* Hence if we must make a choice we will abandon the humanistic tradition for the greater advantage which will come through the plodding and careful methods of science.[1]

From *Walden Two* (1945) to *Beyond Freedom and Dignity* (1971), Skinner has remained consistent in regarding human nature itself as the proper subject of a science of behavior and in rejecting the "inner man" that was given to us by the Greeks and the unnecessary concepts of "dignity" or "worth" that accompany the inner

1. B.F. Skinner, "The Image of Man," The New School Conference on Methods in the Sciences and Social Sciences, 1954; Italics added.

man: "When science begins to bear down on the question of the individual, you must accept determinism or reject the entire scientific worldview."

But as Martin Gardner has pointed out in his iconoclastic book, *In the Name of Science*, not all that is done in the name of science is properly called science. In the case of the behaviorist approach to psychology, this distinction between scientism and science has been lucidly spelled out by Amedeo Giorgi, a pioneer in the application of phenomenology to experimental psychology:

> Science becomes scientism when methods successful in one area are transferred uncritically to another domain where its legitimacy is at best questionable. Psychology turned to established and more prestigious sciences to imitate them. But the established sciences were physics, chemistry, biology—each of which was developed within an implicit ontology suitable for nature but not for the human person. The natural sciences were never *intended* to study man as a person. One need not leave the realm of science to study man adequately. We need only to broaden science itself.[2]

Giorgi summarizes the main features of the natural scientific approach that is uncritically carried over to psychology as "empirical, positivistic, reductionistic, quantitative, deterministic, verifiable and predictive."

In his book *Psychology as a Human Science*, Giorgi states that instead of modeling itself on the natural sciences, the human sciences, including psychology, should have gone directly to the life-world, discovered its questions and methods from there, and only then tried to ascertain to what extent the human and the natural sciences have methods, concepts, and answers in common. The natural scientific approach applies an analytical process which breaks down the whole into its elements or parts whereas the approach of the human sciences would understand the whole as part of a larger-structured context. The actual and the present would then become the point of departure for uncovering relationships, contexts, and meaning. Natural science considers Man as *part of the world* but studies him without reference to his intentional relations *to* the world. The human sciences recognize that

2. Symposium on "Science and Scientism: The Human Sciences," Trinity College, May 15-16, 1970.

Man is also one *for whom the world exists*. Natural science derives its theories and hypotheses from a vital level of integration below the human structural level and looks at the human in terms of pathological cases or traditional laboratory studies. The human sciences, being holistic, study Man at his highest level of functioning, the unequivocally human, to which facts obtained at lower levels of function are only relevant if a human context is implicitly present.

This also implies that the human sciences are intersubjective not only as between scientist and scientist but also as between investigator and subject. Equal in their humanity, they must relate through a nonmanipulative structure based upon appeal and cooperation with research designs that will be open-ended, leaving the final closure to the subject. In contrast to the positivist, reductionistic, analytic, and quantitative approach of the natural sciences, the human sciences must be concerned with meaning, qualitative differences, intentional relations, and investigating human phenomena in a human way. The meaning that the *subjects* bring to the situation thus becomes coconstitutive of the results.[3]

Giorgi rightly recognizes in the *philosophy* with which B. F. Skinner approaches his psychological research a classic example of scientism. "Were it not for the unwarranted generalization that all control is wrong," writes Skinner, "we should deal with the social environment as simply as we deal with the nonsocial." As Skinner recognizes no distinction between natural science and human science, so he recognizes no distinction between dealing with the human and the nonhuman. His two-pronged attack on freedom and dignity is based on a simplistic either/or. Either the individual has an inner, autonomous center completely uninfluenced by what is outside him or her or the individual is totally determined by the environment. A variant of the same is Skinner's assertion that "any evidence that a person's behavior may be attributed to external circumstances seems to threaten his dignity or worth." He has no conception of that "finite freedom" of which Paul Tillich speaks in which a person possesses freedom precisely in the midst of limitation and conditioning. Skinner misses entirely the understanding of dignity as what one *is* and

3. Amedeo Giorgi, *Psychology as a Human Science. A Phenomenologically Based Approach* (New York: Harper & Row, 1970), pp. 176 f., 191 f., 198, 203–205.

sees it simply as a matter of what one *does*: "We recognize a person's dignity or worth when we give him credit for what he has done." Not only does natural science take over one by one the functions of "autonomous man" as it better understands the role of the environment, but the very goal of science is "the destruction of mystery" through the fuller explanation of behavior.[4] Skinner is, indeed, paradigmatic of that analytical, reductive, and deriving look which, Martin Buber says, predominates today between person and person.

> This look is analytical, or rather pseudo-analytical, since it treats the whole being as put together and therefore able to be taken apart—not only the so-called unconscious which is accessible to relative objectification, but also the psychic stream itself, which can never, in fact, be grasped as an object. This look is a reductive one because it tries to contract the manifold person, who is nourished by the microcosmic richness of the possible, to some schematically surveyable and recurrent structures. And this look is a deriving one because it supposes it can grasp what man has become, or even is becoming, in genetic formulae, and it thinks that even the dynamic central principle of the individual in this becoming can be represented by a general concept. *An effort is being made today radically to destroy the mystery between man and man. The personal life, the ever near mystery, once the source of the stillest enthusiasms, is levelled down.*[5]

Buber is not, he explains, attacking "the analytical method of the human sciences, a method which is indispensable wherever it furthers knowledge of a phenomenon without impairing the essentially different knowledge of its uniqueness that transcends the valid circle of the method." Skinner not only impairs the human being's uniqueness. He dismisses it out of hand. Nor does he recognize that there is any valid knowledge that can transcend the circle of his method.

In contrast to Nicolas Berdyaev, who insists that a compulsory good is not good, Skinner entirely dismisses character, personal-

---

4. B. F. Skinner, *Beyond Freedom and Dignity* (New York: Alfred A. Knopf, 1971), pp. 42, 44, 58.

5. Martin Buber, *The Knowledge of Man: A Philosophy of the Interhuman,* ed. with an Introductory Essay (Chapter 1) by Maurice Friedman (New York: Harper Torchbooks, 1966), "Elements of the Interhuman," trans. R. G. Smith, pp. 80 f; Italics added.

ity, motivation, and intention in favor of the redesign of the environment through which we shall progress "toward a world in which people may be automatically good." "The problem is to induce people not to be good but to behave well." By the same token, Skinner can recognize nothing in any moral injunction other than a purely extrinsic desire to escape the punishment that society or other people mete out for stealing, or killing. Since he sees *all* control as exerted by the environment and the task of human kind as designing better environments rather than better humans, he necessarily dismisses as unreal any intrinsic morality, or unconditional imperative, hence any morality worth the name. He recognizes that his view cannot be proved, yet claims that it is in the nature of scientific inquiry that evidence should shift in favor of the image of the human as totally determined by genetic endowments and by environment. He attacks the "inner man" as an unnecessary hypostatization. Without noticing it, as it were, he does away at the same time with the whole person, the unique human being, the person who can respond spontaneously as well as react to the control of the environment. Yet he claims that the technology he proposes is "ethically neutral" and that "there is nothing in a methodology which determines the values governing its use"! The human studies Skinner dismisses contemptuously and out of hand: "What, after all, have we to show for nonscientific or prescientific good judgment, or common sense, or the insights gained through personal experience? It is science or nothing."[6]

The result of all this is a conscious change in the human image and with it art and literature. "We shall not only have no reason to admire people who endure suffering, face danger, or struggle to be good; it is possible that we shall have little interest in pictures or books about them." Since "being good" will be a matter automatically taken care of by the controlled environment, Skinner need not concern himself with the difference between a real value decision as to what is good in this situation and "the things people call good." He combines crude cultural relativism with a slightly complexified pain–pleasure calculus in which individuals can be induced to identify their own good with that of others and with the survival of their culture. He asserts the necessity of intentional de-

6. Skinner, *Beyond Freedom*, pp. 66–69, 82, 101, 113–115, 160.

sign of a culture and the control of human behavior as essential
for the human species to develop and for culture to progress; yet
he has no criteria for what development or progress may mean,
any more than he has any answer to the question he himself raises
as to who is going to do the controlling and what will guide their
control. Here, too, he says that what is essential is changing the
environment rather than the persons. He recognizes no *value*
problem concerning the direction in which the environment
might change. His only criteria are "Will it work?" and "Will it
survive?" or perhaps be replaced by some other culture which
"may make a greater contribution to the future."[7]

Skinner looks forward with excitement to what humans can
make of themselves when the two processes of biological and cultural evolution are speeded up through design and control, and he
imagines to himself "a world in which people live together without quarrelling, maintain themselves by producing the food, shel-
ter, and clothing they need, enjoy themselves and contribute to
the enjoyment of others in art, music, literature, and games, con-
sume only a reasonable part of the resources of the world and add
as little as possible to its pollution, bear no more children than can
be raised decently . . . and come to know themselves accurately
and, therefore, manage themselves effectively." But accuracy and
effectiveness are no answer to the basic value question of who will
set the guidelines for the designed social environment and by
what criteria.

Skinner asseverates that "it is not difficult to demonstrate a
connection between the unlimited right of the individual to pursue happiness and the catastrophes threatened by unchecked
breeding, the unrestrained affluence which exhausts resources
and pollutes the environment, and the imminence of nuclear
war."[8] But what will replace the individualism that he attacks?
Skinner anticipates his Walden Two utopia; but the Nazis, the
most thoroughgoing antiindividualist and totalitarian state in the
history of mankind, have given us a preview of quite a different
kind. Only the most highly organized collectivism with the fullest
possible social engineering and design of the social and physical
environment made possible that miracle of scientific ingenuity:

7. Skinner, *Beyond Freedom*, pp. 153, 163 f., 168, 173, 175, 180-183.
8. Skinner, *Beyond Freedom*, pp. 208, 214 f.

the extermination of up to eleven million people as if they had been insects!

The fact is that Skinner is a sawed-off dualist: he buys uncritically the dualism of inner and outer. Bergson and Jung opt for the inner; he opts for the outer. "Without the help of a verbal community," he writes, "all behavior would be unconscious. Consciousness is a social product. It is not only *not* the specific field of autonomous man, it is not within range of a solitary man." That there might be nonsolitary individuals who are nonetheless persons who can respond to what is outside of them from the ground of their own uniqueness does not even occur to Skinner as a possibility. He dismisses his critics as merely so many rearguard actions in the retreat of those who wish to retain an autonomous "inner man" against an environmentally controlled "outer man." The "essence of man," the "humanity of man," "man as Thou not It," or "as a person not a thing," really means, translates Skinner, the "autonomous man—the inner man, the homunculus, the possessing demon, the man defended by the literature of freedom and dignity."[9] But the person, as Thou, to take one of his examples, does *not* mean an inner or absolutely free person; it means the human being as person finding his or her personhood precisely in open, mutual relationships with other persons and with the nonhuman world.

"Science"—by which we should read Skinner's own scientism—"does not dehumanize man," writes Skinner, "it dehomunculizes him, and it must do so if it is to prevent the abolition of the human species."

> To man *qua* man we readily say good riddance. Only by dispossessing him can we turn to the real causes of human behavior. Only then can we turn from the inferred to the observed, from the miraculous to the natural, from the inaccessible to the manipulable.[10]

If the human being is only the object, who is the existential subject that does the knowing in this science? Even what Skinner writes of the investigator and controller is from without, as an object, rather than from within, as a subject, an experiencing person.

9. Skinner, *Beyond Freedom*, pp. 192, 198, 200.
10. Skinner, *Beyond Freedom*, p. 209.

A formidable reply to Skinner from the realm of psychology itself is Isidor Chein's book, *The Science of Behavior and the Image of Man*. "At the heart of the issue of the nature of psychology," writes Chein, "is the issue of the image of man." Chein contrasts two basic types of image—the human as helpless, powerless reagent and the human as active, responsible agent, and he opts for the latter as against the former. One does not passively permit oneself to be shaped by one's environment; one injects oneself into the causal process, shaping both what is around one and oneself. "If Man is said to respond to his environment, the word 'response' is to be taken in the sense that it has in active dialogue rather than in the sense of an automatic consequence." This statement is similar to the distinction I make in *The Life of Dialogue* between "responding" and "reacting":

> When Buber speaks of the free man as free of causation, process, and defined being, he does not mean that the free man acts from within himself without connection with what has come to him from the outside. On the contrary, it is only the free man who really acts in response to concrete external events. It is only he who sees what is new and unique in each situation, whereas the unfree man sees only its resemblance to other things. But what comes to the free man from without is only the precondition for his action, it does not determine its nature. This is just as true of those social and psychological conditioning influences which he has internalized in the past as of immediate external events. To the former as to the latter, he responds freely from the depths as a whole and conscious person. The unfree person, on the other hand, is so defined by public opinion, social status, or his neurosis that he does not "respond" spontaneously and openly to what meets him but only "reacts." He does not see others as real persons, unique and of value in themselves, but in terms of their status, their usefulness, or their similarity to other individuals with whom he has had relationships in the past.[11]

In place of the image of the responding, responsible human being there dominates, not only among psychologists but among an astonishingly large number of those concerned with guidance, counseling, and psychotherapy, a "robotic image of man" resting

11. Maurice Friedman, *Martin Buber: The Life of Dialogue,* 3rd rev. ed. with new Preface and expanded Bibliography (Chicago: University of Chicago Press Phoenix Books, 1976), pp. 67 f.

"on the false assumption that...every determinant of behavior is either a body fact or an environment fact." In powerful reinforcement of Giorgi's critique of scientism, Chein charges that "psychologists maintain the image of Man as a passive corporeal entity governed by a thermodynamic principle because of their philosophical precommitments and in flagrant disregard of contradictory information."[12]

Freedom to Chein rests on the simple premises that volitions—human desires and motivations—have behavioral consequences and are not themselves reducible to variables of physical environment or physiological process. Like the Gestalt psychologists, Chein holds that the unique aspects of a totality do not emerge from the combination of the components, "since the totality plays a role in determining what the components will be." The alternative to this image, declares Chein, is to reduce psychological science to a concern with "psychological trivia arbitrarily torn out of the context of their natural setting." This setting includes the fact that motivation implies a mission, a commitment to accomplish something. Strict behavioralists who avoid inner feeling and emotion as "mentalistic poison" pay the price of losing much of human beings and what makes them do what they do. Scientism is committed to a reductionism which goes beyond the parsimoniousness of science to a preselected set of primitive terms and propositions, usually drawn from physics, chemistry, or physiology, which are held to dogmatically in complete disrespect for the "unparsimoniousness of nature." In addition, scientismists limit themselves to clearly understandable, verifiable forms even when these forms do not fit the case, thus betraying the scientific goal and purposes for the sake of maintaining the scientific form.[13]

In contrast to scientism, Chein puts forward a clinicalist image of the human. The "clinicalist" is open to human context and human meaning as they are found in the concrete, the particular, and the unique—hence, in the "image of the human" as opposed to the "construct of the human," a contrast I shall discuss later. A desire to comprehend every instance "in all of its particularity and unique individuality" leads the clinicalist to be suspicious of

12. Isidor Chein, *The Science of Behavior and the Image of Man* (New York: Basic Books, 1972), pp. 6 f., 9, 17.
13. Chein, *Science of Behavior*, pp. 20, 22, 26, 43, 268, 277, 309 f., 316.

any fixed scheme of classification, consistent theory, or statistic evidence. "He rejects fiducial probabilities because the very concept abandons the uniqueness of the particular case." "Evidence," to the clinicalist, is the phenomenal given itself, explained, when necessary, in terms of "the subjective compellingness and fittingness of an account in terms of temporal-situational context." Predictability of nontrivial behavior is, to the clinicalist, "*prima facie* evidence of constraints that distort normal behavior"; the clinicalist regards laboratory situations as "so abnormal that no generalizations from them are warranted." The clinicalist gains more from reading Dostoievsky, Mann, Proust, and Shakespeare than all of the pages of the *Journal of Experimental Psychology*; for "a good example of seeing human behavior in its complexity may be worth more in developing principles of grasping particularities than scores of statistically significant generalizations about highly circumscribed behaviors occurring under laboratory conditions."[14]

In his criticism of the scientismic approach to psychology, Chein points out the obvious but nonetheless consistently overlooked fact that behaviorist psychologists as active knowers and interveners cannot be included in their own images of the human as passive being:

> The class *Man* includes the psychologist who adopts the image of Man as an impotent being; this psychologist, like everyone else, cannot live by this image. He may try to apply it to everyone else, but he cannot apply it to himself as a basis of action. He thus professes a faith in an order of law that applies to everyone else, but, implicitly at least, he reserves to himself a special order of law. He knows that he can intervene in events, but he claims that no one else can—and this in the name of science![15]

14 .Chein, *Science of Behavior*, pp. 310–313.
15. Chein, *Science of Behavior*, p. 17. For a fuller critique of Skinner in particular and scientism in general, see Maurice Friedman, *The Hidden Human Image* (New York: Delacorte Press [hardback] and Delta Books [paperback], 1974), Chapter 3, "Science and Scientism," pp. 31–65. This current chapter, "Scientism: B. F. Skinner," is based on selections from "Science and Scientism."

Chapter 5

Psychologism: Sigmund Freud and Carl G. Jung

T HAT the human being has a soul, or psyche, belongs to the age-old wisdom of humankind. What is new about today's Psychological Man is that the psyche is now converted into the more impersonal "mind," that its main determinants are seen as residing in an impersonal and largely repressed "unconscious" mind, and that individuals, thus relatively depersonalized, are seen as existing, in the real sense of the term, not in their relation to the environment or to other people or to the world, but in their minds. Thus, Psychological Man usually means, to a greater or lesser extent, psychologism—the referring of both reality and value to the psyche. If psychologism be defined as the tendency to convert events that happen between oneself and others into psychological happenings or categories, then we must say that all modern psychology, psychotherapy, and psychoanalysis run the risk of falling into precisely this. The very attempt to look at the person in abstraction from his or her relations to others, as a more or less isolated psyche, means this.

Sigmund Freud

Far from seeing the human being as an essentially rational animal, as the ancient Greeks did, Freud holds that the ego only comes into existence as a splitting off from the id, resulting from identifications with the parents in the first years of life. The character of the ego, to Freud, is nothing other than a precipitate of abandoned object-choices. The word "object" here is particularly appropriate; for Freud does not see the cathexis as an essential relation with another person, but as an instinctual relation with oneself through the other person. It is like a closed circuit in which the other person is the intermediate transmitter, but never really the initiator or receiver.

Conscience, to Freud, is the tension between the ego and the ego-ideal. Although the superego condemns and criticizes the ego, a great part of the sense of guilt remains unconscious, "because the origin of conscience is closely connected with the Oedipus complex which belongs to the unconscious." This means not only that there may be neurotic and irrational guilt—and Freud's illumination of this area is certainly one of his greatest contributions to our contemporary image of the human—but also that the superego as such is allied with the passions of the id rather than with the reason of the ego. In melancholia, for example, it is "a pure culture of the death-instinct" that holds sway. The ego struggles against the tendencies of the id, but the superego behaves as if the ego were responsible for these impulses and chastises it.[1]

Freud goes from the divided, sick person that he sees before him—a type of person that is very typical of our age—to a definition of human nature as such. Freud's picture of Man as id, ego, and superego is a *construct* of the human rather than an *image* of the human. It is a synthetic combination of analytical subcategories which systematically excludes from its view the wholeness and uniqueness of the person. What I mean by "person" here is not individuals seen from the outside, as Freud sees them, but the actually existing persons, seen from within, who know themselves, to some extent, as an "I" and not as an "it." Freud has an "ego," but he has no true "I," no actual subject; for as soon as one tries to make the "I" into an object, it ceases to be "I." This Freud never seems to notice, perhaps because he believes that the ego is "lived" by impersonal, instinctual passion. Id, ego, and superego alike are objects to Freud. Yet objects do not exist without

1. Sigmund Freud, *The Ego and the Id,* authorized translation by Joan Riviere (*The International Psycho-Analytical Library*, ed. Ernest Jones, No. 12, 4th ed.; London: The Hogarth Press and the Institute of Psychoanalysis, 1947).

a knowing subject—and that subject is Freud himself! Freud's construct of Man displaces the center of human existence from the person into separate factors which enter into but cannot in themselves constitute human wholeness.

It is not surprising that this construct of Man leads directly to psychologism. Genital love is Man's greatest gratification, says Freud, but through it one becomes to a very dangerous degree dependent on a part of the outer world, namely, one's chosen love-object, and this exposes one to most painful sufferings if one is rejected by it or loses it through death or defection. Some people protect themselves by turning away from the sexual aim, and with it the uncertainties and disappointments of genital love, to a general love of all mankind. The "unchangeable, undeviating, tender attitude" which results "has little superficial likeness to the stormy vicissitudes of genital love," but it is nevertheless derived from it. With a bold stroke, Freud takes Saint Francis of Assisi— perhaps the most famous image of humble love in Western civilization—as his prime example of "using love to produce an inner feeling of happiness." Freud scolds Saint Francis because his love was indiscriminate, for "not all men are worthy of love." Thus, Saint Francis is not an image of the human, after all, because the love of others he seems to represent is neither possible nor desirable!

Freud extends this attack to "Love thy neighbor as thyself." I cannot love my neighbor as myself, he says, for my neighbor is not worthy of my love. Who then is? Only one who "is so like me in important respects that I can love myself in him" or one who "is so much more perfect than I that I can love my ideal of myself in him" or "the son of my friend, since the pain my friend would feel if anything untoward happened to him would be my pain." In other words, to be worthy of love, the other must be a function of myself. Freud *deduces* the true motive of Saint Francis's love from his general theory of sex and sublimation. He is unconcerned with the actual life of the man whose love of Brother Sun, Sister Water, Brother Fire, and Brother Wolf has been for countless persons through the centuries an image of the possibility of loving others without referring them in the first instance to oneself. In the place of Saint Francis, Freud offers us a love which centers entirely around the self and yet is held up for us as a mature "object love" as opposed to Francis's immature narcissism![2]

Freud's touching plea for the individual against the claims of one's own superego and that of the culture shows that Freud does not, in the end, look on the human being merely from without, as a psychological mechanism, but also from within as a being with some value of one's own, and therefore with some claim to happiness. The reality of unconscious compulsion makes it impossible to assert the existence of full, conscious freedom. But it is equally impossible to reduce the person to a purely deterministic system. The human reality—of the well person as well as of the ill—is a complex intermixture of personal freedom and psychological compulsion, a paradoxical phenomenon that can be understood only from within. In Freud's image of the human, in contrast to my own view, there is no place for freedom and spontaneity— with one curious, yet all-important, exception. However Freud may explain it theoretically, the goal of psychoanalysis is the liberation of the individual from past fixations and traumas so that one may be free to respond to and live with the reality of the present.

There is an important theoretical grounding for this exception worked out in the course of Freud's later thought. It rests, first of all, on the fact that, despite his reduction of conscience to the fear of castration, the constructs of id, superego, and ego are not regarded by Freud as psychogenic explanations, but as structures of the mind that is already developed. It rests, second, on the fact that the ego is the reality-tester. In its function of helping the individual to adjust to reality and to modify or compromise between the demands of superego and id, it already implies the existence of real freedom. A corollary of this fact is Freud's tendency to regard consciousness itself as freedom, especially when it succeeds in recognizing repressed material and integrating it into the ego. The goal of Freudian psychoanalysis—"Where id was ego shall be"— itself describes a movement from psychological determinism to personal freedom. Finally, the movement from psychogenic determinism to freedom may be seen in the development of the "reality principle" from a utilitarian extension of the "pleasure principle" in Freud's early thought to an independent arbiter of

2. Sigmund Freud, *Civilization and Its Discontents*, trans. Joan Riviere (New York: Doubleday Anchor Books, 1958).

reality in *The Ego and the Id* and to an acceptance of one's own death and of the tragic limitations of human existence in *Civilization and Its Discontents*.[3]

To Freud, more than to any other single person, goes the credit and the blame for ushering in the age of the Psychological Man. On the credit side are the deeper insights into human passions and conflicts, into the complex inner divisions and internecine strife of Man in general and of Modern Man in particular. Also on the credit side is that moral concern which makes Freud desire to limit the harsh reign of the superego in favor of the more moderate combination of repressions and instinctual satisfactions which a liberated and mature ego can afford. Freud's juxtaposition of the reality principle and the pleasure principle and later of the love instinct and the death instinct afford him a delicately balanced realism which accepts the tragic limitations of life yet believes in the melioristic possibilities afforded by reason when it operates in psychoanalysis as a neutral scientific instrument of inquiry.

On the debit side of the ledger must be entered that overwhelming and overweening individualism which makes Freud reduce the social relationships between persons to secondary products of individual, instinctual gratifications. Even more serious for the image of the human is that psychologism which translates the meaning of human existence into internal, psychic categories and dimensions. Along with this goes that unmasking which reduces all conscious motivations to unconscious determinants.[4]

Carl G. Jung

In the analytical psychology of Carl Jung, the danger of psychologism is doubled. For Jung, self-realization is the goal, and the means toward that goal is a turning inward to a larger-than-

3. I am indebted for this last insight to the penetrating seminar of Paul Ricoeur on "The Reality and the Pleasure Principle in Freud," given for the Council on Existential Psychology and Psychiatry, October 31–November 1, 1964.

4. For a full-scale discussion of Freud, see Maurice Friedman, *To Deny Our Nothingness: Contemporary Images of Man,* 3rd rev. ed. with new Preface and Appendix (Chicago: University of Chicago Press Phoenix Books [paperback], 1978), Chapter 11, "Sigmund Freud," on which this section is based.

life-size Self to be integrated in the depths of the Objective Psyche, or Collective Unconscious. When the person is thus focused on these inward processes, there is the danger that everything else and everyone else consciously or unconsciously becomes the means to the end of that person's individuation, or integration, the function of that person's becoming. Jung emphasizes the inner in such a way that the outer becomes either an obstacle to or a function of the inner. In the face of this approach, it is not possible to say with the poet Richard Wilbur, "Love is for the things of this world," much less "for the people of this world."

Carl Jung consciously endeavored in his psychology to create what I have called in *To Deny Our Nothingness* a "Modern Gnostic" mythology that includes a terminology essentially original to Jung: the "anima" and the "animus" as feminine and masculine parts of the soul, the "shadow" as the suppressed, irrational, and therefore negative part of the soul, the distinction between the personal unconscious and the collective unconscious, which latter contains the great psychological archetypes that Jung sees as universals, and the process of individuation as the shaping of an autonomous center in the unconscious through which the numinous contents of the collective unconscious can be integrated into a personal, if still largely unconscious, wholeness.

Jung proceeds from a simplistic, neo-Kantian theory of knowledge which elevates the psyche from an indispensable corollary of knowledge to being both the creator of what is known and itself the highest reality. Man "himself is the second creator of the world, who alone has given to the world its objective existence." The understanding of "the empirical nature of the psyche" is "a matter of the highest importance and the very foundation of. . .reality" to the person of the twentieth century, writes Jung, "because he has recognized once and for all that without an observer there is no world and consequently no truth, for there would be nobody to register it." In contrast to other modern advocates of "experience," Jung does not value all experiences, but only those found within, and particularly within the unconscious.

In Jung's autobiography, *Memories, Dreams, Reflections,* we find Jung, from the first, an isolated, divided person with a powerful inner world of fantasies, visions, and dreams which he identifies with "Personality Number Two." If this inner division led him to bring "inner" and "outer" into some contact, it also led him to accept a lifelong conflict between them. He tended to regard the inner as the good and the outer as either secondary and instrumental or bad. Many of Jung's statements in his autobiography exemplify the seemingly irresistible tendency of psychologism to regard other people as merely a means to the fulfillment of one's own inner destiny:

> Other people are established inalienably in my memories only if their names were entered in the scrolls of my destiny from the beginning, so that encountering them was at the same time a kind of recollection.
>
> From the beginning I had a sense of destiny, as though my life was assigned to me by fate and had to be fulfilled. This gave me an inner security. . . . Often I had the feeling that in all decisive matters I was no longer among men, but was alone with God.
>
> I have offended many people, for as soon as I saw that they did not understand me, that was the end of the matter so far as I was concerned. I had to move on. I had no patience with people—aside from my patients. I had to obey an inner law which was imposed on me and left me no freedom of choice. . . . For some people I was continually present and close to them *so long as they were related to my inner world.* . . . I had to learn painfully that people continued to exist even when they had nothing more to say to me. Many excited in me a feeling of living humanity, but *only when they appeared within the magic circle of psychology;* next moment, when the spotlight cast its beam elsewhere, there was nothing to be seen. I was able to become intensely interested in many people; but *as soon as I had seen through them, the magic was gone.* In this way I made many enemies. A creative person has little power over his own life. He is captive and driven by his daimon.[5]

In his discussion of "The Development of Personality," Jung sets the true person, who has attained individuation, in contrast to convention, conformity, and the collective. Although he sees convention as a necessary stopgap, he leaves no question in our minds that the great person, the image of the human for all persons, is the one who defies convention for the sake of one's own inner vocation and one's own inner destiny. To be a person is to

5. C. G. Jung, *Memories, Dreams, Reflections,* recorded and ed. Aniela Jaffe, trans. Richard and Clara Winston (New York: Pantheon Books, 1961), pp. 5, 48, 357; Italics added.

have a vocation, Jung writes, and "the original meaning of 'to have a vocation' is 'to be addressed by a voice'." Jung sees the true personality as trusting in one's voice "as in God," but the voice comes not from God but from oneself, one's own inner destiny: "He *must* obey his own law, as if it were a daimon whispering to him of new and wonderful paths. Anyone with a vocation hears the voice of the inner man: he is *called*."

This does not mean, of course, that one consciously addresses oneself. Rather, just as Jung saw himself as split into two personalities, so he sees the human individual in general as split into a conscious ego and an unconscious ground which is the potential arena of the true Self. He leaves us in no doubt as to which of these two is the dominant reality: "Only the tiniest fraction of the psyche is identical with the conscious mind and its box of magic tricks, while for much the greater part it is sheer unconscious *fact*, hard and immitigable as granite, immovable, inaccessible, yet ready at any time to come crashing down upon us at the behest of unseen powers." He also leaves us in no doubt as to which of these is the source of value: it is the unconscious which calls and guides, the conscious which listens and obeys, or, if it fails to obey, pays the price of neuroticism:

> The neurosis is thus a defense against the objective, inner activity of the psyche, or an attempt, somewhat dearly paid for, to escape from the inner voice and hence from the vocation. For this "growth" is the objective activity of the psyche, which, *independently of conscious volition*, is trying to speak to the conscious mind through the inner voice and lead him towards wholeness. Behind the neurotic perversion is concealed his vocation, his destiny: the growth of personality, the full realization of the life-will that is born with the individual.[6]

In this statement, we have the curious doctrine of a "life-will" which is realized "independently of conscious volition," which means independently of the will. For this to make any sense at all, Jung must be positing another "will" in the depths of the unconscious psyche, and in effect this is just what he does. In *Memories, Dreams, Reflections*, as we have seen, he attributes the fact that he

6. C. G. Jung, *Collected Works,* Vol. XVII, *The Development of the Personality,* trans. R. F. C. Hull (New York: Pantheon Books, Bollingen Series, 1954), p. 183; Italics added.

could not be really interested in other people to his *daimon*, his guiding genius, while speaking of himself as the helpless victim. However much Jung may set the impersonal, collective unconscious in contrast to the modern collective as that which is realized only by the liberated, individuated person, it is curiously like totalitarianism in its reference of reality and value to a universal which allows room for individuality but not for true uniqueness:

> The psychic substratum upon which the individual consciousness is based is universally the same, otherwise people could never reach a conscious understanding. So in this sense, personality and its peculiar psychic makeup are not something absolutely unique. The uniqueness holds only for the individual nature of the personality.[7]

"The inner voice is the voice of a fuller life, of a wider, more comprehensive consciousness," writes Jung. Only through responding to this law of one's being and rising to personality does one attain to one's life's meaning. But if one only becomes a personality through consciously assenting to the power of the inner voice, this assent still means the sacrifice of oneself to one's vocation. "That," says Jung, "is the great and liberating thing about any genuine personality." This means again that one must choose between one's conscious will and one's unconscious will, and the latter, the voice of the unconscious, Jung freely identifies with "the will of God."

How, we may ask, can integration of the personality, or individuation, be a goal in itself, independent of the way in which individuated persons move to meet their world? What guidance does obeying the inner voice offer in distinguishing between the authentic and the inauthentic in the concrete context of one's life relationships? What direction of movement as a person in the world is implied as the result of the unification of conscious and unconscious, good and evil? Is Jung's individuation in the last analysis an image of authentic existence for contemporary human beings or a substitute for one that makes one's concrete existence of secondary importance? How can psychic experience take the place of the traditional God as a voice, an address, a guidance when "God" is consistently identified by Jung with the individu-

7. Jung, *The Development of the Personality*, p. 179.

ated person, and the new mystery that he proclaims is the mystery of God become Man?

> The goal of psychological, as of biological, development is self-realization, or individuation. But since man knows himself only as an ego, and the self, as a totality, is indescribable and indistinguishable from a God-image, self-realization—to put it in religious or metaphysical terms—amount to God's incarnation.[8]

Whatever else "conscience" is, it has always been held to be the voice that prompted one to distinguish intrinsic right from wrong in concrete situations. Now this voice is put aside, along with the elemental seriousness of those situations and of one's desire to respond to them in the right way. In their place is the "inner necessity" which need not take either conscience or the situation seriously since both belong to the relatively less real and less valuable world of one's relations to others. Yet human existence is, in important part, made up of these very relations. To make them extrinsic and instrumental inevitably means to destroy one's personal wholeness by dividing one into an essential inner self and an inessential social self.

Submission *to* and deliverance *from* convention are an either/or for Jung that admits of no third alternative. The persons who at the same time try to follow their own way and adjust to the group inevitably become neurotic. The "wholeness of self" which the individuated person attains is the integration of the inner self, a wholeness that reduces the person in his or her relation to other persons to a mere *persona*, a mask, or social role, with at best only secondary significance. Thus, in his teaching as in his life, Jung is not really able to unite "inner" and "outer" and overcome the conflict between them. Instead, he demands a fundamental choice between them which makes the "outer" the instrument and material for the "inner."

Jung's turning away from the existential immediacy of lived life to "universal human validity" has the inevitable effect of depersonalizing the human being, of removing that freedom and that stamp of personal wholeness which make one a person. "It is

8. C. G. Jung, *Collected Works*, Vol. XI, *Psychology and Religion: East and West*, trans. R. F. C. Hull (New York: Pantheon Books, Bollingen Series, 1958), p. 157.

perfectly possible psychologically, for the unconscious or an archetype to take complete possession of a man and to determine his fate down to the smallest detail." Not only does Jung see God as acting out the unconscious of the person, but as *forcing* the person "to harmonize and unite the opposite influences to which his mind is exposed from the unconscious."

> Whatever man's wholeness, or the self, may mean *per se*, empirically it is an image of the goal of life spontaneously produced by the unconscious, *irrespective of the wishes and fears of the conscious mind.* It stands for the goal of the total man, for the realization of his wholeness and individuality *with or without the consent of his will.*[9]

How there can be any personal wholeness, individuality, or spontaneity in the face of a conscious self taken over and compelled by the unconscious is incomprehensible to me.

In Jung's psychology, individuation is attained through the integration in the unconscious of the four faculties—thought, feeling, sensation, and intuition. Particularly central in this process of individuation is the "shadow," the suppressed part of the self. The shadow challenges the whole ego-personality and therefore usually meets with resistance. "To become conscious of it involves recognizing the dark aspects of the personality as present and real." If one does not make the shadow conscious, one invariably projects it onto one's environment, seeing all evil as outside of oneself. For that very reason, one is all the more threatened by the danger of its being unmasked within. Projections isolate the person from his environment by changing a real relation to it into an illusory one. The world is transformed "into the replica of one's own unknown face," and the subject "dreams a world whose reality remains forever unattainable."

The shadow represents first and foremost the personal unconscious and is therefore more easily recognized than the anima or animus which usually exist as archetypes of the collective unconscious. When the shadow appears as an archetype, it, too, is realized only with great difficulty: "It is quite within the bounds of possibility for a man to recognize the relative evil of his nature, but it is a rare and shattering experience for him to gaze into the

9. C. G. Jung, *Answer to Job,* trans. R. F. C. Hull (New York: World Publishing, Meridian Books, 1960), p. 183; Italics added.

face of absolute evil," says Jung in *Aion*. The first stage in the analytic process, for Jung, is the integration of the shadow, or the
realization of the personal unconscious, without which a recognition of anima and animus is impossible. As in all therapy, a therapist is necessary, and other people too, but only as functions of
one's inner integration:"The shadow can be realized only
through a relation to a partner, and anima and animus only
through a relation to the opposite sex, because only in such a relation do their projections become operative.[10]

By identifying the self with an autonomous center within the
unconscious and referring to that "self" not only the conscious
ego-personality, but also relations to other people and God, Jung
falls into psychologism in the most exact sense of the term. "The
goal of psychic development is the self," writes Jung in *Memories,
Dreams, Reflections*. One might as easily say, "The goal of the self is
psychic development," since he has defined the self in just this
way. The self is the center and the goal for Jung, but it is located
in the unconscious psyche, and not in that larger sphere of personal existence that has to do, in all seriousness, with other selves
and the world. Jung holds that we must recognize the unconscious
as the "core" upon whose contents we cannot pass any final judgment because of the inadequacy of our rational understanding.
Thus, it is not the wholeness of the self, but the unconscious, instinctual part of the person that constitutes the real essence of the
self for Jung: "Self-knowledge is of prime importance, because
through it we approach that fundamental stratum or core of human nature where the instincts dwell."[11]

Sometimes it seems that Jung's psychologism lies in the fact
that he refers everything to it. Even the rumors of "flying saucers" are taken by Jung as Modern Man's mandala symbol of the
wholeness of the self. The worldwide stories of flying saucers are
"the symptom of a universally present psychic disposition,"
namely, the anticipation that the cleavage in the psyche will be
surmounted in unity. Sometimes, in contrast, it seems that Jung's
psychologism lies in the fact that there is no reference beyond the

10. C. G. Jung, *Collected Works*, Vol. IX, Part II, *Aion: Researches into the Phenomenology of the Self*, trans. R. F. C. Hull (New York: Pantheon Books, 1959),
pp. 10, 22.
11. Jung, *Memories, Dreams, Reflections*, p. 331.

psyche itself—which is, perhaps, another way of saying the same thing. God, too, is a "psychic reality like the unconscious," an archetype that already has its place in that part of the psyche which is preexistent to consciousness. This gives God, and the other archetypes, an autonomy from the conscious mind, but they are nonetheless psychic.

Jung arrives, in fact, at the peculiar position of holding the unconscious to be more psychic than the conscious. "Consciousness is phylogenetically and ontogenetically a secondary phenomenon. It is time this obvious fact were grasped at last."[12] Jung sees our dreams as statements that the unconscious makes to us. But a statement is only such when it is conscious, and this means that the conscious mind not only listens and responds to the unconscious, but collaborates in and elaborates all its "statements." On the other hand, the very nature of a statement is to refer beyond itself; yet Jung robs it of just this reference in favor of its immanent psychic significance. By so doing he can dismiss all independent philosophical and religious significance in favor of the psychological:

> The whole problem of opposites in its broadest sense, with all its concomitant religious and philosophical aspects, is drawn into the psychological discussion. These aspects lose the autonomous character they have in their own field—inevitably so, since they are approached in terms of psychological questions; that is, they are no longer viewed from the angle of religious or philosophical truth, but are examined for their psychological validity and significance. Leaving aside their claim to be independent truths, the fact remains that regarded empirically—which is to say, scientifically— they are primarily *psychic phenomena*. This fact seems to me incontestable.[13]

If this position is not solipsistic, it is at the very least a Berkelian idealism that holds that *esse est percepii*, to be is to be perceived. Although Jung does not claim that a God that cannot be known in the psyche does not exist, he says that for all practical purposes such a God does not exist since we can only know the existence of what is psychic.

12. C. G. Jung, *Collected Works*, Vol. VII, *Two Essays on Analytical Psychology*, trans. R. F. C. Hull (New York: Pantheon Books, 1953), pp. 237, 348.
13. Jung, *Two Essays on Analytical Psychology*, p. 305.

If we applied this same criterion to the reality of the existence of other persons, we would arrive at the position—by no means inconsistent with Jung's Psychological Man—that they exist only insofar as they are reflected in our own psyche. We do not know them in the impact of their unknowable otherness but only in their reflections within our own conscious and unconscious minds. If we applied it to science, there would be no objects to know, only the knowers knowing them. In fact, Jung holds that whatever the psyche "may state about itself, it will never get beyond itself. All comprehension and all that is comprehended is in itself psychic, and to that extent we are hopelessly cooped up in an exclusively psychic world." Jung does not seem to apply this constriction to the unconscious which, if he were consistent, he would see as as unknowable apart from the conscious psyche as anything else is. On the contrary, he sees the unconscious archetype as "a real force charged with a specific energy," which is at once the subject and the effective cause of those psychic statements which he claims to be universal. "It is not the personal human being who is making the statement, but the archetype speaking through him." Jung concedes that "the ego and its will have a great part to play in life," but it is, for all that, a lesser part: "What the ego wills is subject in the highest degree to the interference, in ways of which the ego is usually unaware, of the autonomy and numinosity of archetypal processes."[14]

Jung makes a very interesting qualification of this psychologism in these same pages. He begins with the observation that he does not mean to imply that *only* the psyche exists, but that, "so far as perception and cognition are concerned"—hence, for all practical purposes—"we cannot see beyond the psyche." Yet he goes on to say that our senses probably cannot perceive all forms of being. "I have, therefore, even hazarded the postulate that the phenomenon of archetypal configurations—which are psychic events *par excellence*—may be founded upon a *psychoid* base, that is, upon an only partially psychic and possibly altogether different form of being." By this Jung means spiritual reality, an "uncomprehended absolute object which affects and influences us." This is, so far as I know, the only time that Jung has recognized the possibility that the unconscious is not necessarily psychic.

14. Jung, *Memories, Dreams, Reflections,* pp. 217, 351 f.

Jung's psychologism becomes most acute in his psychology of religion. In *Psychology and Religion: East and West* he states, "Not only does the psyche exist, it is existence itself."[15] He defines religious experience, by the same token, "as that kind of experience which is accorded the highest value, no matter what its contents may be,"[16] and by value he means psychic value. In contrast to the rationalistic point of view of the eighteenth century, "the psychological standpoint appeals much more to the man of the twentieth century." The charge of "psychologism," he says at the same time, "does not understand the empirical nature of the psyche." It would be an anachronistic regression, Jung holds, for twentieth-century individuals to solve their conflicts either metaphysically or rationalistically instead of psychologically.[17] Yet he fails to recognize how his notion of "the empirical" is in fact a metaphysic that unites the subject and the object and leaves no room for objective empirical fact in the ordinary sense of that term.

In *Answer to Job* Jung's psychologism reaches the absurd lengths of psychoanalyzing God. "From the human point of view Yahweh's behavior is so revolting," he writes, "that one has to ask oneself whether there is not a deeper motive hidden behind it. Has Yahweh some secret resistance against Job?"[18] According to Jung, "he pays so little attention to Job's real situation that one suspects him of having an ulterior motive which is more important to him." Jung sees God, indeed, as projecting his shadow side "with brazen countenance" and remaining "unconscious at man's expense." Even Freud never took so literally the unmasking of motives characteristic of Psychological Man! In *Answer to Job* Jung rejects the charge of "psychologism" on the curious grounds that he regards the psyche as *real*—and then offers abundant evidence that the charge is justly made. That he falls into the logical error of seeing reality as either physical or psychic is clear from such statements as, "God is an obvious psychic and nonphysical fact, i.e., a fact that can be established psychically but not physically," and "Religious statements without exception

15. Jung, *Psychology and Religion: East and West*, p. 12.
16. Jung, *Psychology and Religion: East and West*, p. 62
17. Jung, *Psychology and Religion: East and West*, pp. 309 f.
18. Jung, *Psychology and Religion: East and West*, p. 38.

have to do with the reality of the psyche and not with the reality of physis."

The only action that Jung recognizes as real is from the unconscious and never from any independently other person or reality. Hence, he states, "God acts out of the unconscious of man." "It is only through the psyche that we can establish that God acts upon us," and "Only that which acts upon me do I recognize as real and actual." Jung wishes, to be sure, to treat the archetypes of the collective unconscious as subjects possessing "spontaneity and purposiveness, or a kind of consciousness and free will," but it is not so clear that he is prepared to treat other persons in this way. Even the Holy Scriptures are "utterances of the soul," and God is indistinguishable from the unconscious, or more exactly from the archetype of the self within the unconscious. It is this "God" which spontaneously produces the symbols of wholeness and which forces the person "to harmonize and unite the opposing influences to which his mind is exposed from the unconscious."[19]

Our concern in all this is not Jung's psychology of religion per se but the image of the Psychological Man that is reflected in it, an image that takes Jung to the amazing lengths of denying that there is any effective action upon the person except that which comes through the unconscious. Poor a servant as Freud's ego is, it is at least exposed equally to the reality of the environment and to the inner world of superego and id.

The Jungian will point out, of course, that you cannot relate genuinely to others without first removing the "projections" which distort one's image of them and that when you have removed these projections and become individuated, you will then go out and have a true relationship with the world. But I believe that the means must be like the end if the end is to be reached. If I relate to you now in order to become whole, I doubt that I shall be able to come back later and relate to you as if the relationship were of value in itself. When it was pointed out to me, in connec-

19. Jung, *Answer to Job*, pp. 191 f., 178, 199 f., 18, 178. (*Answer to Job* is also included in *Psychology and Religion: East and West.*) For a full-scale treatment of Jung, see Maurice Friedman, *To Deny Our Nothingness*, Chapter 9, "Carl Jung," on which much of this chapter is based.

tion with a criticism that I published of Jung, that Jung was enormously concerned with others because in others we find our own shadows, animas, and animuses, I replied that it was precisely this that I objected to: that he was not concerned with the other in his or her otherness, or uniqueness, but primarily in terms of the becoming of one's self. I do not think that there is such a thing as personal wholeness, or integration, minus a direction—and that direction is your unique direction, discovered ever anew in your response to the world that calls you out. I would go even further and say that we are not given to ourselves for certain purposes, such as the recognition of our own "hang-ups." There *is* a proper time for concerning oneself with one's projections, introjections, shadow, anima, and animus. But even our hang-ups, projections, introjections, and complexes begin in relationship with others and only later become our "shadow."

Psychologism is a habit of mind. It is the tendency to divide the reality that is given to us into two parts—one of which is an outer world into which we fit ourselves and the other of which is an inner psyche into which we fit the world. This is an understandable division. Much of our lives is lived in terms of it. But the wholeness that is possible for us as human beings can never be found by regarding the outer as a mere reflection of the inner, but only by overcoming the division itself. The real person has to live with that inner brought into relation to the outer. If we have "vocation," it is because we are called, and that call cannot come to us only from within. Even if the call comes in mystic ecstasy or in a dream, we do not have the right to say that it is simply *in* us. We do not actually exist divided into "inner" and "outer" except for certain useful purposes. In reality we are a whole in every moment in streaming interaction with everybody and everything.

By robbing us of the simple contacts with what is not ourselves and the touchstones that emerge from them, psychologism robs life of its finest reality. This is a reality which we cannot sustain and maintain, to be sure, a reality which does not relieve us of the task of working with and on ourselves when we are brought back to ourselves. Nonetheless, the possibility is there of finding real life not by leaving our inwardness behind but by bringing it with us as a whole in our response to whatever comes. This is not a question of "inner" versus "outer." We need all our inwardness, for it is an integral part of our wholeness as persons. Our wholeness is not a state of being but a presence, an event, a happening that comes into being again and again in our contact and response.[20]

20. For a fuller discussion of psychologism, per se, see Maurice Friedman, *The Hidden Human Image*, Chapter 15, "Aiming at the Self: The Paradox of Psychologism and Self-Realization," pp. 274–285.

Chapter 6

Aiming at the Self: The Paradox of Humanist Psychology and the Human Potential Movement

"I believe," wrote James Agee, "that every human being is potentially capable within his 'limits,' of fully 'realizing' his potentialities; that this, his being cheated and choked of it, is infinitely the ghastliest, commonest, and most inclusive of all the crimes of which the human world can accuse itself. ...I know only that murder is being done against nearly every individual on the planet."[1]

The concept of self-realization has its earliest philosophical roots in Aristotle's doctrine of entelechy, according to which every individual being needs to realize his or her own *telos,* or goal. Since then it has developed through innumerable variations of humanism, mysticism, vitalism, pragmatism, psychologism, and existentialism. The concept of self-realization lies at the heart of Sartre's "project"; of Heidegger's realization of one's ownmost, not-to-be outstripped, nonrelational possibility; of John Dewey's ethics of potentiality; and of the thought of such varied psychologists and psychoanalysts as Rollo May, Carl Rogers, Medard Boss, Erich Fromm, Karen Horney, and Abraham Maslow. As a holistic approach to the person, an approach which sees his or her future actuality unfolding from the present possibility, it represents a decisive step forward toward the human image. Nevertheless, this approach is not concrete enough or serious enough to

1. Quoted with no reference in George B. Leonard, *Education and Ecstasy* (New York: Delacorte Press, Delta Books, 1968), p. 24.

grapple with the problem of finding authentic personal direction. Values cannot be based on self-realization, as Karen Horney proposes in her "ethic of self-realization," with its assumption of an already given "real self" contrasted with the pseudo-self erected by neurotic pride and striving for perfection.[2] Neither are we much helped by Erich Fromm's criteria of the "mature and integrated personality" and "the truly human self"; for the real meaning of each of these terms depends upon one's image of what is human and one's sense of one's own personal direction. In *Man for Himself,* Fromm claims that *"there is no meaning to life except the meaning man gives his life by the unfolding of his powers by living productively"* and that the one task that matters is "the full development of our powers within the limitations set by the laws of our existence." But to know what is meant by living productively and by the full development of one's powers, one must *already* have meaning in life, meaning that can be actualized through one's meeting with life. At the same time Fromm's definition of "a genuine ideal as any aim which furthers the growth, freedom, and happiness of the self" vitiates his repeated emphasis on spontaneous relations to others by making self-realization the goal and relations to others the means to that goal. We cannot define ourselves or our potentialities apart from the direction we give them, apart from what we become in relation to others.

In *The Heart of Man,* in probably conscious response to those who have accused him of ignoring the repressed negative aspects discovered by depth psychology, Fromm discusses "the most vicious and dangerous form of human orientation." This is the love of death, malignant narcissism, and symbiotic-incestuous fixation: three orientations which combine in their extreme form into a "syndrome of decay" that prompts destruction and hate for their own sake. In opposition to the necrophilic person, Fromm posits a *"biophilic ethics"* which is clearly his own image of the human:

> Good is all that serves life; evil is all that serves death. Good is reverence for life, all that enhances life, growth, unfolding. Evil is all that stifles life, narrows it down, cuts it into pieces. Joy is virtuous

2. Karen Horney, *Neurosis and Human Growth: The Struggle Toward Self-Realization* (New York: W. W. Norton, 1950).

and sadness is sinful. . . . The conscience of the biophilous person is not one of forcing oneself to refrain from evil and do good. It is not the super-ego described by Freud, which is a strict taskmaster, employing sadism against oneself for the sake of virtue. The biophilous conscience is motivated by its attraction to life and joy; the moral effort consists in strengthening the life-loving side in oneself.[3]

Attractive as this emphasis is, it does not bring us appreciably closer to a direction-giving image of the human than does the "productive orientation" of Fromm's *Man for Himself*, to which Fromm refers. Not even the status which Fromm gives this image by his claim that "the pure biophile is saintly" can rescue it from the fatal ambiguity of what is meant by "life." Fromm cannot capture the human in the sheer love of life since the human being's relation to life is different from that of the rest of life. Life is not worth loving and enjoying unless implicit in the concept of life is living well. Growth is not necessarily a good unless implicit in the concept of growth is growth in a direction that realizes positive values. Fromm's syndrome of growth does indeed imply such values—love, independence, openness—but for that very reason his scheme is circular. His ethics of growth rests on another set of ethics, which in turn he seeks to ground in the ethics of growth.

In *Man for Himself*, Fromm recognizes that what Man *is* cannot be understood without including what Man *ought* to be. "It is impossible to understand him and his emotional and mental disturbances without understanding the nature of value and moral conflicts." Yet he defines the source of values in purely pragmatic terms, the good being what contributes to the mature and integrated personality, vice being what destroys it.

> The character structure of the mature and integrated personality, the productive character, constitutes the source and the basis of "virtue." . . . "Vice," in the last analysis, is indifference to one's own self and self-mutilation. Not self-renunciation nor selfishness but self-love, not the negation of the individual but the affirmation of his truly human self, are the supreme values of humanistic eth-

3. Erich Fromm, *The Heart of Man: Its Genius for Good and Evil*, Vol. XII of *Religious Perspectives*, ed. Ruth Nanda Anshen (New York: Harper & Row, 1964), p. 47.

ics. If man is to have confidence in values, he must know himself and the capacity of his nature for goodness and productiveness.[4]

Fromm presents us here with a succession of terms to each of which we have a positive emotional response—"mature," "integrated," "productive," "affirmation of his truly human self"— but to none has he given concrete content. He defines values in terms of "the mature and integrated personality" and "the truly human self." Yet these terms themselves imply values and would have to be defined in terms of values. Thus, Fromm offers us one set of explicit, conscious values which are merely instrumental and another of implicit, assumed values the source of which he does not explore.

Fromm bifurcates "conscience" into an authorization conscience that demands submission out of fear—not too different from Freud's conception of the conscience as the introjection of the censure of the father—and a humanistic conscience which is "the guardian of our integrity." The humanistic conscience "is the voice of our true selves which summons us back to ourselves, to live productively, to develop fully and harmoniously—that is, *to become what we potentially are.*" But what is meant by the "true self" and by becoming "what we potentially are"? Fromm knows the beneficial results of authentic existence, but he cannot point to such existence itself. Thus, he falls into the trap of psychologism, self-realization, and aiming at the self.

The image of the human distinguishes between our potentiality and the direction we give to our potentiality. Such terms as self-fulfillment, self-expression, and self-realization are comforting to many in our age who vaguely feel that they are living without expressing themselves; yet they offer little real help toward reaching an image of the human, for they leave unanswered the question of what direction one must take in order to "realize" or meaningfully "express" the self. If we had only one set of potentialities, then the question could be simplified to one of realizing them or not realizing them. But our potentialities are, in fact, legion, and until we bring them under the guidance of a personal direction, they are likely to conduct themselves as the demons who named

4. Erich Fromm, *Man for Himself: An Inquiry into the Psychology of Ethics* (New York: Rinehart, 1947), p. 7.

themselves thus before Jesus, rather than as angelic bearers of abundant life. To give our potentialities direction means to decide—not consciously, but again and again through the response of our whole being—what is the more and what is the less authentic choice in a particular situation, what is the more and what is the less authentic attitude and response, what way is *ours* because it is true for us and because we have committed ourselves to be true to it. Albert Schweitzer had not only to choose whether to be an organist, a theologian, or a missionary doctor in Africa, but also, and more significantly, to choose whether to become one sort of person or another sort of person. We become ourselves through each particular action; we choose ourselves in each act of becoming. Actually, we cannot know our real potentialities in the abstract at all. All we can know are generalizations about ourselves from past situations in which we have had other and different resources. Our actual resources are inseparably bound up with what we are as *persons,* with our direction as persons, and with what calls us out in the concrete situation. We cannot foresee these. Potentiality is not in us as an already existing objective reality. We know it only as it becomes actuality in our response to each new situation.

The Viennese logotherapist Viktor Frankl, serves as a useful contrast to the psychologists mentioned above. The main cause of neuroses in our age, he suggests, is the existential frustration that arises from not being able to find a meaning in life. The therapist cannot give a meaning to the patient. "It is up to the patient himself to 'find' the concrete meaning of his existence." In conscious opposition to Sartre, Frankl sees this meaning as one that is discovered, not invented. Potentialities, too, Frankl sees as inseparable from the demand that life places on us to make meaningful and valuable and, thus, existential commitments. The individual has many possible choices, but at any given time only one of them fulfills the necessity of his or her life task. Responsibility and maturity mean choosing one potentiality which shall be actualized, one which is worth actualizing, and relegating the rest to nonbeing. "Thus the problem really just begins when potentialism ends."[5]

5. Viktor Frankl, "On Logotherapy and Existential Analysis," *American Journal of Psychoanalysis,* Vol. XVII, No. 1 (1958); Viktor Frankl, "Beyond Self-

Although Abraham Maslow is best known for making "peak experiences" and self-actualization the goals of his psychology, he recognized, as Brewster Smith has pointed out, that not only do self-actualizing people tend to be altruists but also that "their basic needs can be fulfilled only by and through other human beings, i.e., society." What is more important, he stated, is that "Self-actualizing people are, without one single exception, involved in a cause outside...themselves...some calling or vocation in the old sense." That means that they do not aim at becoming self-actualizing persons but instead are involved in their work. It is Maslow who turned the by-product into the goal by identifying self-actualization as the result of a fully human psychology. I must agree, therefore, with Brewster Smith's conclusion that, "This, of course, is only a restatement of the Christian wisdom that he who would find his life must lose it—that happiness is a by-product that eludes direct pursuit" and with his further assertion that this is an enduring truth about selfhood and its fulfillment which needs to be fitted into a conceptually articulated self-psychology.[6]

The word "self" has no meaning, I submit, apart from the way in which we bring our deep responses to life situations. Jesus said, "He who finds his life must lose it." But if you set out to lose your life *in order* to find it, you will not really have lost it and therefore *cannot* really find it. This is the paradox of aiming directly at self-realization as a goal instead of allowing it to come as a by-product of living itself. If I follow Fromm and other psychologists who tell me that it is important to have good relationships with other people that I may be a mature and productive person, then the relationships are merely functional, and I shall not even become the person I aim at being. Only when I forget myself and respond with *all* myself to something not myself—only then do I even have a self; for only then does my true uniqueness emerge. It is, of course, possible for a relationship that starts out as merely functional to end by being organic. In that sense, Fromm's advocacy

Actualization and Self-Expression," *Journal of Existential Psychiatry*, Vol. I, No. 1 (1960).

6. M. Brewster Smith, "On Self-Actualization: A Transambivalent Examination of a Focal Point in Maslow's Psychology," *Journal of Humanistic Psychology*, Vol. XIII, No. 2 (Spring 1973), pp. 28, 30.

of good relationships with other people "may well prepare the proper climate for the burgeoning of the deeper relationships," as my editor friend, Richard Huett, has said to me. But this depends upon our forgetting our original motivation at some point and getting caught up in the relationship as something of reality and value in itself.

The road beyond potentialism is the direction-giving human image. Real values, the values that are operative in our lives, are brought into being through our decisions made in response to the specific situations that we meet. These values become touchstones of reality for us. We carry them forward not as abstract principles but as basic attitudes, as life-stances that we embody and reveal in ever-new and unexpected ways. They remain with us, latent in the deepest levels of our being, ready to be evoked and given form by the situations that call us out. These basic attitudes are the images of the human that unite one moment of live dialogue with another; for it is not abstract consistency of principles or ideals but faithfulness in responding to the present with the touchstones that live in us from the past that gives unity and integrity to our lives as persons.

In contrast, therefore, to those psychotherapists who seek to derive a direction-giving image of the human from the concept of self-realization, we must recognize that self-realization cannot be made the goal either of therapy or of life, however indispensable it is as a by-product and corollary of a true life. Self-realization is corrupted into psychologism, in fact, precisely at the point where one aims at oneself. This is the age-old paradox. We are called upon to realize ourselves. Yet to aim directly at so doing is always self-defeating. You begin with yourself, but you do not aim at yourself, as Martin Buber says in his little classic, *The Way of Man*. You must recognize the contribution of your inner contradiction to the conflict between you and other people, yet you must not bog down in being preoccupied with yourself. Once we make ourselves the goal—even if we do so in the hope of becoming more of a person and thereby being able to help other people more effectively—we embark on a path that is not likely to lead us beyond ourselves to genuine dialogue with others. Instead, we are more and more apt to view our relations with others in terms of our own progress toward becoming whatever we feel we should become.

At the end of a one-day seminar that I led, I suggested that the people present break up into small groups, one of which I joined as a participant–observer. In that small group there were two people, a woman and a man, who had the same complaint—that they continually observed themselves in all that they were doing and therefore never did anything freely, spontaneously, with their whole being. "My problem is that I am really a very good psychological analyst, and I know it," said the woman. "I bring it to all of my relations in life," she added, "and therefore I never feel anything that catches me up." She brought to my mind Virginia Woolf confessing with shame in her diary that she could never meet a friend without thinking, "How can I use her in my novels?" The man leading the small group asked her, "Is there any place where you do, in fact, come out of this?" "Yes," she answered, "if I go to a ballet, or if I get angry." Here at least—caught up by beauty or taken over by anger—she forgot herself and broke out of the vicious circle.

Even this hope seemed denied to the man in question. After my talk to the group as a whole, he asked me, "Isn't the most important thing to discover your conflicts, your defensiveness, and work on that?" "Yes," I replied, "that is true. Yet you may never get beyond that." He had been with enough groups, he continued, to become aware that he was a defensive person. His problem, he realized, was that he did not hear things as they were said and respond to them spontaneously but heard them only in reference to his own feeling of being vulnerable. He wanted to get out of this by focusing on the fact that he was defensive, but this was equally self-preoccupation. The story he told our small group—of his one and only encounter experience in which he got everyone so angry that they stripped him naked and threw him into the hall—was told so matter-of-factly and impersonally that even this sharing could not break him out of the circle. He was wrapped up in his image of himself. "Rake the muck this way, rake the muck that way, it is still muck" said the Rabbi of Ger. "What does Heaven get out of it? While we are brooding over our sins, we could be stringing pearls for the delight of heaven!"

Many of the ever-growing number of people who are associated with what is called the human potential movement would probably object to our call to go beyond potentialism and aiming at oneself. Between 1965 and 1974, well over a hundred growth centers sprang up in all parts of America, as well as in England, in Japan, and elsewhere. The forms of these centers, to which by now more than a million and a half people have come, are variegated in the extreme. The techniques used may include sensory awareness, relaxation, breathing exercises, direct confrontation, theater games, gestalt exercises, guided fantasy, and nonverbal communication.

In most encounter groups the here and now is emphasized and past experiences, including early trauma, are minimized. A corollary of this emphasis is the focus on personal responsibility for one's fate as opposed to accepting historical explanations or excuses. Rather than harping on past experiences and magnifying mistakes and inadequacies, encounter groups focus upon capacity for love and joy and other positive aspects of living. Yet this is equated by many facilitators with concentration on the future and on one's potential rather than on the present and the unrepeatable reality of this group.

Jack Gibb, cofounder with Lorraine Gibb of TORI and one of the pioneers in "T groups," distinguishes therapy from training groups by the fact that the latter focus upon personal growth and increased human potential rather than upon remedial or corrective treatment, upon interpersonal data rather than upon analysis of the unconscious, upon group processes and intermember interactions rather than upon leader–patient relationships, upon trying out new behavior rather than achieving new insight or motivation.[7] William R. Coulson, one of the leaders of the La Jolla Program, sees encounter groups as a natural corrective to the goals of education in our society. By teaching students to hide their feelings, to be knowledgeable rather than ignorant, to say only what can be said well, and to show only those sides of themselves that are guaranteed approval, schools leave a learning gap that encounter groups fill. Schools do not teach us to express negative feelings or positive ones or to communicate creative thoughts and half-formed ideas that cannot be clearly articulated.[8]

One of the most important claims that encounter and marathon

7. Jack R. Gibb, "Sensitivity Training as a Medium for Personal Growth and Improved Interpersonal Relationships," *Journal of Interpersonal Development*, Vol. I (1970), p. 7.

8. William R. Coulson, *Groups, Gimmicks, and Instant Gurus: An Examination of Encounter Groups and Their Distortions* (New York: Harper & Row, 1972), pp. 25 ff.

groups make is that they promote the achievement of pure, intimate human contact through mutual self-disclosure, emotional expression, and acceptance of self and others—all of which leads to further development of the capacity to love and be loved. Carl Rogers attributes the phenomenal growth of the intensive group experience to the discovery by ordinary people "that it alleviates their aloneness, and...brings persons into real relationships with persons." Freed to become aware of our isolation amid affluence and the role-interacting-with-role, mask-meeting-mask character of most of our life, we learn also that this tragedy of life is not necessary, that we can modify our existential loneliness through the "intensive group experience, perhaps the most significant social invention of this century."[9] One wonders if many people in the encounter movement do not confuse the reciprocal release of pent-up emotions and deeply repressed feelings with genuine relationship. Openness in communication is an important part of genuine dialogue, to be sure, but many encounter leaders seem to be mostly concerned about each person expressing his or her feelings honestly and expect real mutuality to emerge of itself from this self-expression.

In the encounter movement, too, the search to bring the human image out of hiding often leads only to greater eclipse. I have myself witnessed poor, insensitive, or authoritarian leadership dovetailing with clichéed demands and expectations on the part of the participants plus the tendency of leaders and participants alike to rely on techniques as opposed to moment-by-moment awareness of the concrete situation. Carl Rogers criticizes "the manipulative, interpretative, highly specialized expertise which appears to be more and more prominent in the training of group leaders" and "the 'exercises' which have become such a large bag of tricks for many group leaders."[10] The authoritarianism on the part of such leaders may mesh with a corresponding authoritarianism on the part of participants who not only suspend their own responsibility in the leader's favor but use what they take to be the rules as clubs with which to attack one another. "Group work offers infi-

9. Carl R. Rogers, "Ethical Questions of the 21st Century," unpublished manuscript, Humanist Institute of San Francisco.
10. Carl Rogers, *Carl Rogers on Encounter Groups* (New York: Harper & Row, 1970), p. 157.

nite opportunities to slip into a well-disguised, smoothly rational-
ized authoritarianism," writes Thomas Greening, especially on
the part of trainers and participants eager to pursue a predetermined goal of emotional intensity and sensual awakening.[11]

Basic encounter groups seem to offer many people who are in-
tellectually detached or in some other way cut off from their emotions the hope of getting back to what they really feel. Actually,
many such people are as cut off from the feelings of others as from
their own, in addition to which they are programmed to listen for
cues and to put other people on pegs rather than to really hear
them. They not only miss the feeling with which and out of which
the other speaks, they miss the plain meaning of what he or she
says, the standpoint from which he or she says it, and not infrequently the very words that he or she utters. No wonder that in
trying to cure this condition, people not only turn to feelings but
away from words. The danger of this emphasis on feelings at the
expense of thought is that we may cease to struggle for the word
and take it seriously. There are few places left for the person who
cares about the whole human being, the person who brings himself or herself and wrestles with the word. What such a person
says is all too often reduced by those who have jumped on the
bandwagon of "feelings = reality" to "Those are just words" or
"You intellectuals always think in terms of labels." Those who do
this, I have observed, act as if *their* words are really feelings
whereas the words of those they are attacking are "merely
words."[12]

Our feelings are important, of course. We must go back to them
and start there. When we have a deep and perhaps violent emotional breakthrough, it is a revelation of something hidden in the
depths of our souls, something heretofore, perhaps entirely unsus-
pected. This can mislead us into seeing the emotions that are thus
brought to light as the only reality and into depreciating what before was accessible to the conscious mind. An equal and corollary
danger is to see the breakthrough as complete in itself, instead of

11. Thomas C. Greening, "Encounter Groups from the Perspective of Existential Humanism," in *Existential Humanistic Psychology*, ed. Thomas C. Greening
(Belmont, California: Brooks/Cole, 1971), pp. 84 f.
12. Cf. George Miale, "Is Feeling More Real than Thinking?" *Journal of Humanistic Psychology*, Vol. XIII, No. 2 (Spring 1973), p. 58.

seeing it as a little light lighting up a long, dark road up a mountain and down into a canyon—a road which you have to walk in your everyday life before this "breakthrough" can be made lasting and meaningful.

The concentration on feelings most often means the concentration on individual feelings, the feelings experienced within you and expressed to others. This dualism between inner feeling and outer façade raises serious questions about the claims that are made for the carry-over of encounter group experiences into everyday life. In many encounter groups an individual is taken out of his or her world and gets in touch with feelings that he or she can only express outside of any situation which places a demand on him or her as an active person working together with other persons. Our chances of infusing our stance in the world with genuine personal wholeness are far greater, it seems to me, if we hold the tension of the unique person and the social role in such a way that even in the dialogue with bewildering social hierarchies we become more and more ourselves. "Most sensitivity training, as now practiced, is too short in duration to be of optimal enduring effect," writes Jack Gibb. "The effects of training seem to be more enduring when integrated in long-range programs of institutional change and growth," thereby becoming an organic part of management, organization, family life, or whatever subculture may be involved.[13]

The result of the location of feeling within is that experienced encounter-goers and even experienced encounter leaders often tend to see the expressions of others as being important to the individual mainly as "feedback" that will enable him or her to come still more into touch with inner feeling. It is only one short step to a solipsistic hell in which we imagine that feelings are only in ourselves and that the feelings of others concern us at most only as reflections or projections of our feeling. You may be my "anima," to use Jungian terminology, and I may be your "animus," but there can be no direct contact between us as real persons. It is true that we can feel things within that no one else can feel equally well, but we do so as persons whose thoughts and feelings are tied up in the most immediate fashion with other persons.

13. Gibb, "Sensitivity Training," p. 23.

One of the virtues of the encounter group is that it has room for hostility and anger as well as for positive emotions and does not trap people into repressing the negative because they think they ought not to feel it. Yet even in the encounter group a hidden morality often exists, a morality which leads one to say to oneself, "I ought to feel gut-level hostility," or to say to someone else, "You can't be for real. You haven't expressed any anger or hostility." Even in the rare case where the leader, like Carl Rogers, is willing to allow the participant to remain psychologically on the sidelines and not commit himself or herself to the group, the group is not likely to allow such a member to remain in this stance:

> As time goes on the group finds it unbearable that any member should live behind a mask or front. . . . The expression of self by some members of the group has made it very clear that a deeper and more basic encounter is *possible,* and the group appears to strive intuitively and unconsciously toward this goal. Gently at times, almost savagely at others, the group *demands* that the individual be himself, that his current feelings not be hidden, that he remove the mask of ordinary social intercourse.[14]

How can one know that this particular moment is the right time for that person to get so involved? Maybe the person is very sensibly protecting himself or herself against being psychologically murdered. The person may have taken the true measure of this group and may know intuitively, if not consciously, that it does not have the resources to confirm his or her otherness, whatever its rules, aspirations, and stated intentions. Although I would not assume with Bernard and Constance Apfelbaum that holdouts always "express the inevitable presence of real risk in a group," my own experience as a member of a family therapy team leads me to agree that the holdout may sometimes be the identified patient in the family therapy sense (i.e., the one who is carrying the burden for the whole group and who, if helped sympathetically, may also help rescue the whole group). What the group member needs, first of all, is to trust, not the group, but himself or herself. Only if the leader helps the participant see that his or her reactions to the group contain a grain of truth, will he or she have a ground on

14. Rogers, *Carl Rogers on Encounter Groups,* p. 27.

which to stand, a ground from which "self-disclosure would no longer be so risky." How can encounter leaders assume, they ask, "that if a group member is uninvolved and guarded, it is his problem and not the group's? Does not this imply an unstated assumption that if you can learn to trust the group first, then it becomes trustworthy?"[15] If this assumption is held, then there is a strong pressure on the facilitator to urge members to take the risk, whether it be in the name of mental health, moral commitment, the courage to be, or just not to let the rest of the group down.

The temper of the particular group and the emphases of the facilitator inevitably affect our attitude toward our own emotions so that what we express is not the raw emotion but the emotion shaped by our attitude as a member of this group. This means that there is a particular social matrix for the feeling that makes it different from what it would be if we were alone or with a friend or a member of the family. What you feel about your wife or husband, for example, is going to come out modified by the context of this group or by the leadership style of the facilitator. Your sense of the group's attitude in general and of the attitude of some or all of its members toward you in particular will affect the form, intensity, and even content of the feelings you express. This is seldom recognized. Instead, feeling, like potentiality, is treated as a substantive reality that is in us and only needs to be brought out. The distortion that this causes has been recognized by Sara Kiesler in her research on conformity and on emotion in groups. Group "support" is not always wise, she points out, and "well meaning but ignorant members of the group can compound, rather than help, the problem," if the expression of emotion is not accompanied by the trainer's guidance in examining the emotion. The group climate is otherwise often characterized by ambiguity and frustration; for even while a supportive climate is encouraged, "each member of the group wonders if he will be accepted if he acts as 'openly' as expected."

> There is social pressure to be supportive and loving; there is social pressure to give negative feedback and to disconfirm others' self-perceptions. There is pressure to be "real." At the same time, one

15. Bernard and Constance Apfelbaum, "Encountering Encounter Groups. A Reply to Koch and Haigh," *Journal of Humanistic Psychology*, Vol. XIII, No. 1 (Winter 1973), pp. 53–67.

should experiment with new behaviors. Members try to grow and learn, but the leader fails to supply clear cues, goals or rewards. The very stirred-up state creates a need for cognitive explanation, but no one explanation is obvious. The person must look to the group for emotional labels, and...the emotional state will vary drastically according to the group situation.[16]

Foremost among the factors which can prevent an encounter group from being real are the expectations which some participants bring with them of instant enlightment, revelation, and joy. During one encounter group that I led at Big Sur, Esalen, we went around the room at the beginning asking each person what he or she hoped for in coming to the weekend. After hearing some of the others refer to my books, one woman said, "I don't want any lectures [No one had any in mind]. I was here six months ago for a seminar with Will Schutz, and I got joy. I am a social worker, and I've come back to be recharged. I've got to get joy again this weekend." Such insistence on outcome and result means, quite simply, the unwillingness to start from where the group is and by the same token the impossibility of finding a genuine direction of movement in the present.

We cannot avoid the route of feeling, yet expecting and demanding feeling can get in the way of true spontaneity, of our really being open and really meeting one another. It may lead, indeed, to that supreme contradiction in terms—"planned spontaneity." It takes the most sensitive listening to distinguish between those feelings that really grow out of the group being together and those that arise as part of the effort to be "groupy." It takes a great deal of listening to allow what happens to come forth spontaneously—not inhibited by the self-images of the participants, which tell them in advance what their strengths and weaknesses are supposed to be, but also not inhibited by the group pressure to get down to the "true self" and express the emotions that the group holds to be "real." Putting the paradox another way, to deal directly with feelings is often to deal indirectly with them. Talking about feelings does not necessarily mean expressing them. At times, group members have said to me, "You are not showing your hostility, or your anger," and I

16. Sara Kiesler, "Emotion in Groups," *Journal of Humanistic Psychology,* Vol. XIII, No. 3 (Fall 1973), p. 25.

have replied, "Certainly I am! I don't have to say 'I'm angry' to express anger." In fact, if I say I feel angry, already I am likely to be a little less angry; for by putting a label on my emotion, I have to some degree taken myself out of the situation.

Rogers recognizes this danger of hothouse spontaneity quite explicitly and links it with the "old pro" phenomenon, those veterans of previous encounter groups who "feel they have learned the 'rules of the game' " and subtly or openly try to impose these rules on newcomers.

> Thus, instead of promoting true expressiveness or spontaneity, they endeavor to substitute new rules for old—to make members feel guilty if they are not expressing feelings, or are reluctant to voice criticism or hostility, or are talking about situations outside the group relationship, or are fearful to reveal themselves. These "old pros" seem to attempt to substitute a new tyranny in interpersonal relationships in the place of older conventional restrictions. To me this is a perversion of the group process. We need to ask ourselves how this travesty on spontaneity comes about.[17]

Another "travesty on spontaneity" to which Rogers points is the way in which some facilitators make the group reach the emotional openness that they desire:

> I am well aware that certain exercises, tasks set up by the facilitator, can practically force the group to more of a here-and-now communication or more of a feelings level. There are leaders who do these things very skillfully, and with good effect at the time. ... At its best it may lead to discipleship (which I happen not to like): "What a marvelous leader he is to have *made* me open up when I had no intention of doing it!" It can also lead to a rejection of the whole experience. "Why did I do those silly things he asked me to?" At worst, it can make the person feel that his private self has been in some way violated, and he will be careful never to expose himself to a group again.[18]

What began as a chance to recover the freshness of being together with others without performance expectations and with the possibility of making mistakes is in danger of becoming an institution, Coulson points out, "with new rules of procedure, recognized

17. Rogers, *Carl Rogers on Encounter Groups*, p. 55.
18. Rogers, *Carl Rogers on Encounter Groups*, p. 48.

centers for doing it, gurus, formulas, known truths, hierarchies in charge, and credentials for being a practitioner." "To be frank, encounter groups are now drowning in gimmickry."[19]

We would like to live more intensely, more vitally, more fully. We would like to touch and contact others. We would like to share love and joy. Sometimes within encounter groups this is exactly what happens. But the more we aim at this goal, the more one part of us will be looking on from the sidelines, anticipating and measuring results, and for that very reason not living fully in the present. Our problem is that we are divided within ourselves, that we are not in genuine dialogue with one another, and that we live immersed in a deep existential mistrust. These sicknesses of our human condition cannot be overcome simply by the will to wholeness, openness, and trust or by the magic of technique.

By far the most forceful and eloquent statement of the paradox of the hidden human image as it has been manifested in many encounter groups is that of the psychologist and educator Sigmund Koch:

> The group movement is the most extreme excursion thus far of man's talent for reducing, distorting, evading, and vulgarizing his own reality. It is also the most poignant exercise of that talent, for it seeks and promises to do the very reverse. It is adept at the image-making maneuver of evading human reality in the very process of seeking to discover and enhance it. It seeks to court spontaneity and authenticity by aritifice; to combat instrumentalism instrumentally; to provide access to experience by reducing it to a packaged commodity; to engineer autonomy by group pressure; to liberate individuality by group shaping. Within the lexicon of its concepts and methods, openness becomes transparency; love, caring, and sharing become a barter of "reinforcements" or perhaps mutual ego-titillation; aesthetic receptivity or immediacy becomes "sensory awareness." It can provide only a grotesque simulacrum of every noble quality it courts. It provides, in effect, a convenient psychic whorehouse for the purchase of a gamut of well-advertised existential "goodies": authenticity, freedom, wholeness, flexibility, community, love, joy. One enters for such liberating consummations but inevitably settles for psychic striptease.[20]

19. Coulson, *Groups, Gimmicks, and Instant Gurus*, pp. 5, 56, 165.
20. Sigmund Koch, "The Image of Man Implicit in Encounter Group Theory," *Journal of Humanistic Psychology*, Vol. XI (1971), pp. 112–117.

Koch attacks the debasing, schematizing, and vulgarizing of language that the encounter movement has produced and still more "the reducing and simplifying impact upon the personalities and sensibilities of those who emerge from the group experience with an enthusiastic commitment to its values." Even more than behaviorism he sees the "entire, far-flung 'human potential' movement" as "a threat to human dignity" which obliterates the content and boundary of the self by transporting it into "public space." Self-exposure functions as a therapeutic absolute in the work of the movement, he claims, whatever the leaders consciously intend. The threads which Carl Rogers identifies in the encounter process are really "a kind of Pilgrim's Progress toward the stripping of self" (e.g., cracking masks, positive closeness, here-and-now trust, and feedback). The uncritical approval of any kind of feedback, says Koch, makes "the chances for simple-minded callow, insufficiently considered or reductive shaping" of the individual by the group high. Given the common factors of an adventitiously assembled face-to-face group, the encouragement by the leader of frank, direct, and uninhibited feedback, and the assumption that self-disclosure as facilitated by trust leads to the enhancement or realization of human potential, these criticisms must apply, says Koch, not just to some but to all encounter approaches. While not denying that some approaches or leaders are "less 'bad' than others," he sees the danger in all encounter groups of "simplistic lexicons" through which joking or wit is interpreted as evasiveness; sleepiness, boredom, or torpor as withdrawal; a raised voice as hostility; blocking as defense; and abstract statement as intellectualist concealment, or "mind-fucking."

In a reply to Kock, Gerard Haigh, past president of the Association for Humanistic Psychology, suggests that encounter groups do not necessarily violate the uniqueness of persons because encounter groups are not programmed to fit a predetermined model. Although Rogers and others predict what may happen in encounter groups, "the humanistic approach to leadership is not to make the group process happen as predicted but rather to let it happen as it will." Whereas group facilitators in training often try to make things happen as a way of assuaging their anxious uncertainty about their own effectiveness and some "old hands" even employ techniques which have proved effective in the past, most leaders, Haigh holds, are nearer the "facilitating awareness" pole of the continuum. Most facilitators approach the task "in the spirit of discovery, trying to allow the participants to unfold in their own way, or not to unfold, if they wish." The beauty of encounter groups, approached in a spirit of discovery, is that they provide an endless opportunity to revise, expand, and deepen our image of the human and our ways of growing toward it.[21]

21. Gerald V. Haigh, "Response to Koch's Assumptions about Group Process," *Journal of Humanistic Psychology,* Vol. XI (1971), pp. 129–132.

PART THREE

Obscuring and Revealing the Human Image in Existential Psychology and Family Psychiatry

Chapter 7

Existential Psychotherapy: Rollo May

Existential Psychotherapy and Humanistic Psychology

EXISTENTIAL psychotherapy and humanistic psychology are two separate streams that have developed independently of each other in America and yet have converged in significant ways, particularly in the theory and practice of Carl Rogers. What characterizes both schools is an emphasis upon the wholeness of the person, coupled with an equal emphasis upon the full reality of the therapist–client relationship. Beyond that they have often diverged.

Like existentialism itself, existential psychotherapy is a temper uniting diverging schools of thought rather than an essentially unified approach. More eclectic than existentialist philosophies—because they are more pragmatically and less philosophically oriented—even the individual theories of existential psychology and psychiatry often tend to be more of an interplay of trends than a single trend. Humanistic psychology, as we have seen in our discussion of the Human Potential Movement, has tended to emphasize becoming, self-actualization, self-realization, and human potentials, whereas existential psychology and psychiatry, like all existentialism, has represented a movement from the general to the particular, from the abstract to the concrete, from the static to the dynamic, and from the detached, "objective" knower to the engaged, involved, and responsible knower.

Beyond that, both streams converge again in an emphasis upon authenticity—the realization of values in human existence. Both streams, particularly through the figures of Rollo May and Carl Rogers, have made an important contribution to revealing the hidden human image. Because of their emphasis upon "healing through meeting" we are reserving our discussion of May's *Love and Will* and of most of Rogers' writings on therapy to our subsequent volume *Dialogical Perspectives in Psychotherapy*.

Rollo May and Existential Psychotherapy

Existential psychotherapy, according to Rollo May, has developed in response to the "ontological hunger" of those who ask the ultimate questions about Man, neurosis, health, and fulfillment. It is based on the assumption that it is possible to have a science of Man which does not fragmentize Man and destroy his humanity at the same time it studies him. In contrast to the tendency to make technique an end in itself, existential psychotherapy should have flexibility and versatility, "varying from patient to patient and from one phase to another in treatment with the same patient." This means the recognition that the patients' commitment, their basic decision about their lives, precedes their knowledge of themselves. In fact, they cannot even permit themselves to get insight or knowledge until they are ready to take a decisive orientation to life and have made the preliminary decisions along the way. "Existential therapists are particularly concerned... with responding to elements of *will* and *decision* in the patient's utterances," but it is the patient and not the therapist who must make the decision. Patients must be aware of the tragic possibility that they will fail and not regard the therapist as a magic helper who will see that nothing harmful will happen to them. This includes the possibility of suicide. "I am doubtful," says May, "whether anyone ever takes his life with full seriousness until he realizes that it is entirely within his power to commit suicide but chooses himself not to."

May follows Tillich in seeing neurosis as a way of shrinking the possibilities of existence in order to preserve that centeredness which is essential to the existing person. If the common neurotic danger in Freud's day was that of the person who is afraid to participate in the lives of others and lives "in narrowed reactions and shrunken world space," in our day the danger is more often that of dispersing one's self in participation and identification with others until one's own being is emptied. May approves of Buber's emphasis in one sense and Sullivan's in another "that the human being cannot be understood as a self if participation is omitted." May recognizes too that acceptance by and trust in another person is a necessary condition for one's awareness of oneself as "I am." His central emphasis, however, is on this subjective awareness, rather than on the relationship. For May, both the method and the goal of psychotherapy center in this self-consciousness which enables one to transcend one's immediate situation and know that it is *he* who is experiencing it or to whom it is happening. Applied to sexuality this means that sexual impulses are always conditioned by the *person* of the partner. "What we think of the other male or female, in reality or fantasy or even repressed fantasy, can never be ruled out." The therapist's task is to help transmute the patients' awareness that they are threatened into the consciousness that *they* are the ones who are threatened, or, in the language of Martin Heidegger, that they are the subjects who *have* a world. Only whey they see the world and their problems in relation to themselves will they be able to do something about them. Only when they recognize that they are capable of turning against themselves and denying themselves will they be able to affirm themselves. This is true in particular of suicide and death: "The capacity to confront death is a prerequisite to growth, a prerequisite to self-discovery and self-consciousness." May accepts Freud's death instinct to the extent of recognizing that one can never love completely the people to whom one is devoted and there will always remain some element of destructiveness. By the same token, one can never know if one's decision is really the right one, yet one must make it anyway. All of life is a risk since all of life means reaching out into the future. "This risk inheres in self-consciousness."

"The goal of therapy," says May, "is to help the patient actualize his potentialities. To do this the therapist must recognize neurosis as a creative adjustment to the threat to centeredness, and he must recognize anxiety and guilt as containing constructive possibilities if they are accepted and understood by the patient." May distinguishes, of course, between existential guilt and anxiety and neurotic guilt and anxiety. The former are not repressed, do not express themselves in symptom formation, and are not necessarily destructive. Even the unconscious experiences must be understood as a part of the unity of the patients that has been blocked off because they cannot as yet permit themselves to actualize these experiences. When they are able to admit that they can know and communicate only partially, they can use anxiety and guilt as a constructive part of relationships in which they have greater openness and humility than before. May does not agree with Helen Merrell Lynd that shame is more basic than guilt. On the contrary, he thinks that shame waters the matter down. Like fear in relation to anxiety, he thinks that it has to do with specific incidents (whereas to Lynd shame is pervasive and general even as anxiety is to May and Sullivan).

Normal guilt leads us not only to make good our injuries to the order, as Martin Buber says, but also to being open, humble, loving in relationships with other human beings. But for this very reason Buber's concept of "meeting," or "encounter" (as *Begegnung* is also translated), is central to psychotherapy, according to May. In encounter, therapists are open to the worlds of their patients and experience what the patients are experiencing. To do this they must be more than well-trained technicians. They must be real human beings. "To be able to sit in a real relationship with another human being who is going through profound anxiety, or guilt, or the experience of imminent tragedy taxes the best of the humanity in all of us." These encounters do not go so far as to enable patients to become themselves simply through our accepting them, as Carl Rogers seems to say. Acceptance by their therapists *frees* patients to confront the question of the experiencing of their own being, but the crucial question is still what the patients, in their awareness of and responsibility for their existence, do with the fact that they can be accepted.

May sees the awareness of one's own being as occurring basically on the level of grasping and being conscious of one's self. "Though the social realm is a necessary condition of the experience, the experience itself is not to be explained *essentially* in social categories." May describes this experience as " an experience of *Dasein,* realized in the realm of self-consciousness," in which *Dasein* means one's being there as a subject who exists through constantly transcending itself in relation to its world. May's difference from Buber and the existentialists of dialogue is that the ground of self-being is for him *prior to* meeting whereas Buber sees the self as developing the unique ground on which it stands and from which it related precisely *through* the meeting of I and Thou.

This does not mean that May fails to give the existential encounter between therapist and patient its dues. Like many other existential psychotherapists, May replaces the Freudian concept of "transference" by Buber's concept of "meeting" and "encounter," "an event occurring in a real relationship between two people," as May puts it. "When we are dealing with human beings," writes May, "no truth has reality by itself; it is always dependent upon the reality of the immediate relationship." If therapists abstract themselves from their relationships with their patients and do not participate in the relationships with real personal involvement, they will not even see the other persons as they are. May goes so far as to define the therapist as "existential to the extent that, with all his technical training and his knowledge of transference and dynamisms, he is still able to relate to the patient as 'one existence communicating with another,' to use Binswanger's phrase." A prime difference between Freud's "transference" and the meeting of therapist and patient is that the latter, "far from being a revival of an ancient interpersonal relationship...works through the very fact of its novelty."

For existential psychotherapy, consequently, technique follows understanding. Technique and data must be subordinated to the encounter between therapist and patient. Therapists must understand the patient as being-in-their-own-world and must create a situation in the consulting room in which the patient can understand and experience this. Important in the creation of these creative encounters is *presence*. "*Presence*"—a term which is central both to Gabriel Marcel and to Buber—"implies that the encounter between the patient and therapist is taken as a real one in its total meaning." Existential truth, to May as to Buber, "always involves the relation of the person *to* something or someone."

May makes a distinction between *knowing* the patient and knowing *about* him or her that is very close to Buber's distinction between the knowing of the I–Thou relationship and the knowledge of I–It:

What we are talking about is an experience every sensitive therapist must have countless times a day. It is the experience of the in-
stantaneous encounter with another person who comes alive to us
on a very different level from what we know *about* him. . . . We may
know a great deal about a patient from his case record. . . . But
when the patient himself steps in, we often have a sudden, sometimes powerful, experience of here-is-a-new-person. . . *The grasping
of the being of the other person occurs on a quite different level from our knowledge of specific things about him.*

This does not mean I-Thou instead of I-It but rather an alternation between the two in which the I-Thou remains dominant,
giving form and meaning to the raw material of I-It:

Nothing we are saying here in the slightest deprecates the importance of gathering and studying seriously all the specific data one
can get about the given person. This is only common sense. But
neither can one close his eyes to the experiential fact that this data
forms itself into a configuration given in the encounter with the
person himself. . . . When we seek to know a person, the knowledge *about* him must be subordinated to the overarching fact of his
actual existence.

In this connection May cites Ludwig Binswanger, who, as we
shall see, is directly indebted to Buber for his insight into the dual
mode of I and Thou, the being-with-each-other of loving:

Knowing another human being, like loving him, involves a kind of
union, a dialectical participation with the other. This Binswanger
calls the "dual mode." One must have at least a readiness to love
the other person, broadly speaking, if one is to be able to understand him.[1]

Consistent with his definition of the goal of therapy as the realization of the patient's potentialities, May defines *guilt* as the per-
sistent denial of potentialities. We are not always in a position to
realize our potentialities, but our existential guilt, and with it our
neurosis, enters in when we *deny* them. May quotes the *Dasein-*

1. Rollo May, "Contributions of Existential Psychotherapy," May's second
Introductory Essay in Rollo May, Ernest Angel, and Henri F. Ellenberger, eds.,
Existence: A New Dimension in Psychiatry and Psychology (New York: Basic Books,
1958; New York: Simon & Schuster, Touchstone Books [paperback], 1967),
pp. 37 f.

sanalyst Medard Boss on this point: "If you lock up potentialities you are guilty against (or indebted to) what is given you in your origin, your 'Core.' In this existential condition of being indebted and being guilty are founded all guilt feelings, in whatever thousand and one concrete forms and malformations they may appear in actuality." To May, in fact, this is only one form of existential, or ontological guilt, for he recognizes an equally basic guilt arising from the fact that one perceives one's fellows through one's own limited and biased eyes. "This means that he always to some extent does violence to the true situation of his fellow, and always to some extent fails fully to understand and meet the other's needs."

May's first aspect of guilt as failure to realize one's potentialities can only be understood in the context of May's treatment of ontological guilt in general. Following the pre-Socratic philosopher Anaximander, May holds that guilt is a universal existential reality, present in every human being. It is involved in consciousness as such and is a part of the limitation of our finite expression. Our failure to realize our potentialities is only one aspect or expression of this deeper structure.[2]

May recognizes a number of dangers in the relation of existentialism to psychotherapy. One of these is the danger Sartre has warned against of therapists dominating their patients through their own subjectivity. This comes when therapists lose sight of the fact that they are seeing the patients through their own limited and biased viewpoints and absolutize their own perceptions and understandings. Another is the danger of trying to analyze *being*. An individual's being is shown "in his right to exist as a person, his possibilities for self-respect and his ultimate freedom to choose his own way of life." To try to analyze these evidences of being rather than assume them is to violate the fundamental being of the clients themselves, to call into question their existence as human beings. May also recognizes the danger of confusing analysis of existence with existence itself. Concern with existence does not

---

2. The last three sentences are based upon a personal communication from Rollo May in response to my statement about his approach to existential guilt in my book, *To Deny Ôur Nothingness*. Aside from this, the whole of this section on existential psychotherapy is based on May's second introductory essay to *Existence*, "Contributions of Existential Psychotherapy," pp. 37–91.

give ready-made phenomenological categories a privileged position over against the categories of Freud or any other psychologist. "The temptation to use existential concepts in the service of intellectualizing tendencies is especially to be guarded against," May points out. "Since they refer to things that have to do with the center of personal reality, these concepts can the more seductively give the illusion of dealing with reality."

May sees the question of repression as essential for psychoanalysis, and on this issue he sides with Freud. Those who do not believe in the tendency to repress the unpleasant, despairing element will hold that the patient grows "naturally" toward health if given the right soil and security. May believes, in contrast, that "the critical issues of psychoanalysis lie precisely in the phenomenon that the human being can deny, repress, 'lie' to himself, and indeed *has* to do so to survive unbearable threats to his security, the self-system which he built up in childhood." Psychotherapy affords the relationship in which this process of progressive denial of "knowing what we know" is reversed. But the "healing" that reverses this denial of consciousness does not take place through "meeting" alone. Everyone in therapy has to make a journey home alone. All must sooner or later confront and experience for themselves the basic conflicts in their own childhood family constellation. "Therapy gives a world of trust and understanding in which confronting becomes possible, but the therapist cannot protect her (the patient) from this kind of aloneness."

Chapter 8

Phenomenology and Existential Analysis: Sartre, von Weizsäcker Boss, and Binswanger

Existential Phenomenology: Temporality, Distancing, and Immediacy

A distinctive contribution of existential psychotherapy, Rollo May points out, is that it places time in the center of the psychological picture and in so doing replaces the Freudian emphasis on the past, the realm of natural history, with the concern for the future, that mode alone in which the self, personality and—I would add—the image of the human can be understood. Particularly impressive in *Existence*, the anthology which May coedited, are the essays that analyze schizophrenia, hallucinations, and the world of the compulsive in terms of temporality and of such other phenomenological categories as spatiality, loss of distance, and causality. In "Findings in a Case of Schizophrenic Depression," the French phenomenologist Eugene Minkowski demonstrates what happens to a man whose sense of the future is blocked. "Each day life began anew, like a solitary island in a gray sea of passing time." The normal synthetic view of time disintegrates and life is lived "in a succession of similar days which follow one another with a boundless monotony and sadness." As a result, "the individual life impetus weakens, the synthesis of the human personality disintegrates," and "there remains only the person face to face with a hostile universe."

Erwin Straus describes the confrontation with a hostile universe in other terms. In his essay in *Existence*, "Aesthesiology and

Hallucinations," he undertakes to analyze the relation of all the senses to one another in order to reconstruct the world of the well person and that of the ill. Hallucinations, in his account, are "deformed modalities," "pathological variations of the basic relation I-and-the-*Other*." The reciprocity of tactile experience is annulled. Voices address one yet remain anonymous. A world of hostile powers assaults one sexually yet remains at a distance. The barriers of one's intimate life are leveled off and the innermost sphere of his existence invaded. Straus's conclusion is as disturbing to our ordinary way of feeling, or rather of not feeling, about the schizophrenic as it is to our ordinary way of thinking about him or her: "The schizophrenic does not withdraw from reality into a land of dreams; he is immersed in an alien reality with physiognomies which in the severest cases paralyze all action and cut off all communication."

In his central theoretical work, *The Primary World of Senses,* Straus goes beyond any merely descriptive phenomenology of temporality and spatiality to an anthropological grounding of the whole world of senses, time, and place in a primary movement and a primary distancing. Both the Here and the Now are particular delimitations of the totality of my self-world relation. "In the Now, I experience my self-world relation and my self as that which becomes." Distancing arises out of this becoming, out of reaching and desiring. The articulation of distances depends on my Here and Now, and direction depends upon distance. The unity of time and space "would not be possible without openness into the future," and this implies both sensing and moving. Distance is the spatiotemporal form of sensing, "the form of a process of becoming which is open to the future and which itself is not yet fully determined." Psychosis by the same token is a deformity of distance and movement. It may take the form of the passivity of depersonalized individuals whose hallucinations are the result of the world pressing in on them and of all sympathetic communication being suspended or of the groundlessness of those who have no firm stance, no hold on themselves which enables them to limit themselves, as over against their world. Depressed persons are alienated both in time and space. "Frozen in unmoving time," they look at the world as if from above, unable to enter into relation with it.

The combination of primal distancing and primal relation which is central to Martin Buber's philosophical anthropology is also present in Straus's "primary world of senses" as well as in Viktor von Weizsäcker's untranslated *Der Gestaltkreis* ("The Unity of Perception and Movement") both of which thinkers Buber refers to in "Distance and Relation" (*The Knowledge of Man*). Individual sensations of touch and vision do not produce communication, Straus points out. "Because I *am* in communication, a particular given here and now can determine me." To exist is to exist in the world but also opposite it, directed toward it, and meeting it in its counterdirection. Every sensing subject has a Here which is of equal dignity with the There and which enables it to move toward the There in communication with the *other*.

> Community, mutual understanding, and communication and connections between living beings founded on the relations of the together-with and towards-each-other, which do not eliminate the monadic autonomy of the partners, their duality or plurality- ....Community demands distance which continues even during the most perfect forms of togetherness, of nearness, of the "we."...The encompassing *other* which becomes visible to us in seeing, makes possible the communion between us; it mediates between Me and You....All communication, lingual included, is based in the being-with-another of mobility, of meeting and fleeing in a common surrounding world....In primal and basic communication I am not a knower and the other is not the object of my knowledge. He is not a thing singled out from a neutral background as an object of special interest. I discover the other, my fellow man or fellow creature, as a partner in my waking motor intentions, as a being which can come near me or withdraw from me.[1]

The distinguished neuropsychiatrist Kurt Goldstein, although emphasizing the unity of togetherness rather than the distance, makes a statement closely similar to that of Straus in his discussion of "the sphere of immediacy," which represents the deepest character of the world as opposed to the subject–object world in which "we experience only isolated parts of ourselves and the world." By surrendering ourselves to the world with which we come in contact, we achieve the immediacy which "makes unity

1. Erwin W. Straus, *The Primary World of Senses,* trans. Jacob Needleman (New York: The Free Press of Glencoe, 1963), pp. 178–289.

possible between the world and ourselves, particularly in our relationship to other human beings." These experiences of immediacy disturb the stability of the ordered world, particularly when our expectations of a response are disappointed. "Our well-being and possibilities for self-realization are endangered, our very existence and that of the world," for they are all based on the sphere of immediacy. Although order is necessary for the attainment of knowledge, "the impulse to *seek* for knowledge originated fundamentally in the sphere of immediacy."

> Through it, human life acquires its dynamic character. In this sphere is not only the source of all creativity, the development of friendship, love and religion, but also those possibilities for failure, sorrow and anxiety which are part of our life. While being in the sphere of immediacy may involve danger, we deliberately take this risk, since only thus can we realize ourselves fully.[2]

Existential Analysis: Jean-Paul Sartre, Viktor von Weizsäcker, Medard Boss, and Ludwig Binswanger

Like the term psychoanalysis, existential analysis sometimes means an objective attempt to understand the mental illness of a patient and sometimes a practical attempt to heal. Most existential analysts assume that understanding is the necessary groundwork for healing, but some of them do not particularly stress going beyond the analysis itself. This analysis usually takes the form, not of an inquiry into origins and causes, as in Freud, but of a phenomenological description and an attempt to capture the patient's world design. The phenomenological approach developed by Wilhelm Dilthey and Edmund Husserl, each in his own way, holds that the knowers in the human studies, including psychology, cannot be merely detached scientific observers but must also participate themselves, for through their participation they discover both the typical and the unique in the aspects of human life that they are studying. At the same time, they must suspend the foregone conclusions and the search for causality that characterize the approach of natural scientists in favor of an open attempt to discover what offers itself.

2. Kurt Goldstein, *Human Nature in the Light of Psychotherapy* (New York: Schocken Books, 1963), "Foreward—1963," pp. x–xiii.

The existential psychoanalysis of Jean-Paul Sartre is essentially a phenomenology of this sort. Sartre rejects the Freudian unconscious which magically acts as its own censor in such a way that it knows what it must keep itself from knowing. "Psychoanalysis introduces intersubjectivity into my subjectivity," says Sartre, "and posits a lie without a liar. How could the patient *resist* the analyst," Sartre asks, "if he did not know on some level what the analyst was driving at? He must be conscious of the drive that is to be repressed *in order not to be conscious of it.*" This means that psychoanalysis "has established between unconscious and consciousness an autonomous consciousness in bad faith."

In contrast to Freud, Sartre puts forward the self which, in the middle of all facticity, inescapably remains responsible for itself, for the person which it becomes through its own project, and for the image of the human which it chooses for itself and for all human beings. Whereas empirical psychoanalysis may see individuals as wax molded by their history and seek to determine the *complex* which causes their later development, existential psychoanalysis seeks to determine the *original choice* and recognizes nothing *before* the original upsurge of human freedom. Sartre also rejects the hypothesis of the unconscious in favor of a psychic act which, just because it is coextensive with consciousness, lacks those shadings and connections that would enable it to become an object of knowledge. What is more, the fact that the psyche is itself determined by the original choice limits the possibility of investigation. The "project-for-itself can be experienced only as a living possession." The original choice to which existential psychoanalysis leads back accounts for the original contingency which cannot be reduced to any general concept or complex, such as the libido or the will to power. From the start it is absolute concreteness which remains unique. It can be particularized in behavior but not made more concrete. Sartre illustrates this approach with such phenomenological categories as the hole and the slimy, which to him are not symbols for repressed sexuality but original projects.

Viktor von Weizsäcker gives more actual insight into the subject in *Gestaltkreis*; for instead of asserting absolute freedom, as does Sartre, he sees the task of existential analysis as the recognition of the struggle between "having to do" and "wanting to do," the outcome of which is the decision that leads to action. In this struggle, what is wanting in the mentally ill is often not the ability to do, but the ability to will. Thus, instead of saying of the patients that they *would* if they only *could*, as a deterministic psychoanalysis might, it would often be more exact to say that they *could* if they only *would*. Von Weizsäcker also has a subtler understanding of the I as an essentially unstable subjectivity whose continuity and identity is threatened not only in the great crises of mental illness but also, less dramatically, in the ordinary flow of everyday life. The subject is composed of one-time occurrences, but it has to perpetuate itself over and beyond these. It must perpetually be restored in spite of instability and crisis. This ephemeral character of the subject accounts for the fact that there is so much fear of subjectivity. Yet the re-erection of the subject which follows every crisis proves its strength and resilience. This restoration, however, can never make the subject a simple unity to itself; for it continually finds itself in another world when waking and dreaming, enjoying and reflecting, lying down and dancing, composing and performing. These "are all so different from one another that one may describe the one as infinitely strange in relation to the other."[3]

Through our openness to phenomena, says Edmund Husserl, the chief philosophical exponent of phenomenology, we may attain an "eidetic" insight into ideal forms or essences and thus discover human nature, not by disregarding its particular manifestations, but through them. Both Martin Heidegger and Jean-Paul Sartre retain Husserl's phenomenological method, with its corollary of the knowing ego and the known phenomena, while rejecting his idealism. Heidegger, in particular, claims not only to dispense with all universals but to be able to reach, just through the analysis of existentalia (as he calls them), the fundamental ontological reality. To Heidegger the subjects cannot be thought of apart from their world nor the world apart from the subjects who are there in it. Both Medard Boss and Ludwig Binswanger found their existential analysis upon Heidegger's

3. Viktor von Weizsäcker, "The Unity of Perception of Movement," in *The Worlds in Existentialism: A Critical Reader*, ed. with Introductions and a Conclusion by Maurice Friedman (Chicago: University of Chicago Press Phoenix Books, 1973), pp. 404 f.

view of the self as existing precisely through its continual transcending of itself in relation to its world. Binswanger stresses the
world-design that results from this self-transcendence, whereas
Boss rejects "the world design" as an unduly subjectivistic reading of Heidegger and stresses instead Heidegger's later teaching
of Man as the shepherd of being who brings all things into the
light of being through his relationship to them. Beyond this,
Binswanger seems more concerned with the phenomenological
understanding of his *Daseinsanalytik*, Boss more with the therapy.

In sharp contradistinction to the subjectivity of both Sartre and
Binswanger, says Boss, "Heidegger expressly mentions man's *immediate* ability to understand himself and what he encounters (i.e.,
things and other human beings) in the unity of the 'there,' in the
world-openness of his horizons." The way one handles or becomes aware of something discloses and illuminates the world.
The fact that the world is one's world does not stand in the way of
one's existing with others and of one becoming immediately
aware of them as what they are. One's "being-there" (*Dasein*) discloses the meaning of what one encounters, and *Dasein* is always
found *with* what it encounters. As a result, "man depends on
what he encounters as much as the encountered depends on the
disclosing nature of man for its appearance." It is the essence of
existence to be with others, and my world is necessarily one which
one shares with others.

> We never exist primarily as different subjects who only secondarily
> enter into interpersonal relations with one another and exchange
> ideas about the objects all of us perceive. Instead, as any direct ob-
> servation shows, we are all out there in the world together, primar-
> ily and from the beginning, with the same things shining forth in
> the common light of all our existences.[4]

Here Boss gives a more basically social interpretation of
Heidegger than does Rollo May. The implication of this sociological approach to psychiatry is that "no psychopathological symptom will ever be fully and adequately understood unless it is
conceived of as a disturbance in the texture of the social relationships of which a given human existence fundamentally consists."

4. Medard Boss, *Psychoanalysis and Daseinsanalysis*, trans. Ludwig Lefebre (New
York: Basic Books, 1963), pp. 55 f.

Applied to psychotherapy, this means that transference too must be regarded as a genuine relationship in which the partners disclose themselves to each other as human beings. The patient's love of the therapist is not "really" love of the parent. "It is the love of the analyst himself no matter how immature and distorted it may appear because of the limitations of perception imposed on the patient by his earlier relationship to his real father." Boss sees the therapist as the one who possibly for the first time in the patient's life really understands and accepts the patient even though he is stunted by neurosis. "The analyst permits him to unfold more fully his real and essential being within a safe, interpersonal relationship." Existential analysts discard everything which is an obstacle to an immediate understanding between them and their patient—the psychoanalytic libido theory and the labored psychoanalytic interpretation of symbols. The healing factor in psychoanalysis is not "living out," therefore, but an increasingly full appropriation of all of one's life-possibilities. Unless the patient becomes aware of and acknowledges as his own all his possibilities of relating to what he encounters, no authentic responsibility is possible. But these possibilities must be carried out only "in accord with the most productive unfolding of a patient's whole existence, including the welfare of those whom he encounters."

Boss has an exalted view of the role of the therapist, who becomes, in his reading, the very image of Heidegger's authentic human being. In order for the emotional interhuman relationship between analyst and patient to be adequate, the analyst must have "matured into the freedom of selfless concern for his patients." This "means that the analyst has all his own sensual and egotistical tendencies at his free disposal and can keep them from interfering secretly or openly with his genuine concern and selfless love for the patient." Being human, the analyst "is called upon to disclose both things and men," to bring them into the full light of being, as Heidegger would say.

> This knowledge increases his sensitivity to all the obstacles which generally reduce the potential relationships of a patient to a few rigid and inauthentic modes of behavior. Such sensitivity in turn enables the Daseinsanalyst to carry out an "analysis of resistance," wherein the patient is tirelessly confronted with the limita-

tions of his life and wherein these limitations are incessantly questioned, so that the possibility of a richer existence is implied.[5]

Boss compares man's special manner of being-in-the-world to the shining of a light, in the brightness of which all things can appear and reveal themselves in their own, proper nature. This openness to the world makes possible the direct and immediate understanding between human beings. Even the mere act of perceiving another already involves us in his or her particular world-relatedness. "Thus from the very first encounter between the therapist and patient the therapist is already together with his patient in the patient's way of existing."

Like Heidegger, Boss holds that the world needs Man as the realm of lucidity necessary for the phenomena to manifest themselves. Allowing oneself thus to be claimed and needed is what Man owes to what is and has to be, says Boss. As a result, his definition of existential guilt is, in fact, quite different, in context, from the failure to realize one's potentialities, a definition which Rollo May adduces in Boss's name. What Boss says, rather, is that "all human feelings of guilt...are rooted in this state of owing" which is "man's existential indebtedness and guiltiness." Every phenomenon of the human conscience, according to Boss, can be understood as this summons to discharge the human duty of being "a guardian of everything that has to appear, to be and to unfold in the light of any given human existence." The burden and oppression of guilt "are overcome in the joyous readiness to place himself without reservation at the disposal of all phenomena as the light and clearing into which they can appear and unfold, and as their custodian." The most mature form of human openness, that which is the highest aim of all psychotherapy, is that "ability-to-love-and-trust which permits all oppression by anxiety and guilt to be surmounted as mere misunderstandings." Patients who free themselves from the entanglement of neurotic guilt feelings and willingly accept their genuine existential indebtedness "experience their life really as an anxiety-free, fortunate and meaningful state of being-summoned to belong immediately to the luminating world-openness."

5. Boss, *Psychoanalysis and Daseinsanalysis*, pp. 233–236.

Through his approach to existential guilt, Boss eliminates the necessity for the distinction that May makes between guilt as the result of a failure to realize one's potentialities and guilt as the result of a failure to meet the needs of one's fellows. To Boss, these would be corollaries of one basic existential indebtedness. On the other hand, although Boss says of one's fellows that as human beings they are altogether different from things and are encountered as being-in-the-world even as I am, he does not really offer an understanding of guilt that grows basically out of the interhuman. Rather guilt for him is the same whether it means the disclosing of the nonhuman phenomena or the human. So that if he overestimates Heidegger's sociality in making being-together so completely a corollary of being-there, he nonetheless fails to see the encounter with persons or things in any really mutual way comparable to Buber's I–Thou relationship.

Nor does he recognize the essential and constructive nature of anxiety, as do Tillich and May. "Love does not eliminate anxiety," comments Sabert Basescu on Boss's "anxiety-free" stage. "Rather freedom from pathological anxiety makes love possible." To Basescu, Boss seems to want to return to an unconscious communion with nature in which there is no self and therefore no anxiety. Henry Elkin suggests that Boss's approach to therapy really means "an aura of masterful imperturbability, an ineffable superiority over the tormented and needy patient." This "loving acceptance," says Elkin, "is really an inhuman context very different from that in a true I–Thou relationship. It does not make patients feel accepted in their real selves. On the contrary, their deeper selves remain tormented by loneliness, frustrated hatred, and a guilt which is all the more intensified by the therapist's expressions of goodwill and acceptance." In other words, it leads to the transformation of repressed, destructive hatred into warm feelings of "love"—"the inherently grasping, rapacious power and control-seeking love of the possessive mother or the seductive child."[6]

6. The presentations both of Boss and of his critics are based on the Boss section in Maurice Friedman, *The Worlds of Existentialism,* pp. 426–440. The comments by Sabert Basescu and Henry Elkin were originally printed in Medard Boss, "Anxiety, Guilt and Psychotherapeutic Liberation," *Review of Existential Psychology and Psychiatry,* Vol. II, No. 3 (September 1962), pp. 197 f., 203–207.

Ludwig Binswanger's "fruitful misunderstanding" of Heidegger, to use his own phrase, takes its start from the world-design that results from being in the world and the three realms of one's relation to oneself, one's relation to others, and one's natural environment. Being-in-the-world, according to Binswanger has eliminated the fatal gap between subject and object, or self and world, and thus overcome "the fatal defect of all psychology" which reduces human existence to a mere subject of knowing. Now the way is open, Binswanger claims, for scientifically exact investigations of the modifications in mental disease of the essential structure of being-in-the-world. The result of such investigations is the discovery of the patient's world-design and with it the possibility of understanding from within even those patients with whom the therapist can establish no "empathic" communication. "It is one of the most impressive achievements of existential analysis," writes Binswanger, "to have shown that even in the realm of subjectivity 'nothing is left to chance,' but that a certain organized structure can be recognized from which each word, each idea, drawing, action, or gesture receives its peculiar imprint."

"The real battle is the battle over the image of man," says Ludwig Binswanger of his argument with his lifelong friend, Sigmund Freud. Freud's genetic approach reduces human history to natural history. "Only human existence is genuinely historical." Hence, Freud misses that in Man which is specifically human.

> Freud approaches man with the (sensualistic–hedonistic) idea of the natural man, the *homo natura*. According to this idea, which is possible only on the basis of a complete taking apart of being human as such and a natural-scientific-biological reconstruction of it, psychoanalysis has developed its entire critique and interpretation of the historical experiential material. History becomes natural history, essential possibilities of human existing become genetic developmental processes. Man, being thus reconstructed, is at bottom a driven or drive-dominated creature.... If the primary concern in this is libidinous instinctuality, it is so because sexuality is seen by Freud throughout as the true history-forming force within the individual life-history.[7]

7. Ludwig Binswanger, "The Case of Ellen West," in *Existence: A New Dimension in Psychiatry and Psychology*, ed. Rollo May, Ernest Angel, Henri F. Ellenberger (New York: Basic Books, 1958), p. 314 f.

Freud's one-sided naturalist distortion of the image of the human focuses on what one has to be, says Binswanger, and leaves out what one may and should become, one's own freedom in relation to the psychological given. "Even the neurotic is not only a neurotic and man in general is not only one compelled." Existence does not lay its own ground, Binswanger points out, but it is still left with freedom in relation to that ground. "That Ilse got just that father and that mother was her destiny, received as a heritage and as a task: how to bear up under this destiny was the problem of her existence. Hence, in her 'father complex' were destiny *and* freedom at work."[8]

The real key, Binswanger suggests, is not the Oedipus complex, as it is for Freud, but the world-design that makes such a filial tie possible. This world-design stands outside the contrast conscious–unconscious. "It does not refer to anything psychic but to something which only makes possible the psychic fact." Existential analysis attempts to understand words, actions, and attitudes "from basic modes of human existence prior to the separation of body, soul, and mind, and of consciousness and unconsciousness." The issue between phenomenological analysis and psychoanalysis essentially is whether actions, dreams, and speech directly reveal a meaning taken in the context of the personality, as Binswanger holds, or mask a *hidden* meaning, as Freud thinks, "an unconscious second person." Freud's idea of a *homo natura* is a scientific *construct* based on a destruction of one's experience of oneself. It sees man as world or in-the-world but leaves out one's projection and disclosure of the world, Heidegger's being-in-the-world. As a result the doctor–patient relationship for Freud is also one-sided and irreversible and that between researcher and object of research even more impersonal and finished. This does not mean that *Dasein* is completely free in Binswanger's view. It does not lay its own ground or have power over it. It is "thrown" into its situation and has to be "as it is and can be." Only one who scorns these limits becomes neurotic, whereas one who knows of the unfreedom of finite human existence and obtains power over one's existence within this very powerlessness is unneurotic or "free." "The *sole* task of 'psychotherapy'," Binswanger insists, "lies in assisting man toward this power."

8. Ludwig Binswanger, "The Case of Ilse," ibid., p. 225.

Binswanger cannot be understood on the basis of Heidegger alone, however—not even on the basis of his own particular interpretation of Heidegger. There is an equal admixture of the phenomenological concern with temporality and spatiality, of Kierkegaard's "sickness unto death," and of Buber's I–Thou meeting. Just how Binswanger has brought these varying elements together in his existential analysis is best illustrated in his famous essay, "The Case of Ellen West." Ellen West was not Binswanger's own patient, but he had sufficient access to the records of her case to undertake an exhaustive phenomenological analysis.

Binswanger places an analysis of temporality close to the center of his discussion of Ellen West. Ellen West's existence is ruled by the past, encircled in a bare, empty present, and cut off from the future, writers Binswanger. Robbed of the authentic meaning of her life that only the future can give, Ellen West is driven to fill in time, to fill up the existential emptiness, through an insatiable animal greed that represents a desperate and always unsuccessful flight before the dread of nothingness. Binswanger also analyzes Ellen West in terms of a vertical axis of spatiality—the ethereal world, the terrestrial world, and the world of the tomb, or swamp. He shows how the loss of the ground on which to stand and work left her two conflicting worlds with the inevitable outcome of a dissipation of the ethereal world into empty possibility and the complete triumph of the world of the tomb.

Binswanger described Kierkegaard's concept of "sickness unto death"—the "desperate" wish to be oneself and not to be oneself—as "one of the most important contributions to the purely 'anthropological' understanding of certain clinical forms of insanity, and particularly of schizophrenia." He sees "sickness unto death" as central to Ellen West. As was the case in her earlier defiance of her role as a woman, so now in her desperate conflict between a greed which would make her fat and a wish to be thin, Ellen West betrays the stubborn and defiant wish to be herself and not to be herself. "Fate wanted to have me fat and strong," said Ellen, "but I want to be thin and delicate." Ellen's wish to be thin is calamitous, says Binswanger, because it fixates her in the conflict between her ethereal world and the gloomy, dull, damp world of the swamp. Ellen's dread of becoming fat is only the end of the encirclement process by which her existence becomes closed to new possibilities. Ellen knows herself that she cannot live on if she does not succeed in "breaking the ban" and getting out of her preoccupation with self. Her existence, as a result, is "consecrated to death." Yet Binswanger sees Ellen's "freely chosen death" as in some sense a liberation from her "no exit" hell and a real, if tragic, entrance into authentic existence which "marks the victory of this existence over the power of 'hell'."

Binswanger sees Ellen West's suicide as both "arbitrary act" and "necessary event." "Who will say where in this case guilt begins and 'fate' ends?" One of the most interesting aspects of this case, indeed, is its setting aside the customary notions that suicide is necessarily bad and that, in the case of a mentally ill person, it is necessarily purely a product of the sickness. The essential emptying or impoverishment of Ellen's existence was "nothing but a metamorphosis of freedom into compulsion," writes Binswanger, but her suicide itself was the final desperate breakthrough of the free personality:

> That this existence can once again break through its congealing, that once more it is able to burst the prison of pastness, to exchange it for the world of an authentic present, and so once more to become authentically and wholly itself—this testifies to the power of freedom in general which, to some degree, makes itself felt even in the insidious form of schizophrenia.[9]

One may wonder at Binswanger's confidence in the positive nature of Ellen's suicide, especially given his own statement that "love knows no answer to the question of whether Ellen West's suicide had to take place of fateful necessity or whether she had the possibility of escaping it."

Binswanger also analyzes the case of Ellen West in terms of Martin Buber's I-Thou relationship. Ellen West's defiance and stubbornness exclude her from "the authentic I-Thou relationship of the being-with-one another" and leave her to a world of interpersonal relations consisting of mere togetherness in which each seizes on the weak point of the other and tries to dominate him. Nonetheless, without a germ of true love, without at least

9. Binswanger, "The Case of Ellen West," ibid., p. 311.

that "readiness for Thou" which a number of lifelong relations and attachments showed that Ellen possessed, Ellen would not have suffered as much as she did from the emptiness and poverty of her existence. "To him who is completely empty of love, existence can become a burden but not a hell," writes Binswanger. Correspondingly, Binswanger sees Ellen's suicide as a triumph, despite all, of the dual mode of existence with its knowledge of a relationship beyond the isolated self. Even the way we must look at Ellen's suicide, Binswanger suggests, is given us through the I-Thou relationship which lifts us above the judgmental perspective of the plural mode of existence. The "uniting of human existence with the common ground which I and Thou share" is prior to the dichotomy of freedom and necessity, guilt, and destiny.

"Even the reader of her case history," Binswanger remarks, "must have seen Ellen West not only as an object of interest but also as Thou." In reading this case, one does, indeed, get a vivid sense of Ellen West as a person with a developed inner life and a unique personal attitude and will. Her poetry, her travels, her social work, her experiences as a student, her relations with her cousin whom she eventually married, her pitiful efforts to combat her fear of becoming fat by eating almost nothing and sometimes taking as many as sixty laxatives a day, her touching appeal to her husband when she told him that if he loved her he would kill her, and the terrible choice that he had to make between leaving her in a clinic where no hope of cure or even relief was offered and taking her away to a home situation in which her suicide was almost certain—all these bring Ellen West before us not only as a case study but also as a person, a Thou.

Binswanger describes meeting, or the I-Thou relationship, as a dual mode of love and friendship in contrast to Heidegger's authentic existence for oneself. The singular mode is the autonomous individual, essentially related only to oneself; the plural mode corresponds to the area of formal, impersonal relationships, competition, and struggle. This shades into the "anonymous mode," the mode of the individual living and acting in an anonymous collectivity. Binswanger also speaks of the dual mode as "we-ness" and as "communal love." It is the lack of the *communio* of love and the *communicatio* of friendship, says Binswanger, that leads to *extravagance*—that basic element of schizophrenia that sets up an impossible ideal and progressively narrows the ground of its own existence in relation to this ideal. Only where mere intercourse and traffic with "others" and with one's self has taken over the exclusive direction of one's existence, "only there can height and depth, nearness and distance, present and future, have so much importance that human existence can go *too far*, can attain to an *end* and a *now* from which there is neither retreat nor progress."

The *flightiness* of schizophrenic insanity signifies the impossibility of obtaining a genuine foothold, the impossibility of authentic decision, action, and maturation. "Detached from loving *communio* and authentic *communicatio*, all too far and hastily *driven forward* and *carried upward*, the manic hovers in fraudulent heights in which he cannot take a stand or make a 'self-sufficient' decision." Instead of widening the possibilities of being oneself, the extravagant ideal restricts it within ever narrower limits outside of which it becomes completely dependent and absorbed by the "world." This leads to delusions of being possessed, delivered to, surrendered to the world—all signs of the thrownness of one who exists in the bare present without genuine dwelling or location. "Where . . . existence has surrendered in so large a measure to the Overpowering, it remains totally closed to itself." It is then, like Francesca and Paolo in the Inferno, driven about, disturbed, and harassed. In complete schizophrenic autism, the *Dasein*, in retreating from the world of its fellow, from its coexistors, also forgoes or forgets itself as a self. Such an existence is given over to existential weakness in which "a person does not stand autonomously in his world" but "blocks himself off from the ground of his existence." Instead of taking one's existence upon oneself, one trusts oneself to alien powers which one makes "responsible" for one's fate.[10]

In his basic theoretical work, *Basic Forms and Knowledge of Human Existence*, Binswanger acknowledges an indebtedness to Buber equal to that to Heidegger, and passage after passage in this book bear witness to the importance of Buber's influence. Binswanger sees clearly that the I–Thou relation is an ontological reality and

10. *Being-in-the-World. Selected Papers of Ludwig Binswanger,* ed. with an Introduction by Jacob Needleman (New York: Basic Books, 1963), pp. 166, 169 f., 212–214, 218–220, 343–349, 284–286, 288, 290–292, 294 f., 300.

cannot be reduced to what takes place within each of the members of the relationship. Like Buber, Binswanger sees the self as coming to be in the I–Thou relationship. "It is out of the undivided fullness of being of the Each-Other that I and Thou first emerge to attain their 'selfhood' *in* each other." When people *take* the other *at* the other's weak point, or at the other's word, this is a fall from the being-together of meeting into the mere being-with of the self-sufficient ego. Psychology, in our time, proceeds from this absolutized individual ego and its powers, dispositions, events, processes, activities, tendencies, functions, or acts. In contrast to such purely objectifying psychology, based on the isolated ego, Binswanger sees existential knowledge as having its authentic ground and basis in the loving being-together of I and Thou.

In opposition to those who see the meeting of I and Thou as a means to the end of self-realization, Binswanger recognizes a genuine We of relationship which is more than the sum of two separate psychic or personal entities. He sets this dual selfhood of love in explicit opposition to the disclosure of the world as *mine* that Heidegger posits, and Boss accepts, as the true way of authenticating the self:

> The There of love and the selfhood of the Dasein as love does not mean a disclosedness of the There for my self...but for *our*-selves...the selfhood of love does not amount to a selfhood of the *I*, but of the *We*. The There of the Dasein as love is not disclosedness by which Dasein (as mine) is there "for itself," but, rather, "disclosedness" by which Dasein (as We) is there for our-self, for *you and me*, for *each*—and this, again, not as the sense of the being-there [Da-sein] of the world (of care), but as the being-there [Da-sein] of the "world" of Each-Other.[11]

This means that Binswanger ranges himself with the existentialists of dialogue who see the meeting between person and person as the basic ontological reality as opposed to those existentialists, whether atheist or theological, who see the interhuman as a dimension of the existence of the self. Love "does not claim the Dasein philosophically as existence of selfhood," writes

11. Maurice Friedman, *The Worlds of Existentialism* (Ludwig Binswanger, "Basic Forms and Knowledge of Human Existence), p. 417. This selection, trans. Jacob Needleham for this volume, is the only English translation of Binswanger's *Grundformen und Erkenntnis menschlichen Daseins.*

Binswanger, "but completely 'naively' as We." The I and the Thou make themselves and each other present by making room for the other and for the unique *belonging* to each other, the *homeland* of "I and Thou," the dual We. Dasein is already in its ground a loving meeting. It is this which makes possible "the meeting of lovers as lovers" in which "I and Thou are born as we-both." "Only if Dasein already has the character of meeting, only when 'I and Thou' are already part of its ontological structure, is love between Me and You at all possible." This means that loving meeting exists not only in the specific meetings with the surrounding world as the particular Thou, but that it already *is* as a going forward toward the awaited and as yet unspecified Thou which draws it and for which it seeks. This ontological existence of loving meeting makes it possible to permeate the Care world, or "ready-to-hand" world with the Thou, of love, or as Buber would put it to permeate the world of It with the Thou.

Here Binswanger makes a very important distinction between two uses of the word "heart." That which comes from or goes to the "heart" is an exclusively I-Thou phenomenon. But that which we *take* to heart or which *touches* the heart overflows in the world of the "emotional." The ontological priority of the meeting of I and Thou must not be confused, therefore, with any sort of priority of emotion or of subjectivity, which belong to the singular mode or are, at most, accompaniments of the dual mode. By the same token people cannot enter an I-Thou relationship simply by unburdening their emotions to each other but only by leaving the Dasein as mine or thine for the Dasein as ours, the Dasein as We. Each must *give* oneself to the other and *receive* the other. Only in such giving and receiving does one show one's self-sufficiency positively to the other. "Here self-hood issues only from the We." Taking-part, participation, does not bring the I-Thou relationship; it is rather that relationship which is the ground of taking-part. Like Buber, Binswanger sees this mutual participation not as a "one-sided" act of "empathy," putting oneself in the other's place, or of fellow-feeling, but as "a 'two-sided' receiving and giving based on a 'mutual' readiness for what the future has to offer."[12]

12. Ibid., pp. 416-420.

We can say, therefore, that Binswanger has made a fundamental critique of Heidegger which Boss and most other existential analysts have simply overlooked in their failure to distinguish between that being-with-others (*Mitsein*) which is an obvious part of one's existence as a self (Dasein) and the real being-together-with others (*Miteinandersein*) of dialogue, or meeting (*Begegnung*)—a word which Binswanger uses explicitly in Buber's sense. At the same time, Binswanger's "dual mode" of love is less inclusive and more in danger of becoming a sentimentalized unity than is Buber's dialogue, which includes relations of conflict and opposition so long as they are personal and reciprocal and each affirms the other in his or her own being. What is more, despite his critique of Heidegger, Binswanger's attempt to bring Heidegger's phenomenological ontology and Buber's philosophy of dialogue into one system leaves him straddling the basic division between those existentialists who emphasize the self and those who see the meeting between selves as the basic reality. The basic issue between Heidegger and Buber is whether the reality of the self, and of ontology, is found in the ground of the self and its own "mature resolute existence" or whether it is found "between man and man." If the former, one can make use of existential categories of analysis since they will tell us something of a self that may be regarded in itself; if the latter, the self must be understood in dialogue with other selves, in the *between*, and never as an ontological entity understandable prior to its interhuman relations.

The issue between the two philosophers, therefore, is a much more radical one than the question of whether one may add the I-Thou relationship as one further existential category to those with which Heidegger has already provided us. Rollo May recognizes this in placing his fundamental emphasis upon the *being* of the self as ontologically prior to its encounters with others. Boss makes the issue fuzzy by insufficiently recognizing Heidegger's ownmost nonrelational subjectivity of conscience and of existence toward death. In addition he lumps together the openness toward the world and the generalized being-with of Heidegger as if they included every type of mutual relationship between persons. Binswanger recognizes the issue in explicitly substituting existence as We, or I-Thou, for existence as I; yet his method of analysis remains that of Heidegger. From the standpoint of I–Thou knowing, it is inadmissible to substitute an ontological analysis of dialogue for dialogue itself. The result could only be to reduce dialogue from an ontological reality to an ontic one, from "all real living is meeting" to dialogue as a dimension of the self. We may question, therefore, whether Binswanger has succeeded in his attempted synthesis of Heidegger and Buber.

We may also question Binswanger's claim that existential analysts can communicate even with those schizophrenic patients with whom they cannot enter into an empathic relationship. Phenomenological analysis can certainly help in understanding, but such understanding is not the same as direct communication between one person and another. "To analyze phenomenologically the given being-in-the-world" does not necessarily mean real dialogue or understanding the other as Thou, nor does "the degree of potential and real agreement between my world and his world determine the degree of possible communication," as Binswanger asserts. Binswanger's analytic–synthetic "world-design" cannot capture the uniqueness and wholeness of a person, for these are only revealed in the dialogue between I and Thou. Binswanger's existential analysis is "existential" in the sense that it takes over the phenomenological categories of Heidegger, Kierkegaard, and Buber, but it is not "existential" in Kierkegaard's understanding of the term, namely, as deriving from and pointing back to the concrete existence of the person. Even the I–Thou relationship is used by Binswanger in the service of a phenomenological analysis of the patient's "world-design" (who in the case of Ellen West is not even his own patient). Thus, Binswanger's existential analysis tends to lead to still another *construct of the human* to set over against those given us by the older schools of psychotherapy. It does not in itself lead the hidden human image out of its hiding place.

Chapter 9

The Politics of Dialogue: Ronald Laing

The Existentialist of Dialogue

" " **M** ORE significant than the issue between atheist and theological existentialists," I have written in my chapter on "The Existentialist of Dialogue" in *To Deny Our Nothingness*, "is the issue between those existentialists who see existence as grounded in the self and those who see it as grounded in the dialogue between person and person." Existential and humanistic psychotherapists may also be roughly divided along these lines. Except for Kierkegaard, all existentialists recognize the importance of intersubjectivity. There is, nonetheless, an important difference between those existentialists who regard the relations between subjects as an additional dimension of self but see existence primarily in terms of the self, and those who see the relations *between* selves as central to human existence. Among existentialist philosophers, Heidegger, Sartre, Berdyaev, and Tillich might well fit into the former category, with Buber, Marcel, Karl Jaspers, and Albert Camus in the latter. Rollo May and Carl Rogers both emphasize the centered self or becoming, while both recognize the centrallity of dialogue in psychotherapy. But there are other existential and humanistic psychotherapists who might properly be considered existentialists of dialogue. Among these are Ludwig Binswanger, Ronald Laing, Viktor von Weizsacker, Hans Trub, Leslie H. Farber, Sidney Jourard, and Erving and Miriam Polster, the last six of whom we shall deal with at length in *Dialogical Perspectives in Psychotherapy*.

Dialogue, or the I-Thou relationship of openness and mutuality between person and person, is not to be confused with interpersonal relations in general. Dialogue includes a reality of over-againstness and separateness quite foreign to Sullivan's definition of the self as entirely interpersonal. Moreover, neither Sullivan nor Mead makes any basic, clear distinction between indirect interpersonal relations in which people know and use each other as subject and object—the I–It relation in Buber's terms—and direct, really mutual interpersonal relations in which the relationship itself is of value and not just a means to some individual satisfaction or goal. This latter relationship Buber calls "the interhuman." In interhuman relationships, the partners are neither two nor one. Rather, they stand in an interaction in which each becomes more deeply his or her self as he or she moves more fully to respond to the other.[1]

Ronald Laing and the Politics of Dialogue

Ronald Laing might well have been discussed under the heading of "Phenomenology and Existential Analysis" since, in important respects, he represents a continuation of this trend, particularly as it is represented by Sartre, Merleau-Ponty, and Binswanger. Nonetheless, unlike Sartre and like Binswanger, he recognizes the centrality of meeting, or the I-Thou relationship, and his use of Sartre is very often for the purpose of illustrating the pathology that results from the absence of relationship. What is more, he has gone beyond Binswanger in his direct attempts to use healing through meeting in his work with schizophrenics. In this respect, he represents a continuation of the work of Harry Stack Sullivan and Frieda Fromm-Reichmann. At the same time, he has attempted to construct a theoretical understanding of schizophrenia in *interhuman* and not just *interpersonal* terms, as Sullivan and Fromm-Reichmann have.

In *The Divided Self* Laing criticizes the tendency of psychiatry to take the person in isolation from that person's relation to the other and the world and to substantialize aspects of this isolated entity. Laing proposes instead to found a science of persons on the relationship between I and Thou:

1. See Maurice Friedman, *The Worlds of Existentialism*, Part IV—"Intersubjectivity," pp. 173-235 and pp. 9, 11, 542 f.

Mind and body, psyche and soma, psychological and physical, personality, the self, the organism—all these terms are abstracta. Instead of the original bond of *I* and *You*, we take a single man in isolation and conceptualize his various aspects into "the ego," "the superego", and "the id." The other becomes either an internal or external object or a fusion of both. How can we speak in any way adequately of the relationship between me and you in terms of the interaction of one mental apparatus with another? . . . This difficulty faces not only classical Freudian metapsychology but equally any theory that begins with man or a part of man abstracted from his relation with the other in his world.[2]

One acts toward an organism entirely differently from the way one acts toward a person. "The science of persons is the study of human beings that begins from a relationship with the other person and proceeds to an account of the other still as person." Laing postulates as fundamental that separateness and relatedness are mutually necessary. "Personal relatedness can exist only between beings who are separate but not isolated." Both our relatedness to others and our separateness are essential aspects of our *being*. Psychotherapy, accordingly, is an activity in which the patient's relatedness to others is used for therapeutic ends. Since relatedness is potentially present in everyone, the therapist "may not be wasting his time in sitting for hours with a silent catatonic who gives every evidence that he does not recognize his existence." "Inclusion," in Buber's sense of the term, is an absolute and obvious prerequisite in working with psychotics:

> One has to be able to orientate oneself as a person in the other's scheme of things rather than only to see the other as an object in one's own world, i.e., within the total system of one's own reference. One must be able to effect this reorientation without prejudging who is right and who is wrong.[3]

Laing goes even further than Rollo May in his distinction between knowing the person and knowing *about* the person. One can have a thorough knowledge of ego defects, disorders of thought, and hereditary incidence of manic-depressive psychosis without being able to understand one single schizophrenic. In fact, such

2. Ronald D. Laing, *The Divided Self: An Existential Study in Sanity and Madness* (Middlesex, England: Penguin Books, 1969), p. 19.
3. Laing, *The Divided Self,* p. 26.

data are all ways of *not* understanding the person; for seeing the "signs" of schizophrenia as a "disease" and looking and listening to a person simply as a human being are radically different and incompatible ways of knowing. If we do the latter, however, we must have the plasticity to transpose ourselves into another strange and even alien view of the world without forgoing our own sanity. Only thus can we arrive at an understanding of the patient's *existential position*. None of this means that we see the schizophrenic as really just the same as ourselves. "We have to recognize all the time his distinctiveness and differentness, his separateness and loneliness and despair."[4]

Laing is at his best in his insight into schizophrenia as a deficient mode of relatedness. In order that one may be related as one human being to another, he points out, a firm sense of one's own autonomous identity is required. But this is just what the schizophrenic lacks. Any and every relationship threatens the schizophrenic with the loss of identity, or engulfment. "The individual experiences himself as a man who is only saving himself from drowning by the most constant, strenuous, desperate activity." This main maneuver for this purpose is isolation, as a result of which the schizophrenic substitutes for the polarities of separateness and relatedness of the autonomous individual "the antithesis between complete loss of being by absorption into another person (engulfment) and complete aloneness (isolation)." The schizophrenic does not have the option of a third alternative—a dialogical relationship between two persons each sure of his or her own ground and for this very reason able to "lose himself" in the other.

Although it is lonely and painful to be always misunderstood, this is relatively safe compared to the danger of being understood: "To be understood correctly is to be engulfed, to be enclosed, swallowed up, drowned, eaten up, smothered, stifled in or by another person's supposed all-embracing comprehension." Similarly, all love is intolerable to the schizophrenic for it places him or her under an unsolicited obligation. The last thing therapists should do is to pretend more love and concern for their schizophrenic patients than they have. If their concern for the other is genuinely prepared to "let him be," as opposed to either engulf-

4. Laing, *The Divided Self,* pp. 33 f., 38.

ment or indifference, then there is some hope on the horizon. For the schizophrenic is equally threatened by being turned into a robot, automation, or thing, an *it* without subjectivity. If one is treated as an "it," "one's own subjectivity drains away from him like the blood from the face"; for "he requires constant confirmation from others of his own existence as a person." Yet such a one cannot sustain a person-to-person relationship and will regard the therapist as a robot, feeling that one can thereby appear to be a "person" in contrast. Thus, one who is frightened of one's own subjectivity being swamped frequently is found trying to swamp or kill the other person's subjectivity. By so doing one becomes in actuality less of a person oneself: "With each denial of the other person's ontological status, one's own ontological security is decreased." One's lack of a sense of autonomy means that one feels one's own being to be bound up in the other or the other in oneself "in a sense that transgresses the actual possibilities within the structure of human relatedness." In the face of this situation Laing sees the task of the psychotherapist as appealing to the freedom of the patient. "A good deal of the skill in psychotherapy lies in the ability to do this effectively."[5]

One special form in which the schizophrenic accomplishes this desired isolation from others is through divorcing oneself from one's body, which is felt more as an object among other objects than as the core of one's own being. This keeps the self in a pure I-It relation with other persons. Deprived of any direct participation in any aspect of the life of the world, the self becomes pure observer and controller. Such a schizoid individual is trying, in fact, "to be omnipotent by enclosing within his own being, without recourse to a creative relationship with others, modes of relationship that require the effective presence to him of other people and of the outer world." This shut-up self can only lead, of course, to despair, futility, and a progressive impoverishment of the inner world until one comes to feel one is merely a vacuum.[6]

The isolation of the self is the corollary of the need to be in control. The schizoid individual is afraid of letting anything of oneself go, of coming out of oneself or losing oneself in any experience because one imagines one will be depleted, exhausted, emptied,

5. Laing, *The Divided Self*, pp. 44–47, 49, 52 f., 61.
6. Laing, *The Divided Self*, pp. 69, 75.

sucked dry. Laing analyzes this schizoid condition of the inner self in terms of a deficiency in I-Thou relatedness: "*The reality of the world and of the self are mutually potentiated by the direct relationship between self and other.*" But for the schizoid self, a creative relationship with the other in which there is mutual enrichment is impossible. For this I-Thou relationship one substitutes a quasi It-It interaction which may seem to operate efficiently and smoothly for a while but which is sterile and has no life in it. The schizoid "self can relate itself with immediacy to an object which is an object of its own imagination and memory but not to a real person."[7] Thus, in the case of the schizophrenic, Sartre's "bad faith," which introduces the structure of intersubjectivity into the intrasubjective, or psyche, is identical to Buber's description, in the second part of *I and Thou*, of the Thou that strikes inward when there is no longer any genuine relationship to any really other Thou.[8]

Laing's *Self and Others* goes beyond *The Divided Self* in its understanding of forms of interpersonal action. Writing in 1961, Laing declared that the most significant theoretical and methodological development in the psychiatry of the previous two decades was the growing dissatisfaction with any theory or study of the individual which isolates him from his context. Our identities are complementary, Laing points out; for "every relationship implies a definition of self by other and other by self." "A person's 'own' identity cannot be completely abstracted from his identity-for-others." In fact, other people become a sort of identity kit through which one can piece together a picture of *oneself*. This very fact leads to the temptation of seeking confirmation from others by "seeming," Laing asserts, using Buber's categories from *The Knowledge of Man*. It also leads to a collusion between persons in which they shore up each other's false identities. It is essential that the therapist basically frustrate the self's search for a collusive complement for false identity. Put positively, "one basic function of genuinely analytical or existential therapy is the provision of a setting in which as little as possible impedes each person's capacity to discover his own self." Put negatively, "the therapist's intention is not to allow himself to collude with the pa-

7. Laing, *The Divided Self*, pp. 82, 86.
8. Cf. Laing, *The Divided Self*, "The Ghost of the Weed Garden," pp. 195–205.

tients in adopting a position in their phantasy-system and, alternatively, not to use the patients to embody any phantasy of his own."⁹

It is in *The Politics of Experience* (1967) that Laing attains the fullest expression of what we might call his "politics of dialogue." Essential to this politics of dialogue is the recognition that although experience is invisible to the other, it is neither "subjective" nor "objective," "inner" nor "outer," process nor praxis, input nor output, psychic nor somatic, and least of all is it "intrapsychic process." My experience is not in my psyche; my psyche *is* my experience. The relations between persons are not merely the interplay of ongoing intrapsychic processes. There is no thing that is between two people, and the "between" itself is not a thing: "The ground of the being of all beings is the relation between them. This relationship is the 'is,' the being of all things, and the being of all things is itself no-thing."¹⁰

Laing bases his approach to psychotherapy squarely on this ontology of the between:

> We all live on the hope that authentic meeting between human beings can still occur. Psychotherapy consists in the paring away of all that stands between us, the props, masks, roles, lies, defenses, anxieties, projections and introjections, in short, all the carryovers from the past, transference and countertransference, that we use by habit and collusion, wittingly or unwittingly, as our currency for relationships.¹¹

But the metapsychology of Freud, Federn, Rapaport, Hartman, and Kris is incompatible with this approach to psychotherapy; for it "has no constructs for any social system generated by more than one person at a time," for social collectivities of experience shared between persons, or a category of "you," such "as there is in the work of Feuerbach, Buber, Parsons."

> It has no way of expressing the meeting of an "I" with "an other," and the impact of one person on another.... How two mental apparatuses or psychic structures or systems, each with its own con-

9. Ronald D. Laing, *Self and Others*, (Middlesex, England: Pelican Books, 1971), pp. 81, 86 f., 123.
10. Ronald D. Laing, *The Politics of Experience* (New York: Ballantine Books, 1968), pp. 20 f., 41 f.
11. Laing, *The Politics of Experience*, p. 46.

stellation of internal objects, can relate to each other remains unexamined. Within the constructs the theory offers, it is possibly inconceivable. Projection and introjection do not in themselves bridge the gap *between* persons.[12]

Laing criticizes even more severely behavior therapy and, by implication, the psychology of B.F. Skinner as the most extreme example of a schizoid theory and practice that proposes to think and act purely in terms of the other without reference to the self of the therapist or the patient. Behaviorism implies behavior without experience, objects rather than persons. "It is inevitably therefore a technique of nonmeeting, of manipulation and control." He sees it, indeed, as one of a number of theories that, not founded on the nature of being human, betray the inhuman and inevitably lead to inhuman consequences if the therapist is consistent:

> Any technique concerned with the other without the self, with behavior to the exclusion of experience, with the relationship to the neglect of the persons in relation, with the individuals to the exclusion of their relationship, and most of all, with an object-to-be-changed rather than a person-to-be-accepted, simply perpetuates the disease it purports to cure.[13]

In contrast to all these theories, Laing insists that "it is the relations *between* persons that is central in theory and practice." We must, says Laing, continue to struggle through our confusion and persist in being human. "Psychotherapy must remain *an obstinate attempt of two people to recover the wholeness of being human through the relationship between them.*"[14] In the last part of *The Politics of Experience*, Laing loses sight of the "between" that transcends the inner-outer dichotomy in favor of a celebration of the inner, for which he rightly cites Jung as the groundbreaker in psychology. Nonetheless, even there he sees the (sometimes romanticized) schizophrenic voyage as "*as natural way of healing our own appalling state of alienation called normality.*"[15]

As an outgrowth of his work with schizophrenics, Ronald Laing has been more and more directly concerned with family ther-

12. Laing, *The Politics of Experience*, pp. 49 f.
13. Laing, *The Politics of Experience*, p. 53.
14. Laing, *The Politics of Experience*, pp. 50, 53.
15. Laing, *The Politics of Experience*, pp. 167 f.

apy. Following the tradition of the existential analysts, Laing has been more concerned with portraying the negative aspects of the family that obscure the human image than with revealing the avenues toward healing that might bring the human image out of its eclipse. In *The Politics of Experience*, Laing defines the family as a "protection racket" in which each person incarnates the nexus of the family and acts in terms of its existence. Since the person is essential to the nexus and the nexus to the person, the danger to each person is the dissolution or dispersion of "the family." As a result, each member of the family may act on each other member "to coerce him (by sympathy, blackmail, indebtedness, guilt, gratitude, or naked violence) into maintaining his interiorization of the group unchanged." Any defection from the nexus is accordingly punished, with the worst punishment being exile or excommunication: group death. In numerous studies of families of schizophrenics in England and America, "*no* schizophrenic has been studied whose disturbed pattern of communication has not been shown to be a reflection of, and reaction to, the disturbed and disturbing pattern characterizing his or her family of origin."[16]

In *The Politics of the Family*, Laing offers a somewhat subtler analysis of the families of schizophrenics. What is internalized in the individual, he points out, is not the individual members of the family but the sets of relations between them, the *family as a system*. Since "each family member incarnates a structure derived from relations between members," each person's identity rests on a shared "family" inside the others who, by that token, are themselves in the same family. A crisis occurs if any member of the family wishes to leave by dissolving the "family" in himself or herself since the "family" may be felt as the whole world and the destruction of it as worse than murder and more selfish than suicide. This leads to an acute dilemma for the person who feels himself or herself threatened by the family: "If I do not destroy the 'family,' the 'family' will destroy me. I cannot destroy the 'fam-

16. Laing, *The Politics of Experience*, pp. 64, 87, 114. Laing sees his own researches (R. D. Laing and A. Esterson, *Sanity, Madness and the Family* [London: Tavistorck Publications, 1964; New York: Basic Books, 1965]) as matching the studies of the families of schizophrenics conducted at Palo Alto, California, Yale University, the Pennsylvania Psychiatric Institute, and the National Institute of Mental Health.

ily' in myself without destroying 'it' in them. Feeling themselves endangered, will they destroy me?"

It is not surprising that the "family" comes to serve as a bulwark against total collapse, disintegration, emptiness, despair, and guilt. It is this understanding of the family that leads Laing to his insight into "knots," to which he devotes a whole book and which he himself makes still knottier with his choice of language: "Each person's relations to himself is mediated through the relations between the relations that comprise the set of relations he has with others." Laing's family scenarios are full of inductions, attributions, and double binds.

> What they tell him he *is*, is *induction*, far more potent than what they tell him to do. Thus through the attribution: 'You are naughty,' they are effectively telling him *not to do* what they are ostensibly telling him to do.[17]

Despite this grim picture of the family, Laing's approach to family therapy is still that of healing through meeting. To Laing, diagnosis and therapy cannot be separated. "Diagnosis *begins* as soon as one encounters a particular situation, and never ends." Diagnosis means *seeing through the social scene,* and the way one sees through the situation changes the situation. In contrast to the nonreciprocal static model used by the doctor and the still predominantly medically oriented psychiatrist, Laing offers a reciprocal and dynamic model of therapy: "As soon as we interplay with the situation, we have already begun to intervene willy-nilly. Moreover, our intervention is already beginning to change *us*, as well as the situation. *A reciprocal relationship has begun.*"[18]

In contrast to Sartre, then, Laing does not rule out fully mutual and reciprocal relationships a priori, and he uses Sartre, as we have seen, for illustrations of negative, pathological relationships. On the other hand, Laing is like Sartre in that he is at his most brilliant in describing the negative, while he has great difficulty in articulating the nature of trusting and positive interhuman relationships. The one example of the positive that I remember, in fact, is Laing's emphasis on what it means really to give someone a cup of tea!

17. R. D. Laing, *The Politics of the Family and Other Essays* (New York: Vintage Books, 1972), pp. 4, 13 f., 56, 80.
18. Laing, *Politics of the Family,* p. 40.

Chapter 10

The Family's Role in Hiding the Human Image: Pseudomutuality (Wynne) and Parentification (Boszormenyi-Nagy)

Lyman Wynne and Pseudomutuality

MORE impressive for our purposes than Laing is the American psychiatrist Lyman Wynne, who developed a dialogical approach to family therapy through his family studies of schizophrenia at the National Institute of Mental Health. Wynne was in close contact with Leslie Farber for many years, and he came into contact with Buber during the time Buber gave the William Alanson White Memorial Lectures and the seminars on dreams and the unconscious for the Washington School of Psychiatry in 1957. Wynne began doing family therapy with the idea that it was not really adequate to see individuals and then try to reconstruct the nature of their relationships.

> We'd had the hypothesis, based upon our psychoanalytic training, that we could in theory, "should," be able to establish transference relationship—a transference relationship with each member of the family—and then experience in the heat of the transference and counter transference dialogue, what was characteristic of that person's perception of the world, and then we would kind of piece this together and make a composite family out of it.

Working with Irving Ryckoff and Juliana Day, with Farber as a consultant, Wynne became more and more dismayed about how little they all really knew about the family as a whole. This led them to a dialogical theory of relatedness, a social system of the family, in place of the theory of intrapsychic dynamics. Then Buber's ideas came along and fleshed out some aspects of mutuality.[1]

Wynne's most important contribution to family therapy is his understanding of family relationship and communication in terms of the forms of mutuality. Taking Buber's concept of distance and relation as the philosophical anthropological base of his understanding of the human, Wynne posits two fundamental principles of human existence—moving into relation with other human beings and developing, in a lifelong process, a sense of personal identity. The universal necessity of dealing with both these problems leads to three main "solutions"—mutuality, nonmutuality, and pseudomutuality. Mutuality, to Wynne, is like Buber's I-Thou relationship if one adds to it Buber's recognition that it can and should alternate with the I-It, that it is neither continuous nor forced.[2] Nonmutuality is a relationship in which persons have complementary role-expectations but no real personal meeting. Pseudomutuality is what Buber would call "seeming" applied not to the individual person but to the family.

In pseudomutuality the members of a family are absorbed in fitting together at the expense of the differentiation of the identities of the persons in the relation. In relations of genuine mutuality, in contrast, each person brings "a sense of his own meaningful, positively-valued identity, and, out of experience or participation together, mutual recognition of identity develops, including a growing recognition of each other's potentialities and capacities." In pseudomutuality, such a recognition of personal identity is seen as threatening to demolish the entire relation. As a result, "emotional investment is directed more toward maintaining the *sense* of reciprocal fulfillment of expectations than toward accurately perceiving changing expectations." Old roles provide the structure for the relation, and the relation becomes increasingly empty, barren, and stifling. Thus, the members are caught in a dilemma—divergence is seen as disruptive; yet without divergence, growth of the relation is impossible.

1. Interview with Lyman Wynne in Richard Stanton, "Dialogue in Psychotherapy: Martin Buber, Maurice Friedman and Therapists of Dialogue," Ph.D. dissertation, Union Graduate School-West, 1978, pp. 203 f.

2. Lyman C. Wynne, Irving M. Ryckoff, Juliana Day, and Stanley I. Hirsch, "Pseudo-Mutuality in the Family Relations of Schizophrenics," *Psychiatry*, Vol. XXII, No. 2 (May 1958), pp. 206 f.

Such pseudomutuality characterizes the relations of families of persons who later develop acute schizophrenic episodes. The roles in such a family tend to remain fixed even though the persons who enact them may vary. "The ever-present menace of noncomplementarity within these families leads to pseudomutuality as a way of life." This way of life is maintained through shared mechanisms which prevent the articulation and selection of any meaning that might enable individual family members to differentiate their personal identity either within or outside the family role structure. Family members try to act as if the family could be a truly self-sufficient social system with a completely encircling boundary. They are helped in this by the "rubber fence," a continuous but elastic boundary which surrounds the schizophrenic family system and which stretches to include what can be interpreted as complementary and contracts to extrude what is seen as noncomplementary.

One way that this "rubber fence" is preserved is through indiscriminate approval; another is through secrecy. "Both mechanisms keep divergence from having a recognized and meaningful impact upon the family ideology and role structure." Often it is the family member labeled schizophrenic that is the one who is extruded from the family system. All the family noncomplementarity may be consciously localized in this one person who is regarded as not fitting in, and one, too, may share in this negative valuation of oneself. If one tries to abandon this role, one will make everyone very anxious. "The ostracized or scapegoated person thus takes an important covert family role in maintaining the pseudomutuality or surface complementarity of the rest of the family."[3]

The pseudomutuality of the family renders understandable the formerly baffling behavior of the schizophrenic: "The fragmentation of experience, the identity diffusion, the disturbed modes of perception and communication...are to a significant extent derived, by processes of internalization, from characteristics of the family social organization." This internalized family role structure serves as a kind of primitive superego, as a result of which one becomes flooded with anxiety at precisely those moments when one is starting to articulate a meaningful indication of one's

3. Wynne et al., ibid., pp. 208–211, 213 f.

identity. When such a one enters an acute schizophrenic episode, one is no longer able to dissociate one's differences from the family and becomes anxiously sensitive to the slightest hint of possible noncomplementarity. Even when one's schizophrenia is still potential, one is unprepared in those ego skills and perceptions that might enable one to succeed in occupational or marital roles outside one's family of origin. Instead one is invested in saving the family and oneself from the panic of dissolution. One often sees oneself, in fact, as the person who takes care of the needs and expectations of one's family.

Acute schizophrenic panic and disorganization, it follows, represent an identity crisis in the face of overwhelming guilt and anxiety attendant upon moving out of one's family role structure. Ironically enough, however, the schizophrenic takes the covert family role of allowing other family members to achieve vicariously some measure of individuation. In the chronic state of schizophrenia that follows, pseudomutuality is returned to a greater distance—a safe compromise between expression and failure of individuation, acceptance and rejection of family role, achievement of relation and disruption of distance.

In genuine mutuality, imaginative flexibility and perceptual accuracy are essential to enable the members of the family to accept noncomplementary expectations that may create for a time an element of alienation within the relation. In pseudomutuality, in contrast, "the full impact of alienation and loneliness is avoided, but a sense of relation unsupported by accurate perception of the realities of participation becomes a hollow and empty experience."[4]

Wynne and his colleagues soon added "pseudohostility" to the repertoire—as a defense not against divergence but against recognizing or experiencing potential tenderness, affection, or sexual attraction. To ward off such feelings, which are experienced as dangerous or even engulfing, such families maintain contact through enduringly unresolved bickering and turmoil. The dynamics of pseudomutuality and pseudohostility are very similar. Both "help maintain vulnerable relationships in which it is feared that underlying wishes and impulses, opposite to those overtly expressed, would destroy the relationship."

4. Wynne et al., ibid., pp. 215–220.

Another mechanism which Wynne discusses in a 1965 article is the "trading of dissociations," a situation in which each member of the family deals with that in the other which the other cannot acknowledge. "Thus there can be no 'meeting,' no confirmation, no mutuality, no shared validation of feelings or experience." The result of such a trading of dissociations is a "fixed distancing" in which each family member is painfully aware of his or her own need and wishes for relatedness on a human, feeling level, yet each feels that the others block and do not allow intimacy or affection. Inexorably caught up with one another, they are unable to separate or to develop mutuality. Often this fixed psychological distancing is the result of enduring, shared efforts to exclude from family life certain major kinds of feelings which are experienced as unmanageably threatening. "When such feelings intrude themselves into the child's awareness as he moves into later adolescence or adulthood and . . . becomes exposed to these feelings in extrafamilial settings, he is apt to have an abrupt, shattering breakdown, sometimes schizophrenic in quality."[5]

In his discussion of communication disorders in his 1970 Karen Horney lectures, Wynne points out that families of schizophrenics seek information from one another not to solve tasks but to find out about one another's attitudes toward the family relationship. Such families manifest what Wynne has called "transactional thought disorder," thinking difficulties which are not fully apparent until one looks at communicational sequences between two or more persons. Wynne does not make the family system the sole cause of schizophrenia. "Rather, the instability of personal boundaries, the inability to trust one's own perceptions, and broader difficulties in deriving and communicating meaning would constitute the kind of vulnerability to schizophrenia which we believe may be promoted in certain kinds of family settings." Two "schizophrenogenic" family transactions which Wynne isolates are the injection and the concealment of meaning, both of which tend to undermine the recipients' trust in their own capacity to derive meaning from their own experience and at the same time lead to arguments and denials which bind the persons together in the relationship.

5. Lyman C. Wynne, "Some Indications and Contraindications for Exploratory Family Therapy," in *Intensive Family Therapy: Theoretical and Practical As-*

Whereas projection is basically an *intra*psychic process, the injection of meaning is an observable interchange between persons in which one person puts meaning (ideas, feelings, impulses) directly into another person. "Persons who inject meaning regularly perceive their actions as necessary, helpful, therapeutic, or preventive—for the recipient's own good." This makes this injection difficult to withstand, especially since an attribution is characteristically about a subjective state which the other person has not acknowledged and has, like projections, *some* kernel of truth. Anyone who is in an apprehensive state will be especially vulnerable to the injection of meaning and likely to take in such meanings as part of oneself. "He is then likely to experience his own ideas, which lack confirmation and consensual validation, as tenuous and untrustworthy." The person who is unable to ward off the injection of meaning becomes dependent upon the meaning supplier, especially if the avowed purpose is to help, educate, or heal. Even partially resisted injected meaning has this binding effect because of the exchange of attributions and counter-attributions in which the individuals become meshed. The very wish for sharing meanings can lead to an injection of meanings which, if it succeeds, will *seem* to have produced consensual validation no matter how shaky or even false its underpinnings.[6]

The attribution of ideas, wishes, feelings, or motives is inherently *not* subject to a clear confirmation *or* disconfirmation:

> If the person denies the charge, then the accuser can state or imply in various ways that this disconfirmation is not valid: that the other person is "only" a child, is acting "defensively" (if an adult), or is simply massively ignorant of what is going on. If the person making the attribution or accusation is *also* in a higher status, because of a socially defined relationship, then, of course, these charges about stubbornness, defensiveness, or ignorance are especially difficult for the person in the subordinate status to refute. Such

pects, ed. Ivan Boszormenyi-Nagy and James L. Framo (New York: Harper & Row, Hoeber Medical Division, 1965).

6. Lyman C. Wynne, "Communication Disorders and the Quest for Relatedness in Families of Schizophrenics," *American Journal of Psychoanalysis*, Vol. XXX, No. 2 (1970), pp. 105 f., 109; Lyman C. Wynne, "The Injection and the Concealment of Meaning in the Family Relationships and Psychotherapy of Schizophrenics," in International Congress Series No. 259, *Psychotherapy of Schizophrenia*, Proceedings of the IVth International Symposium, Turku, Fin-

charges imply that the other person does not know his own mind. In order to sustain an important relationship and not to jeopardize further the good-will of the more powerful person, he may either submerge and leave unexpressed and untested his objections or, as seems to happen with potential schizophrenics, he may undergo an erosion in the ability to trust his own perceptions.[7]

Concealment of meaning has a very similar effect. It forestalls separation and individuation by leaving the other person perplexed, mystified, and unable to find solid reference points for consensual validation. Both these modes of communication undermine crucial human potentialities, above all, those for personal autonomy within a context of empathy and mutuality.[8]

The ultimate mechanism for preserving family solidarity is to take refuge in the meaning of meaninglessness. In such families even overt psychosis is not acknowledged as valid or real. "Gradually, the very possibility that the family relationship could provide a context for sharing and clarifying meanings is no longer considered." Family members attend to remote and tangential meanings and become dependent upon special cues or language that can have no meaning to those outside the family. Failure to confirm meaning at the simpler levels of task and message ultimately undermines and makes more tenuous and anxiety-laden the relationship itself. When families of schizophrenics become dominated by the belief that all specific meanings will be disqualified, they are left as a last line of defense for sustaining their sense of relatedness their shared rule that *all* communication will be regarded as meaningless. "Invalidations of meaning now become validations of the 'meaninglessness' which, paradoxically, is the 'meaning' that holds the relationship together." This paradox, according to Wynne, is the nub of the double bind theory as it applies to schizophrenia.[9]

Wynne bases his analysis of communication disorders on "a

land, August 4–7, 1971, *Excerpta Medica*, Amsterdam, pp. 181–185.

7. Wynne, "The Injection and Concealment of Meaning," p. 186.

8. Wynne, "The Injection and Concealment of Meaning," pp. 189, 192.

9. Lyman C. Wynne, "On the Anguish, and Creative Passions, of Not Escaping Double Binds: A Reformulation," in *Double Bind: The Foundation of the Communicational Approach to the Family,* ed. C. E. Sluzki and D. C. Ransom (New York: Grune & Stratton, 1976), p. 247.

striking contrast between two views of interpersonal relationships" which is nothing other than a reformulation of Buber's I-
Thou and I-It relations and the necessary alternation between the
two. In the first—*expressive*—type of relatedness, "meaningful
feelings, including experiences of warmth, affection, and, in the
broadest sense, human contact are sought directly and immediately, without preliminaries, often in a rush of what is called
'spontaneity.' " In the second—*instrumental*—type of relatedness,
the interpersonal relation is experienced as necessary or useful to
fulfill a task but is not valued in itself apart from its utility. Those
relationships which are most stable and most open to renewal include both forms of experience.

Based on this typology of relatedness, Wynne distinguishes
three levels of communication: the specific *message*, the *task* in
which the communicating persons are engaged, and "the more or
less enduring interpersonal *relationship*, which both provides a
context for the task and the message and also is an intrinsic ingre-
dient in the communication process as a whole." Traditional psychiatric diagnosis of schizophrenia, especially as it pertains to
thinking disorders, is concerned with the task and content, or
message, levels of communication, whereas "pseudomutuality"
and "consensus-sensitivity" are concepts that are primarily concerned with the relationship level of communication. The schizophrenic's confusion concerning the structure of spoken and
written language results from recurring severe disturbances in his
or her relationships with other people. "Schizophrenics seem to
have a profound distrust of the conventional meanings of language." Sharing language and tasks with others eventually comes
to be regarded by them as empty, meaningless, and sometimes
dangerous. "Nevertheless, the remarkable fact is that despite a
long and painful history of communicative perplexity and disas-
ter, most schizophrenics remain enduringly responsive to the *potentiality* of relatedness."

Schizophrenics are caught in a painful and sometimes tragic
paradox because of their very desire for relatedness. Their "turning away from conventional task-orientations . . . tragically undermines their potential capacity to establish and renew the very
relatedness which they seek so despairingly." Experiencing the
culture as mechanized and dehumanized, they quite understand-

ably seek for relatedness for its own sake. But relatedness *cannot* be long sustained without reference to specific focal content and actual tasks. Those, on the other hand, who are exclusively preoccupied with specific messages and tasks have an existence which is humanly empty. This is true of many so-called normal persons, such as the "con man," but it has its extreme in the sociopaths, who use relatedness only instrumentally as a means for achieving their particular tasks which they are often quite "slick" in achieving. They continue their exploitative way undaunted by interpersonal rebuffs and do not grasp why they are rejected or avoided when others catch on to the fact that the sociopath is simply using them.

Wynne sums up the dilemma of needing both relational and message-and-task oriented communications in Buber's concept of our twofold need for *both* I–Thou and I–It relationships and quotes at length a passage from Buber's *I and Thou* which has enduringly influenced his own thinking:

> "The world of *It*," says Buber, " is set in the context of space and time.
> "The world of *Thou* is not set in the context of either of these.
> "The particular *Thou*, after the relational even has run its course, is *bound* to become an *It*.
> "The particular *It*, by entering the relational event, *may* become a *Thou*.
> "These are the two basic privileges of the world of *It*. They move man to look on the world of *It* as the world in which he has to live, as the world, indeed, which offers him all manner of incitements and excitements, activity and knowledge. In this chronicle of solid benefits the moments of the *Thou* appear as strange lyric and dramatic episodes, seductive and magical, but tearing us away to dangerous extremes, loosening the well-tried context, leaving more questions than satisfaction behind them, shattering security—in short, uncanny moments we can well dispense with. For since we are bound to leave them and go back into the 'world,' why not remain in it? . . .
> "It is not possible to live in the bare present. Life would be quite consumed if precautions were not taken to subdue the present speedily and thoroughly. But it is possible to live in the bare past, indeed only in it may a life be organized. We only need to fill each

10. Wynne, "Communication Disorders and the Quest for Relatedness," pp. 100–103, 111 f.

moment with experiencing and using, and it ceases to burn. "And in all the seriousness of truth, hear this: without *It* man cannot live. But he who lives with *It* alone is not a man."[11]

Ivan Boszormenyi-Nagy and Parentification

In a 1965 monograph on "Intensive Family Therapy as Process,"[12] the Philadelphia family psychiatrist Ivan Boszormenyi-Nagy points out that psychiatric illness and health obtain new definition in family therapy. The family present conflicting goals of autonomous identity and security through symbiotic fusion. Frequently the family interprets the opportunity for conjoint exploration of problems "as a sanction of their deep wishes for never-ending symbiotic togetherness." In the pathogenic family system, the nature of the primitive interrelatedness among the members is such that it prevents the necessary individuation which could lead to autonomous personality development and eventual separation. Each in fantasy assigns to the other a parental role and thereby blocks the autonomous growth aspirations of the other and of oneself. Collusive complementaries contribute to an endless postponement of individuation. "The experienced and genuinely family-oriented therapist will develop a third ear for each member's unconscious object-assignment designs as well as for each partner's unconscious compliance with the other's narcissistic needs."[13]

One of the key conflicts of many a family's growth and development is the problem of how parents can give more than they have received from their own parents. In healthy families there is an alternation of roles. "In marriage, for instance, one can be parent to the mate in one moment and child in the next moment." But in a pathological family each repels the other because of their fixated, mutually noncomplementary need configurations. Many

---

11. Wynne, "Communication Disorders and the Quest for Relatedness," pp. 122 f. The quotation is from Ronald Gregor Smith's translation of *I and Thou* in its first edition (Edinburgh: T & T Clark, 1937).
12. Ivan Boszormenyi-Nagy and James L. Framo, eds., *Intensive Family Therapy: Theoretical and Practical Aspects* (New York: Harper & Row, 1965), pp. 87–142.
13. Boszormenyi-Nagy and Framo, eds., *Intensive Family Therapy*, pp. 87 f., 90 f., 94.

marriages are essentially lived between each partner and their respective introjects, and this carries over to the children. As a result, no true change of role or definite working-through can occur in any single family member without a corresponding change in the system itself. In what Murray Bowen calls the "undifferentiated ego mass," it is the state of undifferentiatedness itself, and not any particular shared fantasy or *folie à deux*, that constitutes the essence of family pathogenicity. Family relationships are based primarily on deep existential and experiential structures and only secondarily on communication or visible transactions. In the battles of married couples, the family therapist can often sense underneath the words the presence of two warring families of origin.[14]

In *Invisible Loyalties*, the decisive formulation of his relational theory and family therapy, Nagy sets forth one of his most important concepts, that of "parentification," in which the parent has given an unfair burden of parenting to the child, perhaps because of inadequate parenting by his own parents of origin. The rebellion of the so-called delinquent child may, from this viewpoint, be actually an attempt to bring the feuding parents together, and the identified patient in the family, the "schizophrenic," may really be the scapegoat who bears the problems of the family. There may even arise a basic trust among siblings who share in common the parentification thrust upon them by their parents. The delinquent child's actions may bring unconsciously wished-for parental substitutes into the picture, for example, police, court, and school authorities, thus answering the parents' own need for limit-setting authorities. Similarly a child may accept the incongruous role of being sexual partner to one of its parents "because of the unconscious, collusive loyalty expectation that to act otherwise might result in psychological loss or nonsurvival of one or both parents." Thus, it may be the child's supreme effort to hold the family together. In a family where one child is ill, the well child may also make a contribution to family loyalty by playing certain prescribed premature roles and not living an age-appropriate life. Such a child may be a poor performer at school and quite de-

14. Boszormenyi-Nagy and Framo, eds., *Intensive Family Therapy*, pp. 133, 119 f., 122 f.

tached from the world of its peers. "Behind his well-preserved façade he may be struggling with feelings of emptiness, emotional depletion, or depression."[15]

The parentified child is in an especially difficult position in considering new commitments like marriage or parenthood. At the same time feelings of guilt and obligation becloud the child's natural devotion to the parent and lead to deep-seated ambivalence. Even the violence of a bound schizophrenic child may document his unchanging involvement and interminable devotion. Again real or alleged delinquent acts by the child may serve to divert attention from parents' mutual destructiveness as a result of which the key to family treatment with overtly rebellious young people often consists of bringing into the open the ways in which they have remained devoted to their parents. Such parentified loyalty may also be displayed by marriage partners who by mutually rejecting one another and the marriage unwittingly prove their unaffected loyalty to their families of origin. "Impotence, frigidity, and premature ejaculation may all amount to covert attitudes of disloyalty to the mate to underline the invisible loyalty to one's family of origin." "Another form of relational stagnation is an unconscious freezing of the inner self and an *incapacity for commitment* to anyone in a close relationship," even though a pattern of productive functional performance may create an appearance of commitment and responsiveness.[16]

Nagy charts the development of family pathology from the in-love phase of early marriages, where each partner looks to the other as the "idealized" parent who makes up for or provides what one eternally lacks, to the next stage in which, disappointed in each other, the marriage partners turn their hopes to their children. Even though they wish to give their children what they did not have, they still have their own unmet hungers for which they subtly resent the child even while they overgive. At the same time, the sacrificing, martyrlike parent inevitably produces guilt feelings in the child who feels that it must overpay for what is

15 .Ivan Boszormenyi-Nagy and Geraldine M. Spark, *Invisible Loyalties: Reciprocity in Intergenerational Family Therapy* (New York: Harper & Row, Medical Division, 1973). I refer in this chapter only to Nagy because it is he who authorized the main theoretical chapters of *Invisible Loyalties*.
16. Boszormenyi-Nagy and Spark, *Invisible Loyalties*, pp. 165 f., 260, 157 f.

given in such a selfless manner and, even more important, that it is forever bound to live up to the parent's expectations. "All their life such individuals are left with a sense of indebtedness or obligation which can never be repaid." Guilt over failing its familial loyalty is not simply a regressive fixation on the part of the child, anchored in an internal situation. It is, rather, validated by the interpersonal reality of the parents' own messages. In order to keep its guilt down and protect its parents, such a child learns to appease the excessive expectations by preserving its symptom and by sharing with its parents everything it can enjoy in life. It would be unrealistic to expect such a child to progress too far in the face of actual disloyalty and mounting guilt over it.[17]

The loss of a meaningful relationship, either through rejection of the child by the parents or through the child's becoming autonomous and moving away from parents, "always implies the ontic disconfirmation of one's person,"[18] says Nagy. Thus, the threat of separation becomes one of the most important dynamics that must be recognized in Nagy's system of family therapy:

> Man's greatest satisfaction is connected with entering into a relationship, and his greatest pain with unrelatedness or the threat of losing an important relationship. As the chance of raising a family is the most universal source of anticipated happiness, the prospect of losing one's child, even through the child's growth and maturation, can lead to the most penetrating grief.[19]

In an unhealthy family, the separation takes place even while the family is still together through that overpermissiveness in which the parents abandon the children and exploitatively parentify them, appearing to give them freedom of action while actually not giving them concern or limits. This "constitutes the true double bind." Frequently the myths of permissiveness and family togetherness coexist and mutually reinforce each other, as in Wynne's concept of "pseudomutuality." On the other hand, if the parents carry responsible rearing of the child to an extreme, this leads to another form of exploitation through the child's permanent, symbiotically dependent relationship to the parents. Guilt-laden obli-

---

17. Boszormenyi-Nagy and Spark, *Invisible Loyalties*, pp. 161, 115 f., 118.
18. Boszormenyi-Nagy and Spark, *Invisible Loyalties*, pp. 220 f., 189.
19. Boszormenyi-Nagy and Spark, *Invisible Loyalties*, p. 154.

gation to the overdevoted parent makes change and growth so difficult that excess indulgence can lead to as much exploitation as overt child abuse.

Nagy declares the intrapsychic realm meaningless if it is taken out of the context of the I–Thou relationship. Any consideration of need will never by itself lead to definable boundaries of interaction. Human rights must be redefined from a viewpoint of merits in relationships.

> The genuine I–Thou dialogue transcends the concept of the other's being a mere "object" or gratifier of my needs. The mutuality of care and concern is not only experienced by the participants, but it transcends their psychology through entering the realm of action or of commitment to action. The dialogue as defined by Buber becomes one characteristic of the system of family relationships. The experiential reciprocity between two human beings, both of whom are confirmed by their meeting on an I–Thou basis, creates a mutually supportive base among family relationships. Perhaps this is connected with what Buber refers to as the zone of the "between."[20]

The sum of all ontologically and ethically interdependent mutual dyads within a family constitutes a main source of group loyalty. Therefore, the family therapist must be able to conceive of a social group whose members all relate to one another according to Buber's I–Thou dialogue.[21]

20. Boszormenyi-Nagy and Spark, *Invisible Loyalties*, p. 153.
21. Boszormenyi-Nagy and Spark, *Invisible Loyalties*, pp. 7, 381.

PART FOUR

The Human Image as the
Hidden Ground
of Psychology and Literature

Chapter 11

Psychology and Literature

" "THROUGH considering together both literary and non-literary works," I suggest in my book *To Deny Our Nothingness*, "we can gain a deeper understanding of the image of man as the hidden ground in which literature, philosophy, psychotherapy, religion, and social thought all meet." The human image might well be called the matrix from which each of these fields emerges, which they continue to embody within them, and which continues to bind them together in essential ways no matter how stringently the disciplines pertaining to each particular field make it necessary to hold them apart. This ground or matrix must necessarily remain hidden. It can be pointed to through one or the other field or through the meeting between them, but it cannot be disclosed or made manifest since this would always mean translating one discipline or field into another and thereby destroying its integrity. We cannot translate literature into psychology and thereby get the image of the human; for literature and psychology are *both* rooted in the human image. Realizing this, we can at one and the same time take seriously the need for the human image to be revealed, the need for remaining faithful to each of these various ways of knowing the human, and yet the need *not* to take seriously the ultimate overclaim that it alone contains all the important knowledge about its own field. For each field is simply a human and ultimately arbitrary marking off which shades into another field. These fields of knowledge are so many partial ways

133

of trying to get a purchase on the multidimensional reality of the wholeness and concreteness of the human.

Contemporary psychology obscures the human by its implicit claim that it alone possesses the "real" way of looking at guilt, anxiety, and motivation. Literature is usually taken as at best an illustration of psychological concepts, at worst a luxury, an ornament of the superstructure that does not get down to the foundations. Actually literature gives us a *deeper* understanding of most of these phenomena because it is concrete and because it sees persons from within and not just from the outside. We have already seen that Isidor Chein writes of the clinician: "He gains more from reading Dostoevsky, Mann, Proust, and Shakespeare than all of the pages of the *Journal of Experimental Psychology*." For literature, as Chein observes, can give us an example of the particular in all its complexity as opposed to "statistically significant generalizations about highly circumscribed behaviors occurring under laboratory conditions."

The eminent American psychoanalyst Leslie H. Farber goes even farther than Chein. He opts for literature, not only instead of experimental psychology, but also instead of the statements of the psychoanalysts themselves, none of whose competing systems "is—to my present way of thinking—fit for human habitation." Freud took pains, to be sure, to dissociate his theories from those of metaphysics or religion. "Yet, for lack of any other definitions of the fully human, it is virtually impossible nowadays for the psychiatrist *not* to derive his norms and standards from his own theories—thus creating definitions of man out of his fragments of psychopathology." Then, after citing quotations from Karl Abraham, W. Ronald D. Fairbairn, Harry Stack Sullivan, and C. G. Jung, Farber comments:

> Though the creatures described above may bear some resemblance to animals or to steam engines or robots or electronic brains, they do not sound like people. They are, in fact, constructs of theory, more humanoid than human; and, whether they are based on the libido theory or on one of the new interpersonal theories of relationships, it is just those qualities most distinctively human that seem to have been omitted. It is a matter of some irony, if one turns from psychology to one of Dostoyevsky's novels, to find that, no matter how wretched, how puerile, or how dilapidated his char-

acters may be, they all possess more humanity than the ideal man who lives in the pages of psychiatry.[1]

Freud, to be sure, recognized the genius of Shakespeare and Dostoievsky. Yet his followers, in the ranks both of psychoanalysts and of literary critics, have often contented themselves with Freudian analyses of Shakespeare's *Hamlet*, Dostoievsky's *Crime and Punishment*, or Kafka's *Trial*. Then they have turned around and used these analyses as evidence of the way in which literature illustrates the Oedipus complex! Despite their enormous interest in literature, myth, and fairy tales, the Jungians have done essentially the same. Whether in Melville's *Moby Dick*, for example, one says that the harpoons are phallic symbols or falling into the whale's head a return to the womb or whether one sees the whole thing in Jungian terms as a descending into the archetypal unconscious and working through to the individuation of the self, what one tends to do is to reduce the actual novel to the set of meanings that one has brought to it and prevent *its* saying what it is. This also means reducing the dynamic moving event of what takes place between one and the book to something which can be put into a static category.

In the chapters that follow I shall draw on my interpretations presented in *Problematic Rebel* of Melville, Dostoievsky, Kafka, and, to a lesser extent, Camus to show how literature can give us a deeper insight than can psychological theory into a number of problems that stand at the heart of the human condition. These perennial human problems are still more intensified by the alienation of Modern Man, and they come to us, thus intensified, in peculiarly modern guise: anxiety, freedom and compulsion, the divided self, conflict of values, sex and love, guilt and shame. Precisely because such problems are regarded by most educated people today as the exclusive province of psychology, such a turning toward literature can stand together with our concern for philosophical anthropology as a significant contribution to our critique of contemporary psychology.

1. Leslie H. Farber, *The Ways of the Will: Essays toward a Psychology and Psychopathology of Will* (New York: Basic Books, 1966), Chapter 7—"Martin Buber and Psychoanalysis," pp. 131–133.

Chapter 12

Our Age of Anxiety[1]

W HETHER or not we follow W.H. Auden in dubbing the present time as "the age of anxiety," no one would deny that there are a great many evidences of anxiety in our culture, manifestations that are all the more striking given the fact that we have attained a level of technological advance and a standard of living never before known to humankind. The hydrogen bomb, the cold war, racial conflict, the growing pressure on children to compete for grades so that they may have a chance to enter college, down to the anxiety of parents about toilet training and the right balance of discipline and permissiveness—all these are too well known to need elaboration.

Yet these manifestations of anxiety raise the question of whether we should regard anxiety as a product of our culture or our culture as an elaborate mechanism for warding off basic human anxiety, or both. Here we shall part company according to our approach. If we are Freudians, we shall see anxiety as the repression of childhood fears, on the one hand, and as the individual's discontent with civilization, on the other; but in either case we shall see it as a product of guilt connected with the Oedipus complex or the too harsh repression of libidinal instincts. If we are Sullivanians, we shall see anxiety in terms of the dissociation between our images of ourselves and our actual interpersonal per-

1. Reprinted from Maurice Friedman, *The Hidden Human Image* (New York: Delacorte Press, Delta Books [paperback], 1974), Chapter 8, pp. 137-145.

formances, necessitated by the fear of the disapproval of significant others. If we are Jungians, we shall see anxiety as the repression of the "shadow" self, those frightening elements of the self which turn negative and "evil" when we fail to integrate them with the rest of our personality. If we take a sociopsychological approach, we shall see anxiety in terms of competition, "keeping up with the Joneses," "what makes Sammy run." Or we shall talk of the anxiety created as well as allayed by the patterns of social conformity, such as the "Organization Man" and the "other-directed" person.

In contrast to these approaches are those which see anxiety as basically human and culture as either a manifestation or avoidance of this anxiety. For Kierkegaard anxiety begins with the leap from innocence to experience, the fear and trembling which the "single one" experiences in his unique relationship with God, the dread of the person who has fallen into demonic shut-inness, the despair of wishing to be or not to be oneself. For Martin Heidegger anxiety is the primordial phenomenon, which the "They" of culture, ambiguity, gossip, idle talk, cover over and conceal, and by the same token it is that which calls one back to one's "thrownness" and with it one's authentic existence.

> Anxiety throws Dasein back upon that which it is anxious about, its authentic potentiality-for-Being-in-the-world. Anxiety individualizes Dasein for its ownmost Being-in-the-world, which as something that understands, projects itself essentially upon possibilities. . . Anxiety brings Dasein face to face with its BEING-FREE-FOR the authenticity of its Being, and for this authenticity as a possibility which it always is. . . That kind of Being-in-the-world which is tranquilized and familiar is a mode of Dasein's uncanniness, not the reverse. FROM AN EXISTENTIAL-ONTOLOGICAL POINT OF VIEW, THE "NOT-AT-HOME" MUST BE CONCEIVED AS THE MORE PRIMORDIAL PHENOMENON.[2]

Paul Tillich also takes an ontological approach to anxiety and sees, beneath the layers of individual neuroticism, on the one hand, and our specific culture, on the other, the general human anxiety before fate and death, before emptiness and meaningless-

2. Martin Heidegger, *Being and Time*, trans. John Macquarrie and Edward Robinson (New York: Harper & Row, 1962), pp. 232, 234.

ness, and before guilt and self-condemnation. Tillich holds that to exist is to exist face-to-face with nonbeing, by which he means what is changing and passing away—all the negative in existence. The neurotic, according to Tillich, is not the one who is anxious but the one who is not anxious, that is, the one who through one's fear of facing the anxiety of nonbeing cuts oneself off from being as well and cruelly curtails the possibilities of one's own existence.

All of these approaches have enough truth in them to add to our understanding of anxiety, yet none of them can answer the question of whether anxiety is a product of our culture or whether culture is a means of warding off a basic human anxiety. To answer this question we need a new approach that does not choose between the psychological, sociological, and ontological but unites them within a larger framework, the historical. Anxiety in our culture at its basic level means the special role our culture plays in reflecting, concealing, and creating anxiety about authentic existence, an anxiety that derives in turn from the absence of a modern image of the human.

Martin Buber begins his little classic *The Way of Man* by recounting the story of a gendarme who asked a Hasidic rabbi why God, who presumably knows everything, said to Adam, "Where art thou?" "In every era, God calls to every man, 'Where are you in the world?' " replied the rabbi. " 'So many years and days of those allotted to you have passed, and how far have you gotten in your world?' God says something like this: " 'You have lived forty-six years. How far along are you?' " Forty-six years was the age of the gendarme, and the effect of hearing his age mentioned thus was to awaken in him a heart-searching which destroyed his system of hideouts and led him to render accounts so that he might find the unique direction purposed for him in his creation.[3]

When I was forty-six years of age, I received from my Harvard class a printed book in which each of my classmates described "how far along" he was in his world, twenty-five years after grad-

3. Martin Buber, *Hasidism and Modern Man*, ed. and trans. with an Introduction by Maurice Friedman (New York: Horizon Books, 1972), Book IV, "The Way of Man According to the Teachings of the Hasidim," pp. 130–135. *The Way of Man* is also published separately by Citadel Press (Secaucus, New Jersey, 1966) with the subtitle *According to the Teaching of Hasidism*.

uation. When I read from my classmate Cabot that he is head of the million-dollar Cabot industries, that it helped to have the right grandfather, and that he is busy every night of the week on the board of one or another important organization or university, I did not envy classmate Cabot his millions. But I did have to ask myself just what I had done in the quarter of a century since I graduated from Harvard to justify that feeling of superiority to the Harvard "club man" that, as an undergraduate socialist, I took for granted.

I can remind myself, to be sure, that Buber is not talking about success and power. On the contrary, he writes: "Whatever success and enjoyment he may achieve, whatever power he may attain and whatever deeds he may do, life will remain way-less, so long as he does not face the Voice." I can remind myself, too, following Buber's philosophy of dialogue, that "heart-searching" does not mean anything comparative but is the unique demand that is made on me as the person I am in the unique situation in which I find myself. Yet I cannot so easily as that divorce my anxiety about whether my existence is authentic and whether I am answering the true call of my vocation, from the anxiety concerning my place in my culture, my age, my status, my social position, my accomplishments or lack of them. It is not just that both anxieties coexist in me, as they must, I suppose, in a child of this culture, and most especially in the child of immigrants. They become confusedly intermingled through the very conception of being a certain age and of being so far along in the world.

In my book *Problematic Rebel,* I try to find the historical link that joins the basic anthropological, or ontological, reality of human existence, on the one hand, and the special alienation experienced by the persons of our culture, on the other. I call this historical link "the death of God and the alienation of modern man," and I see arising from this alienation the Modern Exile and the "problematic of modern man." The former includes various types of isolation and alienation, and the latter focuses on the intermixture of personal freedom and psychological compulsion, the effect of the absence of the parent on the inner division of the child, the crisis of motives and the problematic of guilt, and the paradox of being a person who, in an era of the "death of God," must still hear and respond to the call that makes him or her a person.

The "death of God" is not just a question of the relativization of "values" and the absence of universally accepted mores. It is the absence of an image of meaningful human existence, the absence of the ground that enabled Greek, biblical, and Renaissance Man to move with some sureness even in the midst of tragedy. The "death of God" is an anthropological-historical anxiety that is still more basic than the *Angst*—or dread—with which Kierkegaard's "knight of faith" is tried and the anxiety that makes Heidegger's individual turn from the "They" to the possibilities of his or her own authentic existence toward death. Indeed, I should go so far as to say that the *Angst* of Kierkegaard and Heidegger are secondary products of this more basic anxiety. Both Kierkegaard and Heidegger reject society and culture for the lonely relation of the "single one" to God or the self to its own authentic existence. Both posit a dualism between the "crowd" or the "They" and the individual. Both reflect the loss of faith in the universal order and in the society that purports to be founded on it.

The "death of God" means the alienation of Modern Man, as Albert Camus has tirelessly pointed out in his discussion of the "absurd." Similarly, the ultimate terror to Herman Melville in *Moby Dick* is the blank indifference of an absolute that excludes us: "Is it by its indefiniteness," Ishmael asks, that whiteness "shadows forth the heartless voids and immensities of the universe, and thus stabs us from behind with the thought of annihilation, when beholding the white depths of the milky way?" While Ahab has a more terrible aloneness and isolation from other people than Ishmael, his exile is less profound than that of Ishmael, who cannot come up against, much less hate, the indifferent evil that oppresses him. An exactly analogous situation has occurred in our times with the scientific extermination of whole populations. Speaking of the Nazis who murdered six millions Jews, Martin Buber said, "They have...so transposed themselves into a sphere of monstrous inhumanity inaccessible to my power of conception, that not even hatred, much less an overcoming of hatred, was able to rise in me."[4]

4. Martin Buber, *A Believing Humanism: Gleanings*, trans. with an Introduction and Explanatory Comments by Maurice Friedman (New York: Simon & Schuster Paperbacks, 1969), "Genuine Dialogue and the Possibilities of Peace," p. 195.

Ishmael's impression as he stood at the helm of his ship "that whatever swift, rushing thing I stood on was not so much bound to any haven ahead as rushing from all havens astern" suggests Modern Man's sense of the earth hurtling through the empty space of the heavens on its meaningless progress to extinction. The "heartless immensity" forces us to realize our own limitedness, our own mortality. When one loses one's limits, one has lost that condition that makes human existence possible. But it is not the infinity of time and space alone that threatens Modern Man. It is one's increasing inability to stand before this infinite. One less and less sees oneself as a self with a ground on which to stand, and at the same time one less and less trusts that existence outside oneself to which one must relate. As a result one cannot accept Pascal's dictum that one is neither all nor nothing. One feels compelled, instead, to the Either/Or of what I call the "Modern Promethean," the rebel who believes that one must destroy the other that confronts one or one will be destroyed oneself.

In Dostoievsky's "Underground Man," the anxiety of the Modern Exile is manifested in a different constellation, that of isolation from others, inner emptiness, and inauthenticity. The Underground Man, Raskolnikov, Svidrigailov, Kirilov, Stavrogin, and Ivan Karamazov are all essentially isolated from others, and their attempts to break out of this isolation, such as Raskolnikov's murder of the pawnbroker woman and Stavrogin's debauchery, leave them more isolated still. It is interesting to compare the different kinds of anxiety that are manifested in Dostoievsky's suicides. The Underground Man has spoiled his life in his funk-hole because of his anxiety before any "real life," as he puts it—his desire to protect himself in his grandiloquent world of fantasy from the dirt and degradation that he considers his inevitable portion in reality. Svidrigailov kills himself out of inner emptiness, isolation, and guilt connected with a child he has raped, whose image he cannot get out of his mind. Kirilov kills himself in an effort to liberate humankind from the fear of death and to make his own will absolute in the place of God's. Yet his actual suicide is a pure concentrate of fear and frozen horror which transmutes him from a human being into a jerking, grotesque monster. It is his anxiety before his own fear of death coupled with his terror before the infinite Other that he can neither accept nor disregard that manifest themselves here. Stavrogin's suicide is the last act in an inauthentic existence. It is anxiety before boredom and inner emptiness, dissociation and vacuity, fixated guilt (he has committed the same crime as Svidrigailov), and the inability to bring himself wholly into any one act or relationship.

Even Dostoievsky's supposedly Christlike character Prince Myshkin ends in a suicide, or more literally "selficide," through his passive identification with the sufferings of the demonic and tormented. Myshkin's attraction to suffering is a desperate release of the inner tension which he cannot bear. Even the element of compassion in it touches one of the deepest sources of anxiety in our culture: It is the hopeless attempt of the one who is unconfirmed oneself to supply an absolute confirmation to others. Myshkin's anxiety leads directly to a self-destruction beyond all mere self-denial, the portion of the one who walks the lonely path of fear and trembling without the grace received from others that enables one to be human.

Franz Kafka's whole work is a profound demonstration of anxiety in our culture. In it is reflected Kafka's own anxiety about his choice between the imprisonment of marriage, on the one hand, and the progressive exile of the bachelor, on the other. Kafka chooses the latter way for himself and his heroes, and they all end with only enough space to bury them. Kafka's heroes move from self-sufficiency to ever more anxious isolation and exile. From beneath their compulsive mastery of their surroundings ever fresh anxiety inevitably breaks forth. Their metamorphosis turns someone who stands on a very narrow plot of ground into someone who has no ground at all. The self is torn out of the social role and the accustomed routine that it has built up for itself.

Absence of confirmation is also a central source of anxiety in Kafka. Had the "hunger artist" found some way open to a direct, meaningful existence, he would not have needed to seek the indirect confirmation of his art. In Kafka's novel, *The Castle*, K. needs to be confirmed in his vocation as "land-surveyor" before he can practice it. To receive it he must make contact with the Castle, which he cannot do; yet without this confirmation from the Castle, he cannot remain in the Village.

All of this leads to "the problematic of modern man": the complex intermixture of personal freedom and psychological compulsion that brings deep anxiety not only to the sick person but to any modern individual who is aware of the discontinuities of a personal existence in which one sometimes acts relatively wholly and spontaneously but very often more as a conditioned reflex or partial compulsion and not infrequently in such a way that one cannot tell which of these two is predominant and how they relate. The relationship between anxiety and compulsion that threatens the sense of being a person must be coupled with the equally important relationship between anxiety and will. The mental illness of Modern Man is not just individual neurosis but the result of one's uprooting from the community in which one formerly lived. It is only an aspect of one's existence as an exile, one's own exile and that of Modern Man.

This anxiety also applies to the modern individual who goes through that crisis of motives in which one can no longer take at face value either other people's motives or one's own. This means a mutual mistrust in which people cease to confirm one another, but it also means a mistrust and fragmentation of the self in which one is incapable of confirming oneself. In Camus' novel, *The Fall*, it is the anxiety before the shattered image of the "man of goodwill" that leads Jean-Baptiste Clamence to abandon any attempt at real existence. An even deeper anxiety leads Joseph K. in *The Trial* to try to handle his case as a business deal, to forget it almost entirely, and than to abandon his position at the bank in favor of futile efforts to circumvent a judgment which he can never comprehend.

How can we live in the face of the anxiety in our culture? Must we choose between accepting those cultural forms that help us to repress this anxiety—only to see it break out afresh in ever new areas—and being so aware of anxiety that it is reflexively intensified and reduplicated? Not necessarily. It is also possible to revolt against our modern exile rather than deny or underscore it. But here, too, the way in which we revolt against it makes an enormous difference as to whether this revolt will result in new anxiety that is greater than we need to bear or in holding our own before anxiety in a way that allows us some margin for a human and even a meaningful existence. The all or nothing of the Modern Promethean represents a romantic revolt which can only in the end make one subject to the very anxiety one is trying to escape, whereas the Modern Job's trust and contending within the "Dialogue with the Absurd" represents a sober, unprogrammatic revolt that accepts the anxiety of our culture yet gains real ground in the face of it. By neither accepting nor cutting ourselves off from the anxiety of our culture but by fighting with it and receiving from it, we may attain the meaning it has to give us.

The answer to our original question then is "Both": Anxiety is a product of our culture and our culture is a means of warding off basic human anxiety. Just for this reason, the Modern Job's stance toward the anxiety of our culture—the stance of trust *and* contending—also means a stance toward the *Angst* of the human condition itself. This is an integral part of the meaning that the anxiety of our culture has to give us.

Personal Freedom and Psychological Compulsion

THE Modern Rebel-Exile is an uncertain figure underneath whose romantic gestures is revealed not only the alienation but the problematic of Modern Man. This problematic in no way invalidates the Modern Rebel, but it transforms his meaning. It is no longer possible to see him as a pure type or to divorce his heroic gestures from the inner conflicts and complexities that bring us into the realms of personal freedom and psychological compulsion, inner division, the crisis of motives, and the problematic of the person in the modern world. One of the most important aspects of this problematic is the complex intermixture of personal freedom and psychological compulsion, a paradoxical phenomenon that can only be understood from within. The characters of Melville, Dostoievsky, and Kafka show more clearly than any case history the impossibility of ignoring the reality of such compulsion, on the one hand, or of reducing the human being to a deterministic system, on the other.

Ahab

What makes Captain Ahab, the central figure of Herman Melville's novel *Moby Dick,* really modern is the deep inner division in him. We are told that Ahab's intense thinking has made him into a Prometheus whose own mind creates a vulture that feeds upon his heart. In Ahab, Melville has depicted the problematic of Modern Man—the alienation, the divided nature, the unresolved tension between personal freedom and psychological compulsion which follow the "death of God."

Melville himself never lets us forget how much of Ahab's Prometheanism must be ascribed to psychological illness. Ahab cannot be dismissed as *merely* projecting evil on the nonhuman world; for Ishmael himself provides us with an enormous accumulation of suggestions that the world is hostile to Man either in a personal-malignant or a cold-indifferent way. What makes Ahab "crazy" is the fact that he personifies this evil in Moby Dick. Melville explicitly ascribes this association of all evil with the White Whale to Ahab's delirium and his "transference," a term which Melville uses in a manner not unlike its modern psychoanalytical usage.

In *Moby Dick* Melville actuallly appears to "psychoanalyze" his hero. We are told of the stages of Ahab's monomania, being constantly reassured throughout that this *is* a monomania. The first stage was the "sudden, passionate, corporal animosity" which led him to drive his knife into the whale; the second stage was "the agonizing bodily laceration" that he felt when his leg was sheared off; the third came when "Ahab and anguish lay stretched together in one hammock" for "long months of days and weeks"; the fourth was that period when "his torn body and gashed soul bled into one another; and so interfusing made him mad"; by the fifth stage he became "a raving lunatic. . . unlimbed of a leg," yet possessing enormous "vital strength." This coupling of impotence and vital strength recurs again and again with Ahab. His sense of impotence is expressed in his terrible rage and frustration, but he is the only really vital person in the whole boat, the only one with full depths of vitality, and this is why everything centers on him. In the sixth stage Ahab hid his madness. "The direful madness" was gone from the outside, but "Ahab, in his hidden self, raved on." His "full lunacy subsided not but deepeningly contracted," and yet, at the same time as his "broad madness" had not been left behind, so "not one jot of his great natural intellect had perished." His vital intelligence is not only preserved in madness but enormously enhanced: "Far from having lost his strength, Ahab, to that one end, did now possess a thousand fold more potency than ever he had sanely brought to bear upon any one reasonable object."

Ahab's madness has given him sources of almost unlimited

strength: He has gone down to a deeper level not only than ordinary persons can reach, but than he himself could reach so long as he was sane. He is, in fact, a sort of negative superman; he has achieved what the rest of humanity vainly strives for: the full working of the mind, the great clarity of intellect, the fullness of passion and vitality—all harnessed in one direction. And the whole process is mad. Yet at just this point we are told: "This is much, yet Ahab's larger, darker, deeper part remains unhinted. But vain to popularize profundities, and all truth is profound." Here, despite all the disclaimers about Ahab's madness, Ishmael clearly tells us that there is reality in this man which, far from our being able to dismiss it, is too deep for us to begin to comprehend.

Ahab's inner division and the complex relation between his personality and his psychological illness come to the surface most clearly during that brief interlude in "The Symphony" in which Ahab recognizes his compulsion for what it is. There he identifies himself, for once, not with the monomaniacal drive to chase the whale, the rage and passion to pursue, but with the person who is driven by that compulsion, the man who is old and tired and knows it. "What mad thing has made me run the seas these forty years!" he exclaims. The very nature of the compulsion that possesses Ahab has always in the past made him identify with it. The symptoms of his inner dualism that he manifests up till now are not so much a sign of the weakness of his resolve, we are told in "The Chart" (XLIV), "but the plainest tokens of its intensity." When Ahab's intolerably vivid nightmares become an insufferable anguish that force him to "burst from his stateroom, as though escaping from a bed that was on fire," the agent is not "crazy Ahab, the scheming, unappeasedly steadfast hunter of the White Whale" who had gone to the hammock. The agent is "the eternal, living principle or soul in him" which, becoming dissociated in sleep, "spontaneously sought escape from the scorching contiguity" of that supreme purpose which "by its own sheer inveteracy of will, forced itself... into a kind of self-assumed, independent being of its own" which "could grimly live and burn, while the common vitality to which it was conjoined, fled horror-stricken from the unbidden and unfathered birth."

> Therefore, the tormented spirit that glared out of bodily eyes, when what seemed Ahab rushed from his room, was for the time

but a vacated thing, a formless somnambulistic being, a ray of living light, to be sure, but without an object to color, and therefore a blankness in itself.

Now, however, in "The Symphony," it is the fully conscious Ahab, rather than a dissociated vacant, inner blankness, who does not identify himself with his compulsion.

> "The madness, the frenzy, the boiling blood and the smoking brow with which for a thousand lowerings old Ahab has furiously, foamingly chased his prey—more a demon than a man!—aye, aye! what a forty years' fool—old fool, has old Ahab been! Why this strife of the chase?"

"Locks so grey did never grow but from out some ashes," Ahab adds, reinforcing the image of an extinct volcano implicit in Melville's earlier phrase, "the burnt-out crater of his brain." Perhaps it is because his volcanic fire has temporarily gone out, or at least burnt low, that Ahab now knows his compulsion for what it is. Ahab's inner compulsion is fate itself for him. "With little external to constrain us," says Ishmael commenting on Ahab, "the innermost necessities in our being, these still drive us on." After Ahab has ceased to identify with his compulsion and before he projects it on God, he has a moment of genuine doubt as to his own self which makes him question whether there really is an "I," a person behind his actions and not some objective, impersonal force.

> "What is it, what nameless, inscrutable, unearthly thing is it, what cozening, hidden lord and master, and cruel, remorseless emperor commands me; that against all natural lovings and longings, I so keep pushing, and crowding, and jamming myself on all the time; recklessly making me ready to do what *in my own proper, natural heart, I durst not so much as dare? Is Ahab, Ahab? Is it I, God, or who, that lifts this arm?*

How startling this confession of weakness on the lips of the man who said, "Who's over me? Truth hath no confines"!

Dostoievsky

The problem of the relation of personal freedom to psychological compulsion cannot be solved by the attempt to reduce the human being to a bundle of instinctual drives, unconscious complexes, the need for security, or any other single factor. Each psychoanalytic school has attempted to find a key to the human, and each, in so doing, has lost the human. Motivation is inextricably bound up with the wholeness of the person, with one's direction of movement, with one's struggles to authenticate oneself. This wholeness of the person in one's dynamic interrelation with other persons Dostoievsky guards as no psychoanalytic theory ever has. In Dostoievsky we never see a metaphysical freedom or free will separate from conditioning factors; rather, we see the free will shining through and refracted by the sickness which shapes and exasperates so many of Dostoievsky's characters.[1] At the age of eighteen Dostoievsky wrote to his brother: "Man is a mystery. Even if you were to spend your whole life unraveling it, you ought not say that you had wasted your life. I occupy myself with this mystery, for I want to be a man."[2] The fact that so many psychiatrists, including Freud, have praised Dostoievsky for his psychological acumen has led some to assume that Dostoievsky either holds a theory of psychological determinism himself or provides

1. Vyacheslav Ivanov sees the relation of compulsion to freedom in Dostoievsky as a lower level of empirical determinism and a higher level of free will that simply uses but is in no wise determined by the lower: "Dostoievsky presents each individual destiny as a single, coherent event taking place simultaneously on three different levels. . . . On the two lower levels is displayed the whole labyrinthine diversity of life. . . the changeability of the empirical character even within the bounds of its determination from without. On the uppermost, or metaphysical, level. . .there is no more complexity or subjection to circumstance: here reigns the great, bare simplicity of the final. . .decision. . . .for being in God; or for. . .flight from God into Not-being. The whole tragedy played out on the two lower levels provides only the materials for the construction, and the symbols for the interpretation of the sovereign tragedy of the God-like spiritual being's final self-determination: an act which is solely that of the free will." (Vyacheslav Ivanov, *Freedom and the Tragic Life: A Study in Dostoievsky* [New York: Noonday Press, 1957]), pp. 38 f. Ivanov's material and metaphysical levels do not so much solve the problem that Dostoievsky presents us as sidestep it. Although we may agree with Ivanov that Dostoievsky's "searching. . .has a single aim: to ascertain that part played by the intelligible act of will in the empirical deed," we cannot agree with any a priori formulation that answers this question in the abstract rather than in terms of each character and each situation. Dostoievsky does not present us with "empirical" and "metaphysical levels," but with an image of the wholeness of Man in all his complexity and contradictoriness.

2. Quoted in Zenta Maurina, *Dostojewskij. Menschengestalter und Gottessucher* (Memmingen: Maximilian Dietrich Verlag, 1952), p. 129, my translation.

evidence for it. Dostoievsky is interested in mental sickness, as Samuel Smith and Andrei Isotoff have pointed out, but not in its genesis á la Freud.

> So far from holding to the doctrine of closed-linked...causation for psychic events, he emphasizes the waywardness and unpredictability of impulse which motivates the actions of his persons....The closeness of his observation, since borne out by psychiatrists, is no evidence that he had the same notions on causation in psychic dynamics as the analysts have developed.[3]

To Dostoievsky the view which reduces free will to psychological determinism is as untrue as that which accords persons a metaphysical free will untouched by conditioning forces. The Underground Man is both free and not free at once. No general theory of psychogenesis and no general knowledge of persons will tell us in advance what will be their actual mixture of spontaneity and compulsion in any particular situation. Hence Dostoievsky's contribution to the problematic of Modern Man is in this respect superior to Freud's psychogenic determinism. This does not mean that Dostoievsky's characters must be taken at face value or even as Dostoievsky himself may have intended them. On the contrary, even in those characters that he intended to make most ideal, like Myshkin, and in those ideas that he most cherished, like suffering, guilt, and the responsibility of each for all, abysses open before us that lead us into the problematic of Modern Man.

Stavrogin and Versilov

Nikolai Stavrogin, the hero of Dostoievsky's novel, *The Devils* or *The Possessed*, has his inner division revealed by his devil-doubles. The question that haunts us throughout *The Devils*, however, is whether Stavrogin's enigmatic character and antisocial actions are to be explained as madness or as attitudes for which he is responsible. After six months in the society of the town where the story takes place, Stavrogin suddenly breaks loose and pulls a gentleman by the nose at his club, kisses the wife of another man at a party in the latter's house, and bites the ear of the Governor, who is trying to help him in a fatherly way. These actions offend

3. Samuel Stephenson Smith and Andrei Isotoff, "The Abnormal from Within; Dostoievsky," *Psychoanalytic Review*, XXII (1935), pp. 390 f.

local society all the more because they seem a tangible expression of the insufferable pride and contempt that people sense in him. When it is discovered that he has "brain fever" and these incidents are retroactively attributed to his "not being himself," people receive his apologies sympathetically but are still embarrassed, and some remain "convinced that the blackguard was merely having a good laugh at us all and that his illness had nothing to do with it."

Stavrogin, like Ivan, has a lackey devil with whom he talks, though almost all indications of this have been omitted from the finished version. Stavrogin assures Dasha in a deleted passage that he does not believe in the existence of this devil, that his devil is himself in different form; that, in fact, he splits himself and talks with himself.[4] But in his conversation with Tikhon, which Dostoievsky also omitted, he not only tells him that he has had hallucinations of the devil for a year, but suggests that even though he speaks of it as aspects of himself, he wonders whether it is not really the devil. In fact, he declares categorically, "I do believe in the devil, I believe canonically, in a personal, not allegorical devil," and raises the same question as his lackey devil—whether one can believe in the devil without believing in God. These hallucinations again pose the problem of the extent to which Stavrogin's actions are to be attributed to madness, and Stavrogin himself says that he should see a doctor, to which Father Tikhon immediately assents. The form of the hallucination is even more important than the fact—the heightening of the "double" that reveals not only the extent of Stavrogin's inner split but also the demonic and even diabolical character of that ignoble and not at all heroic part of himself that confronts him in Peter and still more in his lackey devil.

In his last letter to Dasha, Stavrogin seems to equate losing one's reason with an uncompromising belief in an idea. He does not see that a personality split into opposing extremes, like his own, might also mean madness, though in a different way from the monomania of Kirilov. When he apologizes for the supposedly irresistible impulses that led him to pull Gaganov by the nose and bite the Governor's ear, he says he was "not himself," and

4. René Fülop-Müller and Friedrich Eckstein, eds., *Der unbekannte Dostojewski* (Munich: Piper Verlag, 1926), pp. 355–357, 371–373.

when Liputin implies he was, he turns pale and cries, "Good Lord...do you really think that I'm capable of attacking people while in the full possession of my senses?" Stavrogin turns pale every time someone scores a direct hit. It is easier for him to face the idea that he acted on impulse, under the influence of "brain fever," than the idea that it is his very self that is split so that one part of him acts out these impulses while the other fully knows what it does.

In the St. Petersburg version of the Confession, Stavrogin says, "I suspect that this is all a sickness," and the narrator himself says, "This document is, in my opinion, a product of sickness, a work of the devil that has gained mastery over this gentleman."[5] In the finished Moscow version of the Tikhon chapter, Stavrogin opines that his hallucination of the devil is a product of his inner split. But he repeatedly insists that his actions in relation to Matryosha and Mary were *not* the products of madness. And his evidence for this is always of the same nature, namely, that no idea ever took full hold of him, that he could always control himself "if he wanted to," that he was always completely aware of what he was doing.

> "I tell all this in order that every one may know that the feeling never absorbed the whole of me absolutely, but there always remained the most perfect consciousness (on that consciousness indeed it was all based). And although it would take hold of me to the pitch of madness,...it would never reach the point of making me forget myself....I could at the same time overcome it completely, even stop it at its climax, only I never wished to stop it."[6]

While he waits for Matryosha to hang herself, Stavrogin's breathing stops and his heart beats violently but, at the same time, he looks at his watch and notes the time "with perfect accuracy" and has a heightened awareness of every detail around him. When he sits by the window and looks at the little red spider, he thinks of how he will "stand on tiptoe and peer through this very chink" to see if Matryosha has hanged herself. "I mention this detail because I wish to prove fully to what an extent I was ob-

5. Fülop-Müller and Eckstein, eds., *Der unbekannte Dostojewski*, pp. 403, 409.

6. Fyodor Dostoievsky, *Stavrogin's Confession and the Plan of the Life of a Great Sinner*, trans. S. S. Koteliansky and Virginia Woolf (Richmond, England: L. & V. Woolf, 1922), pp. 44 f.

viously in possession of my mental faculties and I hold myself responsible for everything." A more sophisticated awareness of mental illness would have led Stavrogin not to dismiss so conclusively the possibility that the reputation of being mad that he had in his town was right. His heightened awareness of everything and his complete consciousness of what he is doing and his sense of perfect control might as easily be the mark of some type of schizophrenia, or even of paranoid schizophrenia, as of being responsible and in his right mind. Like the Underground Man, he makes the mistakes of equating consciousness and will and of thinking that because he knows what is happening he is free to stop it.

> "I know I can dismiss the thought of Matryosha even now whenever I want to. I am as completely master of my will as ever. But the whole point is that I never wanted to do it; I myself do not want to, and never shall. So it will go on until I go mad."[7]

The fact that he never *wants* to stop what is happening, even though it leads to madness, may cause us to suspect that his perfect mastery of his will is an illusion.

Stavrogin's split is nowhere more clearly manifested, in fact, than in these scenes in which one part of him acts out to the last extreme his tormented impulses while the other looks on with clinical detachment. In addition to this, his constant insistance that his statements prove that he is "of sound mind" are in themselves enough to raise the question of whether he is. That this is a question that Dostoievsky also wants to leave in our minds we have already seen, and it is significant that the final comment of the book, after "the citizen of the canton of Uri" is found "hanging there behind the door," is again on just this matter of Stavrogin's sanity:

> On the table lay a scrap of paper with the words: "No one is to blame, I did it myself." Beside it on the table lay a hammer, a piece of soap, and a large nail, evidently prepared in case of need. The strong silk cord with which Stavrogin had hanged himself had evidently also been prepared and chosen beforehand. It was thickly smeared with soap. All this was evidence of premeditation and consciousness to the last minute.

7. Dostoievsky, *Stavrogin's Confession*, pp. 56–58, 62 f., 67, 69.

The verdict of our doctors after the post-mortem was that it was most definitely not a case of insanity.[8]

What does Dostoievsky want us to believe—that Stavrogin was insane or that he was not insane? Neither the one nor the other. He wants us to understand Stavrogin as precisely that compound of freedom and compulsion, personal responsibility and impersonal determinism that we find in Dostoievsky's Underground Man and in Ivan Karamazov. Like the Underground Man, Stavrogin confronts us not only with his sickness but with the fact that he is aware of it himself, and this means that there is always more to Stavrogin than the psychological categories that he himself offers us. Dostoievsky has created in Stavrogin a truly independent character who has the right to give us his own conclusions about himself and to demand of us that we meet him as a person—an existential subject—and not just as the object of his or our analyses. We have the right to draw our own conclusions about Stavrogin and in so doing to make use of all the material that Stavrogin and his author offer us, but we do not have the right to substitute our own conclusions for the wholeness and uniqueness of the person who is before us. Stavrogin is not a real person, to be sure, but neither is he a "case." He is a literary creation *and* an image of the human created by an author who has succeeded, as few others have, in using literature as a medium for bringing us man the human being in his or her wholeness. Both Stavrogin's despair and his self-awareness show that there is something more to him than any psychological categories can explain—that, in contrast to Peter Verkhovensky, he is a real human being. Dostoievsky clearly wants us to consider the possibility of Stavrogin's madness, or he would not revert so often to this theme, but he does not want us to conclude that he is mad, for this would mean dismissing him as a person and diminishing his stature as an image of the human. What he wishes us to understand, rather, is the *problematic* of Stavrogin, which cannot be resolved into the easy either–or's of sane or insane, free or compulsive, responsible or irresponsible.

Versilov, the paradoxical central figure of *The Raw Youth*, illuminates Dostoievsky's attitude toward Stavrogin still further; for

8. Fyodor Dostoievsky, *The Devils (The Possessed)* trans. David Magarschak, ed. E. V. Rieu (Harmsworth, England: Penguin Classics, 1953), pp. 668 f.

Versilov inherits many of Stavrogin's traits, including his pride and his uncontrollable impulses, and his personality is as clearly split and subject to extremes as Stavrogin's. When Versilov breaks in two the ikon that the saintly pilgrim Makar Ivanovitch has left to him and his wife, he explains his action in advance, as an almost irresistible impulse brought about by the presence in him of a "second self." Versilov does not mean by his "two selves" merely two opposing tendencies, such as Faust's "two souls," one of which pulls him up to heaven while the other drags him down to earth, but one self that is rational and another that is definitely irrational. His description of this state is similar to Stavrogin's self-analyses with one significant difference: Versilov does not believe that his rational self can control his irrational one.

> "I am really split in two mentally, and I'm horribly afraid of it. It's just as though one's second self were standing beside one. One is sensible and rational oneself, but the other self is impelled to do something perfectly senseless, and sometimes very funny, and suddenly you notice that you are longing to do that amusing thing, goodness knows why. That is, you want to, as it were, against your will: though you fight against it with all your might, you want to."[9]

When Versilov breaks the ikon, his pale face suddenly flushes red, almost purple, and every feature in his face quivers and works. Versilov's bastard son Arkady Dolgoruky interprets this event at the time as a symbolic way of showing that Versilov is putting an end to everything. Yet he adds, "But that second self was unmistakably beside him, too, of that there could be no doubt." In the last chapter Arkady, who is also the narrator, dismisses the notion of "actual madness" on Versilov's part but accepts the theory of "the second self" as "the first stage of serious mental derangement, which may lead to something very bad." His conclusion is again precisely that mixed state of freedom and compulsion, responsibility and sickness that we have seen in Stavrogin. It is indeed the place in which the image of the human and psychotherapy meet:

> Though that scene at Mother's and that broken ikon were undoubtedly partly due to the influence of a real "second self," yet I

9. Fyodor Dostoievsky, *A Raw Youth*, trans. Constance Garnett, Introduction by Alfred Kazin (New York: Dial Press, 1947), pp. 552 f.

ever since been haunted by the fancy that there was in it an element of a sort of vindictive symbolism, a sort of resentment against the expectations of those women, a sort of angry revolt against their rights and their criticism. And so hand in hand with the "second self" he broke the ikon, as though to say, "That's how your expectations will be shattered!" In fact, even though the "second self" did come in, it was partly simply a whim....But all this is only my theory, it would be hard to decide for certain.[10] (602 f.)

It *would* be hard to decide for certain, but what appears clear is that it is not a question of an either–or; in Versilov, as in Stavrogin, we see the sick self and the whimsical person together, inextricably mixed. If we contrast Versilov's analysis of his "second self" with Arkady's, we can see not only what Dostoievsky thinks about the problematic of Versilov and Stavrogin, but also his understanding of the human as such. Versilov assumes that the sane and free self is the sensible and rational one and that the "senseless," "funny," and "amusing" things that he feels impelled to do are the product of a sick and unfree self. Thus, he equates the rational with the sane, the irrational with the sick. Arkady, in contrast, sees the "whim" as a product not of the sick "second self" but of the free person. Like the Underground Man, he knows that the human self is just as much irrational as it is rational and that the very essence of that self is the freedom to do the arbitrary and whimsical, what is *not* sensible and rational. Hence, in a perfectly clear and precise formulation, Arkady states, "And so hand in hand with the 'second self' he broke the ikon," in which sentence the "he" refers to the free and responsible self in contrast to the unfree "second self." In the same way, when he says, "Even though the 'second self' did come in, it was partly simply a whim," he is contrasting the lack of freedom of the "second self" with the freedom of the self that acts on whims, whereas Versilov identifies acting on a whim with being compelled by impulses dissociated from his real self. There can be no question that Dostoievsky's view of the human in general—and of Versilov and Stavrogin, in particular—coincides with Arkady's analysis and not with Versilov's.[11]

10. Dostoievsky, *A Raw Youth*, pp. 602 f.
11. This chapter is based upon Maurice Friedman, *Melville, Dostoievsky, Kafka, Camus*, 2nd rev. ed. (Chicago: University of Chicago Press, Phoenix Books, 1970), pp. 469–472, 129–133, 220–227.

Chapter 14

Fathers and Sons: The Divided Self

T HAT deep inner division which characterizes the problematic of Modern Man can only partially be illumined through
understanding the intermixture of personal freedom and psychological compulsion, for this tells us only of the psychological accompaniment and not of the interhuman reality of which that
psychological division is the product. A deeper insight into the divided self can be obtained through understanding its close connection with the image of the human and the relationship between
parent and child in which that image first arises.

The father is the first and often the most lasting image of man
for the son. It not infrequently happens, however, that the father
is not really present for the son, either because he is dead or absent or inattentive, or because he is in no sense a father, or because he is too weak or despicable for a son to be able to emulate
him. In such a case the need for the father as the image of man remains and often leads to a lifetime search for a father who will
supply an image of man as the actual father has not. Freud and
modern psychoanalysts in general have only seen one aspect of
this father–son relationship and have reduced it to fear of castration, introjection of the father's ideals and conscience, or even
identification. The aspect which they have missed is the need that
the son has for a relationship with the father which will help him
find direction in the choices he must make between one way of life
and another. This need is not for identification but dialogue, and

it is not a conditioned formation or reaction but a free and even spontaneous response. At the same time, the other, conditioned reaction does enter in, and the relationship of father to son, even in the most "normal" cases, must also be seen as a blend of the conditioned and the free, the "psychological" and the personal, as is the problematic of Stavrogin and Versilov, of which we have spoken.

It is illuminating to consider the extent to which the relationship to the father has been at the center of both the life and the writings of the three men with whose work I was particularly concerned in *Problematic Rebel:* Melville, Dostoievsky, and Kafka. Throughout almost all their works, one theme remains constant—that of the son in search of a father who is either dead or absent or who has betrayed him or does betray him. In Newton Arvin's view, Melville, who lost his father at an early age and went to sea to escape from the women in his family, was seeking for the father in all his writings. Melville's own relation to his dead father is mirrored, certainly, in Ishmael and Ahab, Pierre and his father, Bartleby and his employer, Billy Budd and Captain Vere. This is not to say, however, that these relationships have a merely psychological significance. On the contrary, the absence of the father so deeply affected Melville's world view that the most profound metaphysical and existential questions take root in this soil. Ultimately the absence of the father meant for Melville the shattering of trust and the search for the father the search for renewal of trust.

The Raw Youth and The Brothers Karamazov

The theme of fathers and sons is central to *The Raw Youth* and *The Brothers Karamazov*, but it is also present in *Crime and Punishment* and *The Devils*. When Dostoievsky's father was murdered by serfs, Dostoievsky, who knew, like Ivan Karamazov, that he had wished for his father's death, was left with a burden of guilt. Hence, his relationship was less to the absent father whom he longed for and sought, like Melville, or the present father whom he both loved and hated, like Kafka, then to the absent father toward whom he felt hatred and guilt—and also, no doubt, resentment that he was not the father whom he would have wished.

The result is a recurrent bifurcation of the father figure into a hated figure and a respected one, an image that repels and an image that attracts, or a problematic image and a clear one. Raskolnikov relates to both Porfiry and Svidrigailov as father figures; Stavrogin, who also lost his father when he was a child, to both Stepan Trofimovitch and Father Tikhon. In *The Raw Youth*, Arkady Dolgoruky is the bastard son of the nobleman Versilov while legally the son of Versilov's former serf Makar Ivanovitch. During the time he was growing up, Arkady had almost no contact with the aloof and enigmatic Versilov. The plot of the novel is largely centered on his coming to live near Versilov and his attempts to penetrate the mystery and solve the riddle of this fascinating, divided man. His need to do this is the need to provide himself with a sense of patrimony. But it is even more clearly the search by an intense and troubled young man for an image of the father that will give him some guidance and sense of direction. Yet the deeper he enters into relationship with Versilov, the more baffled and put off he is by the contradictions in Versilov's character and in his relationship to the other members of the family. As a result, not only does Arkady find himself reacting against Versilov and periodically breaking with him "forever," but he also becomes aware of a very different quest in his soul: the quest for "seemliness."

This quest is answered by the man who is legally his father—Makar Invanovitch. After relinquishing his wife to his master Versilov, Makar has spent twenty years as a pilgrim and now comes home to the family to die. Like his desire to become rich through self-control, Arkady's conversations with Makar Ivanovitch derive directly from Dostoievsky's plan for "The Life of a Great Sinner." Dostoievsky portrayed a discussion similar to that between Tikhon and the boy three times, in fact: in the meeting of Stavrogin and Father Tikhon, in the conversations of Arkady and the pilgrim Makar, and in the relationship of Alyosha to Father Zossima in *The Brothers Karamazov*. In the original drafts of this last novel, moreover, Dostoievsky even planned a meeting between the learned brother, Ivan, and the *staretz*, or holy man. Father Tikhon, the pilgrim Makar, and Father Zossima are successive attempts by Dostoievsky to represent the "god-man" and in each case this "god-man" serves as father and image of the human for a young man in the process of becoming.

The relation of father to sons is as central to *The Brothers Karamazov* as it is to *The Raw Youth*. Here, too, the father figure is bifurcated—into the depraved sensualist Fyodor Karamazov and the god-man Father Zossima, with the Grand Inquisitor as something of an ideal father figure to Ivan. Fyodor Karamazov, the father of Ivan, Dmitri, and Alyosha, characterizes himself aptly as "the old buffoon." He is sly, greedy, rapacious, sensual, dishonest, masochistic. It is significant that we are introduced to Fyodor at the same time as we are introduced to the other father who dominates the book, the *staretz* Zossima, and that we meet them both at a gathering in the latter's cell in which all three sons are present and in which all the main, interrelated themes of the novel are brought out: Dmitri and the desire to murder the father, Ivan and the death of God, Alyosha and his holy Zossima. The two worlds of *The Brothers Karamazov* are the village and the monastery. These are the natural worlds of Russian rural life of that time, but, at the same time, they are also the symbolic worlds in which the drama unfolds. Fyodor Karamazov is the father of the village world and Father Zossima of the world of the monastery. In the confrontation of these two men in Father Zossima's cell, these two worlds are also brought into confrontation. This meeting takes place in unadulterated fashion, not as that of the sacred and the secular, but as that of the sacred and the profane. Fyodor Karamazov plays out his buffoonery to the full and shows that he is able to bring a challenge of equal force, not in the traditional sense of evil opposing good, but in the much more dreadful sense of meaninglessness opposing meaning, directionlessness opposing direction, a mask opposing a person.

Terrible as he is—and he is one of the most terrible and fully unsympathetic figures in literature—Fyodor Karamazov has a stature in some sense greater than that of anyone else in the book. He is elemental passion, the base Karamazov energy and will to live. Out of him come all three of the sons, even Alyosha, and the cold, inhuman, emasculate bastard Smerdyakov, son of the idiot girl Stinking Lizaveta, whom Fyodor raped as the last stage of depraved sensuality. Fyodor has an energy which exceeds that of any of his sons, but in him it lies formless, stagnant, and corrupt.

Although he neither rears his sons nor provides for them and even cheats them out of what is rightfully theirs, he bequeaths this elemental Karamazov passion to each of them and with it the abyss of shame and the sordid depths of existence. This heritage can be either overcome, as in Alyosha, through going the way of Father Zossima and the "god-man"; or affirmed, as in Ivan, through throwing off every demand that is placed on him and becoming himself the higher law; or acted out, as in Dmitri, by one minute following a lofty impulse and the next minute a base one.

"Why is such a man alive?... Tell me, can he be allowed to go on defiling the earth?" cries Dmitri at the meeting at the monastery in which his father, instead of accepting the reconciliation with Dmitri that was to have been the purpose of the meeting, shamelessly baits him. "Listen, monks, to the parricide," Fyodor cries in response to Dmitri's words. Parricide, the murder of the father, is indeed the primary motif of the novel—a motif which involves in the closest possible way not only Dmitri, who almost murders his father, but Ivan, who wishes his father dead and half knowingly encourages the murder, and the bastard son, Smerdyakov, who actually commits the murder.

Ivan, as Smerdyakov says, is more like the father than either of the other two brothers. On his intellectual side he remains grand and noble, bold and courageous, with only the loftiest passions admitted to his self-image. But the other side of him remains nasty and mean. One part of him identifies with his father and, for that reason, passionately hates him, whereas the other part of him is simply detached or at best emotional only in a lofty and abstract manner. Although he likes to think that his whole being is placed at the service of his ideals, the truth is that the other, baser parts of him uses both his ideals and his detachment in its own service.

The superior Ivan, who is above conventional morality, regards his brother Dmitri not merely as a "reptile," but as a "scoundrel," a "murderer," a "parricide," and a "monster" and constantly refers to him as such. When Katya says to Ivan, "It was you, you who persuaded me that he murdered his father. It's only you I believed!" and informs him she has been to see Smerdyakov, Ivan is unable to bear it and rushes off to see Smerdyakov to force him to tell what transpired between him and

Katya. Ivan's irrational hatred of Dmitri is as much connected with his own feeling of guilt for desiring his father's death as with his jealousy of his rival for Katya's love. At one point Alyosha says to Ivan that he has been sent by God to tell him that it was not he, Ivan, who killed his father even though he has several times told himself that he and no one else is the murderer. Trembling all over, Ivan accuses Alyosha of having been in his room and having seen his "visitor." Once earlier, when troubled by doubts, Ivan asks whether Alyosha had thought that he desired his father's death. When Alyosha softly answers, "I did think so," Ivan says, "It was so, too; it was not a matter of guessing." Yet when he goes to see Smerdyakov and the latter also says that Ivan desired his father's death, Ivan jumps up and strikes the sick man on the shoulder with all his might. After Alyosha confesses that he thought that Ivan wished Dmitri to kill their father and was even prepared to help bring it about, Ivan takes a dislike to Alyosha and avoids seeing him. Ivan is too honest to rationalize his actions altogether, but he is too shaky in his own self-image to bear the truth. A large part of Ivan's thought, in fact—from his saying that "all is lawful" to his sin-carrying and sinless Grand Inquisitor and his all-forgiving Christ—can be seen as arising from his inability to accept guilt and his need to sublimate his guilt-feeling into the semblance of noble motives which will satisfy his conscious mind.

The dialectical and intellectual Ivan is so divided that he cannot admit to his conscious mind what has gone on. He keeps that part of himself which he does not care to recognize in a separate compartment, and he uses his hysteria as a relief from the nervous tension that comes from his inner division and from the fact that he is choosing to let things happen rather than make a real decision. Only in this murky, half-conscious world can he persist in this decisionless state of not taking responsibility and at the same time giving a negative "go ahead" to what one part of him, at least, must know is going on. He hates Dmitri as the murderer of his father, but he is impelled to plan his escape because of the burning and rankling sensation that he is "as much a murderer at heart."

Ivan is unable to cast off his guilt by identifying his self with his *conscious* self only or to accept his guilt by identifying himself with that other, surprising self that emerges into thought and action before his eyes. Ivan cannot bear to look into the foul pit of his own inner life; neither can he turn away from it. Versilov's theory of the second self applies equally to Ivan and with it the ambiguities of responsible freedom and impersonal compulsion that Versilov does not see but his son Dolgoruky does. Ivan is not Smerdyakov, able to act without conscience and without guilt, but neither is he Dmitri, ready to receive the suffering that comes to him as a way of working out of dividedness and guilt to some sort of personal wholeness. After the conflict within him between "god-man" and lackey devil has wreaked its havoc, Ivan is left less rebel than simply divided man. The bifurcation of the father figure means the bifurcation of the son.[1]

1. This chapter is based on Maurice Friedman, *Problematic Rebel: Melville, Dostoievsky, Kafka, Camus,* 2nd rev. ed., pp. 472 f., 238–251.

Chapter 15

Crisis of Motives and the Problematic of Guilt

The Crisis of Motives

THE inner division which results from the alienation of fathers and sons from each other is as much a commentary on the absence of a modern image of the human as on the breakdown of the specific father–son relationship. At the heart of this breakdown, in fact, is the inability of the father to given his son a direction-giving image of meaningful and authentic human existence. The inner division in the son that results expresses itself at times, as we have seen, in the bifurcation into opposing selves and opposing father images. It may also, as we have seen, express itself in a crisis of motives when the son, unable to accept the father, suppresses his awareness of the side of him that resembles his father in favor of an ideal self-image. Ivan Karamazov has two contradictory images of the human, two incompatible sets of motivations: the one represented by his "Grand Inquisitor," a noble man with high humanitarian motives; the other by the lackey devil of his hallucinations, who embodies all the mean and trivial emotions and attitudes which he has not wanted to recognize in himself. In all Dostoievsky's divided men, the inner conflict takes the form of a crisis of motives. Motives which in the past might have been taken at their face value—humility, love, friendship—must now be looked at more carefully. For, as Dostoievsky saw even before Freud, they may, in fact, mask resentment, hatred, or hostility. When Modern Man thinks of the humility of St. Francis, he may also see the masochistic Marmeladov allowing his wife to drag him by the beard, or Dostoievsky's "Eternal Husband" who, after ministering to the sick friend who has taken his wife, tries to kill him in his sleep.

For Nietzsche, too, men dissemble without knowing it, unaware of the ignoble lust that conceals itself behind the noble ideal. Zarathustra labels as "Tarantulas" those socialist and humanitarian "preachers of *equality*"whose demand for "justice" masks a secret desire for revenge. The man "who will never defend himself" is the man of *ressentiment* who "swalloweth down poisonous spittle and bad looks, the all-too-patient one, the all-endurer." The chaste are those who seek in chastity the satisfaction that has been denied them elsewhere.

> And how nicely can doggish lust beg for a piece of spirit, when a piece of flesh is denied it!...
> Ye have too cruel eyes, and ye look wantonly towards the sufferers. Hath not your lust just disguised itself and taken the name of fellow suffering?[1]

Friendship, similarly, is often merely an attempt to overleap envy, and the love of one's neighbor nothing but the bad love of oneself.

> Ye call in a witness when ye want to speak well of yourselves; and when ye have misled him to think well of you, ye also think well of yourselves...
> The one goeth to his neighbor because he seeketh himself, and the other because he would fain lose himself.[2]

That modern psychoanalysis has attempted to find a rational pattern behind these hidden motivations that Dostoievsky and Nietzsche have unmasked in no way reduces the problematic nature of the mistrust that impels such unmasking and of the bad faith—with others and with oneself—that is unmasked. Both the bad faith and the mistrust mean essentially the fragmentation of the self. Modern Man knows his alienation nowhere so intensely as in the alienation from oneself that results from this inner division and conflict. In the modern age it is no longer possible to ac-

---

1. Friedrich Nietzsche, *Thus Spake Zarathustra*, trans. Thomas Common (New York: Modern Library, 1927), pp. 56 f.
2. Nietzsche, *Thus Spake Zarathustra*, pp. 63 f.

cept any person, not even oneself, at "face value." Yet it is equally impossible simply to explain away the reality of a person by reducing that person to the psychologically determined being pictured by one of another school of psychoanalysis. What confronts us again and again in others and in ourselves, in the characters of our literature and in the authors who create them, is the bewildering intermixture of personal freedom and psychological compulsion; and the specific form which this intermixture takes differs with each person and with each unique situation.

Jean-Baptiste Clamence

Perhaps the best illustration in contemporary literature of the crisis of motives that results from this inner division is in Albert Camus' last novel, *The Fall*. Jean-Baptiste Clamence, the hero of *The Fall*, was once a respected lawyer who contributed his services to worthy causes, loved one woman after another, and felt secure in the approval of himself and the world. Then, as with Franz Kafka's K., the world breaks in on his self-assured existence, in this case in the form of a young woman whom he sees leaning against a bridge on the Seine and does not try to save when she jumps in and cries for help after he walks by. This event so undermines his faith in his own motivation that he leaves his work and the society of those he knows and becomes a "judge penitent," confessing to others in order to get them to confess to him. Unable to assert his own innocence, he takes refuge in the common guilt: "We cannot assert the innocence of anyone, whereas we can state with certainty the guilt of all. Every man testifies to the crime of all the others—that is my faith and my hope." To Clamence, as to Kafka, the Last Judgement takes place every day. The foundation of his world is social guilt, and he tries to bring others with him into "the closed little universe of which I am the king, the pope, the judge."

Like Dostoievsky's Underground Man, Ivan's Inquisitor, and T. S. Eliot's Prufrock, Camus' "false prophet" is making a confession from hell. Hell is the nonexistence to which he retired when he found existence insupportable; it is the world without reality and without grace into which he tries to attract others, who he knows will have more nasty things to confess in the end than

those he himself has told. He identifies himself, in both his past
and present unwillingness to commit himself, to risk his life, with
the "you" to whom he has talked throughout the book and whom
we realize at the end is ourselves:

> Are we not all alike...? Then please tell me what happened to you
> one night on the quays of the Seine and how you managed never to
> risk your life. You yourself utter the words that for years have
> never ceased echoing through your mouth: "O young woman,
> throw yourself into the water again so that I may a second time
> have the chance of saving both of us!" A second time, eh, what a
> risky suggestion! Suppose, *chèr maître*, that we should be taken liter-
> ally? We'd have to go through with it. Brrr...! The water's so
> cold! But let's not worry! It's too late now. It will always be too
> late. Fortunately![3]

Jean-Baptiste Clamence's affirmation of guilt is deeply disqui-
eting because in his very acceptance of the split between what he
had once pretended to be and what he is, he surrenders that tension that might have led him back to some form of real existence.
Thus, in the end the crisis of motives becomes inseparable from
the problematic of guilt.

Franz Kafka's *The Trial:* The Problematic of Guilt

Our fullest insight into guilt as an interhuman reality and into
the problematic of guilt that grows out of it comes to us from the
works of Franz Kafka. Kafka's treatment of guilt unquestionably
includes a strong neurotic component, as the relation of son to father in Kafka's writings strongly suggests.[4] Yet it is equally clear
that Kafka is concerned not only with neurotic guilt but also with
real guilt that arises as a corollary of one's personal situation and
one's personal responsibility. "Existential guilt," writes Martin
Buber, is "guilt that a person has taken on himself as a person and

3. Albert Camus, *The Fall*, trans. Justin O'Brien (New York: Alfred A. Knopf,
1957), p. 147.
4. "Nowhere in twentieth-century letters is there a better case for the Freudian," writes Frederick J. Hoffman. "The writings of Franz Kafka are...persis-
tent demonstrations of an anxiety neurosis—a constant flight from anticipated
affective danger." Hoffman links this anxiety with the guilt arising from Kafka's
Oedipus complex. ("Escape from Father," in *The Kafka Problem*, ed. Angel
Flores (New York: New Directions, 1946), pp. 214, 246.

in a personal situation." As such, it cannot be comprehended adequately through such psychoanalytic categories as "taboos," "conventions," and "repression." It is not merely guilt-feelings but an objective reality: "Existential guilt occurs when someone injures an order of the human world whose foundations he knows and recognizes as those of his own existence and of all common human existence.[5]

"Although he imagines that he knows more about himself than did the man of any earlier time," writes Buber, "it has become more difficult for the man of our age than any earlier one to venture self-illumination with awake and unafraid spirit." Buber sees this modern problem of guilt illustrated in two of the figures whom we have seen as representative of the problematic of Modern Man—Stavrogin and Joseph K. Stavrogin, "the man on the outermost rim of the age," " 'commits' the confession as he commits his crimes: as an attempt to snatch the genuine existence which he does not possess." Joseph K. is not able to make confession at all. "Not merely before the world, but also before himself, he refuses to concern himself with an ostensible state of guilt. . . . Indeed, it now passes as proved, in this his generation, that no real guilt exists; only guilt-feeling and guilt convention."[6] Each man in so doing is faithful to the stage that the problematic of Modern Man had reached in his author's lifetime:

> *The Possessed* was written in 1870, Kafka's *Trial* in 1915. The two books represent two basically different but closely connected situations of human history from which their authors suffered: the one the uncanny negative certainty, "Human values are beginning to shatter," and the other the still more uncanny uncertainty, "Do world-meaning and world-order still have any connection at all with this nonsense and this disorder of the human world?"—an uncertainty that appears to have arisen out of that negative certainty.[7]

Although the Court that K. is confronted by is "wild, crude, and senselessly disordered through and through," writes Buber,

5. Martin Buber, *The Knowledge of Man*, "Guilt and Guilt Feelings," trans. Maurice Friedman.
6. Buber, *The Knowledge of Man*, p. 146.
7. Buber, *The Knowledge of Man*, p. 140.

"Joseph K. is himself, in all his actions, of hardly less indefiniteness...as charged with guilt, he confusedly carries on day after day a life as directionless as before." He refuses to confess, not because he is proud, like Stavrogin, but because he does not distinguish himself from others. His statement, "And, if it comes to that, how can any man be called guilty? We are all simply men here, one as much as the other," is his way of denying the existence of personal guilt and escaping "the demand to bear into his inner darkness (of which Kafka speaks in his diaries) the cruel and salutary light." In denying "the ontic character of guilt, the depth of existential guilt beyond all mere violations of taboos," writes Buber, Joseph K. is doing just what Freud wished to do "when he undertook to relativize guilt-feeling genetically."[8]

Guilt, to Kafka, must be understood within the context of two discernible stages in Kafka's thought: the world breaking in on the self, and the self seeking to answer a call. To say that guilt originates with the world breaking into the self is to say that the world in some sense calls one to become oneself through fulfilling one's "calling," that to which one is called, and that it calls one to account when one does not do so. Kafka understands this calling to account, however, in a thoroughly problematic way. The central problem of *The Trial*, that of guilt, cannot be referred simply

---

8. Buber, *The Knowledge of Man*, p. 142. Buber answers the question of "how the absurd confusion that rules in the court is to be reconciled with the justice of the accusation and the demand" with the assertion that Kafka lets "the just accusation of an inaccessible highest judgment be conveyed by a disorderly and cruel court." For Kafka the meaning that reaches one and demands response from one comes to one only through the absurd. Buber's conclusion, nonetheless, has to do not with one's encounter with the absurd but with oneself and one's illumination of one's personal guilt: "Only that man can escape the arm of this court who, out of his own knowledge, fulfills the demand for confession of guilt according to its truth through executing the primal confession, the self-illumination. Only he enters the interior of the Law." Buber's discussion of exististial guilt includes an emphasis upon concrete and specific acts of guilt that seems quite foreign to *The Trial*, where no specific action is ever in question. By the same token, Buber's emphasis upon illumination and confession of one's personal guilt has a far more particular ring than anything in Kafka. Even when Kafka speaks of confession in his diaries, it is doubtful that he means confession of particular acts. Kafka was a man who lived all his life in a shadow world of guilt in which "the profound ambiguity between good and evil," to use Tillich's phrase, far outweighed any specific sense of sin.

to K.'s subjectivity, nor to the frighteningly irregular and corrupt bureaucracy that has him in its "clutches," but to the encounter between the two. The world of Joseph K. gradually changes from the everyday business world that he takes for granted into a mysterious Gnostic hierarchy that, like some gigantic octopus, wraps its tentacles around the whole of reality until it finally crushes him to death—and, most startling of all, does so with his compliance!

"Someone must have traduced Joseph K., for without having done anything wrong he was arrested one fine morning." Thus begins a book which, while it never brings to light even the most trivial offense for which K. might be arrested and punished, increasingly places in question the unambiguous insistence of the hero that he is simply the innocent victim of injustice. K. is arrested on his thirtieth birthday and executed on his thirty-first, biographical coincidences which suggest already that his "trial" is not a judgment on what he has specifically done or left undone but on his life itself. When he is told that the Law does not hunt for crime but is drawn to the guilty, K. says, "I don't know this Law," to which the warder who has arrested him replies, "All the worse for you." When K. then says, "And it probably exists nowhere but in your own head," the warder responds, "You'll come up against it yet," while the other warder comments, "See, Willem, he admits that he doesn't know the Law and yet he claims he's innocent." K.'s very guilt, we may surmise, lies in the fact that he does not know the Law, that his life is closed to the *hearing* of the Law.

Joseph K. has successfully constructed, in fact, a life which excludes "hearing." Between the meaningless routine of his work at the Bank, where he is the chief clerk, and the meaningless routine of his "bachelor pleasures," there is no room for any kind of self-examination. This is the case with his life before his arrest. It is also the case after his "arrest" when he cannot bring himself to take the time needed for recalling his past life in detail. Since after his arrest K. is allowed to carry on his business as usual and since he "cannot recall the slightest offense that might be charged against" him, he begins by dismissing his arrest as an affair of no great importance. The warders cannot say that he is charged with any offense, but they advise him: "Think less about us and of what is going to happen to you, think more about yourself instead." This advice directs us away from any specific guilt on K.'s part to his existence as such. In striking contrast to Kafka himself, however, K. acknowledges no guilt whatsoever and persists in regarding his trial as real only if he recognizes it as such.

The significance of K.'s ignorance of the law—of his having no time for hearing and for self-examination—is indicated not merely by the routine character of his work and his pleasures but still more by his attempt to turn his whole existence into one of professional smoothness and efficiency. K. must always "be prepared," he must always be in control. What makes his arrest a special nightmare to him is that it comes to him when he is unprepared, at home, in bed, not ready to master the situation with smooth professional skill without involving himself personally.

Throughout the opening stages of the trial, K. preserves the demeanor of the detached observer who is somehow not really involved in his own case. Other people seem to him mad and incomprehensible; he is always sane and cool. By the same token, he is constantly impelled to contrast the orderly nature of his own life and the disorderly character of the Court. The conclusion that he draws from this is that what is needed is the sort of strengthening of self-confidence through autosuggestion which is regularly preached to the modern businessman as the gospel of success: "The right tactics were to avoid letting one's thoughts stray to one's own possible shortcomings, and to cling as firmly as one could to the thought of one's advantage." The Court would encounter in him a formidable opponent, a man with "know-how": "These tactics must be pursued unremittingly, everything must be organized and supervised; the Court would encounter for once an accused man who knew how to stick up for his rights."

K.'s guilt, in other words, so far as we can glimpse it, is neither legal nor social, but existential. By this we do not mean, as so many existentialists do, that his guilt is only or even primarily in relation to himself; for his existence is inseparable from his relations to others. But we do mean that he is accountable as a person and not just as someone who fulfills a social role. When the novel opens, he knows his existence only as that of the chief clerk of the Bank. By drawing him forth from the social confirmation that such a role gives him to the solitude in which he has to face his trial just as the person he is, with no help from others, his "arrest" has forced him to become aware of a personal dimension of existence that he would never have noticed of his own free will. The persons with whom K. comes in contact cannot be his allies since he has built his life on the exclusion of the reality of other people and wants to relate to them only insofar as he has mastered them. Every person who meets him is a potential judge, for that person has a reality quite alien to his own existence, a reality that confronts his existence and calls it into question.

The situation of K., who is torn out of the security of his social role into the anxiety of personal accountability, is to some extent the situation of everyone who at one time or another in one's life suddenly finds oneself standing alone without those supports of family, position, and name that are so familiar to one that one has come to take them for granted. So, too, everyone stands, whether one knows it or not, in a situation of continuous personal accountability as long as one lives. No person achieves a plane where one not only may approve of all one has been but may take for granted one's responses to the new, unforeseen situation that awaits one. Our existence in time is characterized above all else by just this necessity of meeting the new face that the moment wears. In other words, the possibility of a final decision that is true of an ordinary trial is not true of our existence itself. "Only our concept of time makes it possible for us to speak of the Day of Judgment by that name," says Kafka in one of his aphorisms; "in reality it is a summary court in perpetual session." If one thinks of guilt not in legal but in personal and existential terms, then it becomes impossible to say, as K. says, that one is completely innocent. The question of whether one's existence is authentic or inauthentic cannot be answered by the sum of one's actions, as K. wishes, nor by any objective standard that detaches guilt from one's personal existence itself. Neither is it merely a subjective or arbitrary matter, but the responsibility of the self in relation to the world. This responsibility cannot be judged from the standpoint of the world alone or of the self alone nor from the standpoint of any third party looking at the world and the self, but only within the relationship itself. "Only he who is a party can really judge," reads another Kafka aphorism, "but as a party he cannot judge. Hence it follows that there is no possibility of judgment in the world, only a glimmer of it." This means, too, that one is accountable for one's existence and is accountable alone, without any possibility of a "joint defense." "You are the problem. No scholar to be found far and wide," says Kafka in a remarkably Zenlike aphorism.[9]

In the course of the book, K. experiences a growing anxiety about his case, an anxiety arising from the failure of his attempts to master the situation. His trial works on K. as an ever greater distraction so that he is no longer able to concentrate on his business or to be really present to the external world which was his life. Speaking psychologically, one might say that Kafka describes a person whose unconscious impulses or anxieties block one's conscious drive for success, a person whose life is more and more preoccupied with and distracted by a guilt that one cannot face. The proceedings and the verdict have an organic continuity with each other since what is in question here is no single crime but a line of inauthentic existence that gradually crystallizes into its own judgment on itself.

The Law is not available to every person at every moment for the simple reason that in the reality of one's personal existence one is not approached at every moment and one is not always ready to go forth to meet what comes. Something is required of one before a decisive meeting can take place, something that K. is unwilling to do, namely, involving one's whole person in one's actions in such a way that one becomes genuinely responsible for them. This in no way contradicts the statement in the "Parable of the Law" that the door is intended just for this person, for what is in question here is not some universal law that applies to people in general, but a unique relationship to reality that is available to no one else. The door is shut at the time of the man from the country's death because with the end of his existence the possibility of the realization of this unique relationship also disappears.

In *The Trial*, Kafka is clearly as concerned about the grotesque absurdity of the world that K. encounters as about K.'s existential guilt. But he is concerned most of all about the confrontation of

9. Franz Kafka, *The Great Wall of China, Stories and Reflections,* trans. Willa and Edwin Muir (New York: Schocken Books, 1946), "Reflections on Sin, Pain, Hope, and the True Way," No. 38, p. 263.

these two, about what happens when the world breaks in on the self as it does on K. Although the world that confronts the self is absurd, it places a real demand on the self that the latter must meet. The self can find meaning in its existence neither through rationalizing away the absurdity of the world nor through rejecting the world's demand because of this absurdity, but through answering with its existence the demand that comes to it through the absurd and that can reach it in no other way. This is the ultimate meaning of the self breaking in on the world, as Kafka develops the theme.

Kafka emphatically denies that his view of life as a judgment is merely a psychological matter. On the contrary, he sees life itself as erected upon inner justification, and the task of such a justification as essential to human existence. By "inner justification" Kafka in no sense means an act of arbitrary self-confirmation or the self's free choice of its own image of the human in responsibility only to itself. On the contrary, he holds that time itself, and our own existence in time, must be justified before eternity. The very fact of being asked about one's life and having to answer—of being called and responding to the call—is the inner meaning of the justification which Kafka sees as the underpinning of human existence. We may even say that this call is at the same time a "calling to account," in the sense that it makes us accountable for our lives. Moreover, when we have tried to avoid this accountability, like Joseph K., then the judgment that follows is a calling to account for our failure to answer the call.

We know ourselves as called but we do not know who calls nor the direction from which the call comes nor the way in which we must answer it. This is the problematic of Modern Man. It is possible, therefore, to say, at one and the same time, that life is a commission and a task and that we do not know who commissions or what our task is. The conclusion from this is not, as Joseph K. thinks, that we are all absolved from guilt, but that we are accountable for our existence in a way that eludes our rational grasp of guilt and innocence. We are guilty for not answering or for answering in the wrong way the call that we could never clearly hear. "Only those fear to be put to the proof who have a bad conscience," said Kafka. "They are the ones who do not fulfill the tasks of the present. Yet who knows precisely what his task is? No one. So that every one of us has a bad conscience."[10]

10. This chapter is based upon Maurice Friedman, *Problematic Rebel: Melville, Dostoievsky, Kafka, Camus,* 2nd rev. ed., pp. 473–475, 425–427, and Chapter 15, " 'The Trial': The Problematic of Guilt," pp. 346–356, 360–364, 367–369, 372 f.

Chapter 16

Sex and Love[1]

T HE paradox of the hidden human image with which we started is that it needs to be revealed yet must also remain, its depth-dimension, concealed. This paradox is complemented and complicated by a second paradox—that many of the contemporary attempts to reveal it only serve to conceal it further, or sometimes reveal surface facets at the expense of causing the depth-image of the human to draw ever deeper into hiding. In no case is this more so than in the case of sex and love. One part of the natural hiddenness of the human which can and should be naturally revealed is sex—or more exactly, sexual relationship, love, and marriage. Yet a large part of the obscuring of the human in our day comes through precisely this area of our existence.

In the 1920s T. S. Eliot expressed this dilemma with great forcefulness in his classic poem *The Waste Land*. The modern Waste Land is a sterile place. It has been violated because of the misuse of sex—because sex has nothing to do with real human emotions or depth and still less with genuine relationship between people. In his early poetry Eliot splits humankind, in almost Freudian fashion, into Sweeney, an embodiment of pure "id," and Prufrock, a man entirely dominated by "superego." Sweeney is hardly human, while Prufrock has lost touch with his vital forces almost entirely. Prufrock cannot summon up passion, for in

1. This chapter is reprinted from Maurice Friedman, *The Hidden Human Image* (New York: Delacorte Press and Delta Books, 1974), Chapter 10, pp. 165–182.

176

the moment of giving himself to another, he is afraid that a chilling response from the other will suddenly make his action seem inappropriate, leaving him ludicrous and exposed. Hence, he is cut off equally from the lust of Sweeney and from the personal relationship of which Sweeney is incapable. Together Prufrock and Sweeney make up the world of *The Waste Land*—consciousness without life and lust without love. Both preclude any relationship between persons. This absence of meeting between persons is distilled in the figure of "Gerontion," the old man finishing out his meaningless existence with "thoughts of a dry brain in a dry season."

> I have lost my passion: why should I need to keep it
> Since what is kept must be adulterated?
> I have lost my sight, smell, hearing, taste and touch:
> How should I use them for your closer contact?

I cannot use my passion in any pure way, for my meaningless existence adulterates it as I use it. I have lost my five senses, the means whereby I came near your heart, but I could not have any real contact with you even if I had not lost them. All that is left to me is the decadence of pure sensation.

In *The Waste Land* Eliot uses the ancient myth of the land cursed by sterility because of the rape of the virgins at the shrine to portray the sterility of modern life, the rape of lust without love. The waste land is the world not only of the animal lust of Sweeney but also of the frustrated and trivialized passion of Prufrock. Above all, the modern violation of sex means isolation: 'I have heard the key / Turn in the door once and turn once only / We think of the key, each in his prison / Thinking of the key, each confirms a prison." Only sympathy, Eliot implies, can begin to overcome the isolation of Modern Man, and with it control, discipline, direction, bringing oneself into the focus of a single intent. Yet this possibility seems to be open only for the exceptional individual. At the end of the poem the waste land is as sterile as before.[2]

Sex, which should be the crown of human relationships, be-

2. For a full-scale interpretation of T. S. Eliot's *The Waste Land,* see Maurice Friedman, *To Deny Our Nothingness: Contemporary Images of Man,* 3rd rev. ed., (Chicago: University of Chicago Press Phoenix Books, 1978), Chapter 2, "Images of Inauthenticity," pp. 31–38.

comes the opposite—the mark of its inauthenticity. Sex touches on the *problematic* of the hidden human image as few things do. One reason for this is that people are inclined to distrust themselves, and they are inclined to mistrust each other. This mistrust arises in part because of the popular Freudian view of Man as a two-layer being whose instincts are likely at any moment to take over control from the rational mind. That ancient dualism in which the body and sex are regarded as evil has been modernized in no less puritanical form by Freud, who tells us that our conscious thoughts *and* feelings are rationalizations for the drive toward fulfillment of libidinal urges which we cannot admit directly to ourselves. How this affects the relationship of men and women is vividly illustrated by Germaine Greer in her colorful book, *The Female Eunuch*:

> As long as man is at odds with his own sexuality and as long as he keeps woman as a solely sexual creature, he will hate her, at least some of the time.... Shakespeare was right in equating the strength of the lust drive and the intensity of the disgust that followed it.[3]

This is not to imply that Freud has not revealed something of the hidden human image in his stress on the dominant role of sex in human motivation. If we cannot join Freud in making the conscious mind so much the superstructure determined by and reflecting our unconscious motivations, we can certainly assert that what Martin Buber called "the world of It" and "the world of Thou" are nowhere so completely intermingled as in sex and love. That would be no problem if the It were transformed by and taken up into the Thou. Often, in fact, we do not know which is in the service of which. Even if we could rid ourselves of the tenacious notion that sex is something innately evil, we would still have the problem of when it is a revealing of the human image and when an obscuring. More terrible still, how often does what seems to be a beautiful and gracious revealing turn out to be a hideous obscuring!

Although it may no longer be true to say that Freud dominates the psychiatric thought of our time, it certainly is true that he

3. Germaine Greer, *The Female Eunuch* (New York: McGraw-Hill, 1971), p. 250.

dominates its approach to sex. While many people might quarrel with the central role that Freud ascribes to libidinal sexuality in the human psychic economy, few look at sex itself in terms basically other than those of Freud—namely, as an irrational, instinctual, and largely unconscious drive that must be understood in the first instance in terms of the biological needs of the individual organism and only secondarily and derivatively in terms of interpersonal relations. The significance of Jean-Paul Sartre's approach to sex lies in the fact that, without any attempt to minimize its significance, he lifts it out of the Freudian categories to which we are accustomed and places it squarely within his own existentialist thought, with its emphasis upon the relation of the subject to itself and to others. This means, in the first instance, that Sartre rejects the Freudian unconscious which magically acts as its own censor in such a way that it knows what it must keep itself from knowing. Sartre puts forward instead the self which, in the middle of all facticity, inescapably remains responsible for itself, for the person which it becomes through its own project, and for the image of the human which it chooses for itself and for all human beings.

This approach of Sartre's deals a death blow to the favorite concept of romantic love—the passion which overwhelms one and by which one has no choice but to let oneself be carried along. Man, to Sartre, is responsible for his passion. Sartre's existentialist "will never agree that a sweeping passion is a ravaging torrent which fatally leads a man to certain acts and is, therefore, an excuse." This does not mean that Sartre has retrogressed to some naive rationalism that ignores the dark, swirling forces in Man's being that have been uncovered by the romantics and by depth psychology. It means, rather, that human existence can never be reduced for him to a psychological state, a pure content of feeling, minus the attitude which the subject has toward that state or feeling. The pederast who admits that he has sexual relations with young boys but denies that he is a pederast is in bad faith, says Sartre; yet his friend, who hopes to liberate him by getting him to admit that he is a pederast, is equally in bad faith, since he wants him to call himself a pederast as one calls this table a table.

To understand Sartre's approach to sex we must understand his approach to intersubjectivity—the relation between subject and subject. "The Other *looks* at me and as such he holds the secret of my being, he knows what I am. Thus the profound meaning of my being is outside of me, imprisoned in an absence." The Other steals my being from me, and I recover myself only through absorbing the other. Nonetheless, I exist by means of the Other's freedom; for I need his the Other's look in order to be. Therefore, I have no security in making him or her into an object. I must instead try to get hold of his or her freedom and reduce it to being a freedom subject to my freedom. This to Sartre, as to Proust before him, is the essence of love. "The love does not desire to possess the beloved as one possesses a thing; he. . . wants to possess a freedom as freedom." I want to to ensnare the Other's freedom within his or her facticity, to possess his or her body through his or her consciousness being identified with his or her body. But "desire is itself doomed to failure"! Pleasure is the death and failure of desire, says Sartre, for pleasure produces a reflective consciousness which destroys the immediacy of desire and makes one forget the Other's incarnation. The very attempt to seize the Other's body, pull it toward me, grab hold of it, bite it, makes me aware of my own body as no longer flesh but a synthetic instrument, and thus destroys my incarnation as well.

What this approach to sex means in concrete situations of human life, Sartre has abundantly illustrated in his novels, plays, and stories. In *No Exit* it is the hopeless situation of a man and two women, one of them a lesbian, shut together in a room where no one can possess another without interference by the third, which occasions, in part, the conclusion "Hell is other people." But even in less contrived situations, even when only two are present, as in the scenes in *The Age of Reason* in which Matthieu is alone with Marcelle, his mistress, or with Ivich, the self-centered young student, the sexual relations between two people are abundant illustration on the thesis "Hell is other people." Not only sexual desire must inevitably fail but love as well. The plot of *The Age of Reason* turns on Matthieu's inability to experience Marcelle's side of the relationship, to imagine that she might want a child and not an abortion when she becomes pregnant after seven years in which he has spent four nights with her regularly every week.

Martin Buber would certainly agree with Sartre that sex is human and not animal and that it cannot be divorced from our relations to others. He is like Sartre, too, in his essentially positive attitude toward sex. Sex is an "urge," or passion, which only becomes evil when we leave it undirected and allow an undirected possibility to turn into an undirected reality. What counts here is not the expression, repression, or sublimation of sexual desire but the response with one's whole being that diverts our powerful desires from the casual to the essential. We are not to turn away from what attracts our hearts but are to find mutual contact with it by making our relationship to it real. We are not necessarily torn between a cruel id and a cruel superego. Where some degree of trust and relationship exists, we may bring our passions into unification of a personal wholeness which is itself a by-product of the ever-renewed act of entering into dialogue. Buber calls this becoming a whole, this shaping of the chaos of matter into the cosmos of personal existence, "a cruelly hazardous enterprise." It is, nonetheless, an enterprise that one can and must undertake. Man is not for Buber what he is for Sartre—"a useless passion."

It would not be possible from Buber's standpoint to treat sexuality in abstraction from human relationships and, specifically, from the interplay and interaction between the I–Thou and the I–It. On the other hand, we must recognize, perhaps even more strongly than Buber himself did, that nowhere is the relationship between these two attitudes so intermingled and confused as precisely in this sphere. Although we need not define bad faith as essentially one's relation to oneself, as Sartre does, we must certainly agree that in this sphere of sexuality, deception, illusion, and bad faith of every kind appear. Here, more than anywhere, monologue loves to mask itself as dialogue—not only because we are all of us "seeming" persons who seek confirmation from the other by trying to appear what we are not, but also because we do not wish to recognize the extent to which we are treating the other as an It and are letting the other do the same to us. Real love, as Buber has pointed out, is not *in* the person but *between* I and Thou. Yet in all the much-discussed erotic philosophy of the age, it is not love between I and Thou that is represented but the precious experience of the I that enjoys the feelings that the other produces in him without giving himself to the other. Love of this sort, love without dialogue, without genuine outgoing to the other, Buber calls Lucifer. "Lame-winged beneath the rule of the lame-winged" Eros, the souls of lovers "cower where they are, each in his den, instead of soaring out each to the beloved partner."

The kingdom of the lame-winged Eros is a world of mirrors and mirrorings.

> Many years I have wandered through the land of men, and have not yet reached an end of studying the varieties of the "erotic man" (as the vassal of the broken-winged one at times describes himself). There a lover stamps around and is in love only with his passion. There one is wearing his differentiated feelings like medal-ribbons. There one is enjoying the adventures of his own fascinating effect. There one is gazing enraptured at the spectacle of his own supposed surrender. There one is collecting excitement. There one is displaying his "power." There one is preening himself with borrowed vitality. There one is delighting to exist simultaneously as himself and as an idol very unlike himself. There one is warming himself at the blaze of what has fallen to his lot. There one is experimenting. And so on and on—all the manifold monologists with their mirrors, in the apartment of the most intimate dialogue![4]

"They are all beating the air," Buber concludes. One only receives the world in the other when one turns to her and opens oneself to her. Only if I accept her otherness and live in the face of it, only if she and I say to each other, "It is Thou," does Present Being dwell between us. The true Eros of dialogue means a knowing of the beloved in the biblical sense of mutual relationship. True lovers have a bipolar experience, a contemporaneity at rest. They receive the common event from both sides at once "and thus for the first time understand in a bodily way what an event is." The lover feels the inclination of the head on the neck of his beloved as an answer to the word of his own silence without losing the feeling of his own self. He does not assimilate the beloved into his own soul or attempt to possess her freedom. He vows her faithfully to himself and turns to her in her otherness, her self-reality, with all the power of intention of his own heart.

This is not Sartre's otherness of the object, or even of the alien subject that makes me into an object, or of the other whose free-

4. Martin Buber, *Between Man and Man*, trans. Ronald Gregor Smith, with an Introduction by Maurice Friedman (New York: Macmillan Paperbacks, 1965), "Dialogue," pp. 28 f.

dom I make subject to my freedom. It is the otherness of the other who lives with me as Thou, who faces me as partner, who affirms me and contends with me, but vows me faithfully to being as I vow her. The ancient Hindu teaching of identity in which "Husband is not dear because of husband but because of the Self in the husband" is not the basis for authentic relationship between the sexes; rather the basis is the full acceptance of otherness. Uncurtailed personal existence first appears when wife says to husband or husband says to wife, not "I am you," but "I accept you as you are." In avoiding sex and marriage as temptation to finitude, Kierkegaard sidestepped the possibility of authentic existence. What is exemplary in marriage is the fact that in it one must mean one's partner in her real otherness because one affirms her as the particular person she is. Indeed, there is scarcely a substitute for marriage for teaching us the "vital acknowledgement of many-faced otherness"—that the other not only has a different mind, way of thinking or feeling, conviction or attitude, "but has also a different perception of the world, a different recognition and order of meaning, a different touch from the regions of existence, a different faith, a different soil." Through its crises and the overcoming of these crises that arise out of the organic depths, marriage enables us to affirm and withstand otherness.[5]

Buber carries "inclusion," or experiencing of the other side of the relationship, into the sexual act itself. He defines "imagining the real" in *The Knowledge of Man* as a bold swinging into the other which demands the intensest action of my being and which enables me to imagine quite concretely what the other is feeling, willing, thinking—to make her present in her wholeness and uniqueness. In love this takes place, not as some Emersonian meeting of soul and soul, but with the whole body–soul person, and includes an experiencing of the other's reaction to the sexual act far more radical than Sartre's incarnation of the other's freedom:

> A man caresses a woman, who lets herself be caressed. Then let us assume that he feels the contact from two sides—with the palm of his hand still, and also with the woman's skin. The twofold nature of the gesture, as one that takes place between two persons,

5. Buber, *Between Man and Man*, "The Question to the Single One," pp. 61 f.

thrills through the depth of enjoyment in his heart and stirs it. If he does not deafen his heart he will have—not to renounce the enjoyment—to love.

I do not in the least mean that the man who has had such an experience would from then on have this two-sided sensation in every such meeting—that would perhaps destroy his instinct. But the one extreme experience makes the other person present to him for all time. A transfusion has taken place after which a mere elaboration of subjectivity is never again possible or tolerable to him.[6]

Erich Fromm follows Buber in emphasizing love as responsibility, but he tends to overvalue will and commitment so much that he leaves no proper room for the erotic. "Every man is Adam, every woman Eve," writes Fromm in *The Art of Loving,* implying that if one commits oneself to the other, one can love any person. This would hardly be compatible with Buber's emphasis on affirming the other as the particular person she is, for in matters of sexual love this affirmation cannot be made with everyone, any more than every sexual attraction can be the ground for an enduring relationship. The Viennese logotherapist Viktor Frankl comes much closer to Buber when he writes:

There is not the least thing to be objected to in the sexual drive as long as it is included in the personal realm: as soon and as long as the sexuality is *personalized,* personalized through us to grasp another man in his being, in his suchness, in his uniqueness and particularity, but not only in his being and his suchness but also in his value, in what he shall become, and that means to affirm him. Love may be defined now as: being able to say Thou to someone— and beyond that to be able to say Yes to him; personal love must now join the sexual drive to the spiritual person, it must personalize it. *Only an I that means a Thou can integrate the It.*[7]

In his widely read book *Love and Will,*[8] Rollo May, in contrast to both Sartre and Buber, shows us sex precisely in the fusion of I–It and I–Thou: "To be human means to exist on the boundary between the anonymous and the personal." The "normal" person in our society finds, amid a plethora of sex, that very sterility

6. Buber, *Between Man and Man,* "Education," pp. 96 f.
7. Viktor E. Frankl, *Das Menschenbild der Seelenheilkunde: Kritik des Dynamischen Psychologismus* (Stuttgart: Hippokrates Verlag, 1959), p. 91; my translation.
8. Rollo May, *Love and Will* (New York: W. W. Norton, 1969).

which Eliot's *Waste Land* foresaw. If the Victorian was guilty for experiencing sex, we are guilty if we don't. The removal of all limits has only increased inner conflict; for "the sexual freedom to which we were devoted fell short of being fully human." The same can be said of the relatively greater education in sexual facts and techniques of our contemporaries compared to the generations that preceded us. Our bookish approach to "ideal marriage" has boomeranged, and the emphasis upon technique in sex has given us a mechanistic attitude toward lovemaking that has left us all the more alienated, lonely, and depersonalized. By a curious inversion, people become more wary of the sharing of tenderness than of physical nakedness and sexual intimacy!

The reasons that May advances for the obsession with sex in our culture are a depressing commentary both on our lack of love and on the emptiness of our lives. In "desperate endeavor to escape feelings of emptiness and the threat of apathy, partners pant and quiver hoping to find an answering quiver in someone else's body." This search for a responding and longing in the other through which to prove their own feelings alive is called love, but it has nothing to do with it. Nor is there any real love present in that compulsion to demonstrate one's potency that leads one to treat the most intimate and personal of all acts "as a performance to be judged by exterior requirements." The ironic result of viewing oneself as a machine to be turned on, adjusted, and steered is the loss of feeling for oneself and one's partner to the point where "the lover who is most efficient will also be the one who is impotent." Another cause of impotence is our compulsively hurried relationship to time. In the age of "short-order sex," sex itself gets shortchanged. "The fact that many people tend not to give themselves *time* to know each other in love affairs is a general symptom of the malaise of our day," says May. Carried far enough this leads to actual impotence—the body's statement that it has been left behind in the compulsive rush to carry out an idea of what we are supposed to want. We *fly* to sex in order to avoid passion, pushed by an anxiety that cannot even know in the moment of intercourse itself any real presentness. Sex in our society, says May, is a technique for a gigantic repression of true passion. Or our obsession with sex results from our repression of death. "Sex is the easiest way to prove our vitality, to demonstrate we are still 'young,' attractive, and virile, to prove we are not dead yet.''

Passion, then, is not identical with sex but is a separate force deeper than it. It may be expressed through sex, but it also may be pushed under by it. What gives the special depth-dimension to passion, according to May, is the "daimonic," which he defines not as something evil but as any force capable of taking over the whole personality. In the daimonic there is an affirmation of one's self that gives one the power to put one's self into the relationship. Without such self-assertion, one is unable to participate in a genuine relationship, a reciprocity in which each acts upon the other. Although May says that this relationship "always skates on the edge of the exploitation of the partner," the give-and-take, the experiencing of the other side of the relationship, prevents it from going over that edge while retaining the vitality of the relationship. It is only when love and will come together that we attain the truly personal, and the personal is never something I possess alone but only in a person-to-person relationship. The "human being has to make the creature with whom he has sexual relations in some way personal, even if only in fantasy, or else suffer depersonalization himself." The need for sex is not so powerful as the need for relationship, intimacy, acceptance, and affirmation. Therefore, exploitation, seduction, and the domination of another's freedom cannot, both Freud and Sartre to the contrary, be the last word in sex and love. In attitude as well as in physical fact, sex means that posture of the ultimate baring of one's self. This mutual baring is not *despite* but *with* and *through* the fact that we are creatures destined to die. "Love is not only enriched by our sense of mortality," writes May, "but constituted by it."

Even our feelings are not private but are part of the dialogue that takes place in love. They "are ways of communicating and sharing something meaningful from us to the world." "Our feelings not only take into consideration the other person," writes May, "but are in a real sense partially *formed by the feelings of the other persons present.*" Every successful lover knows by instinct to pick up the magnetic field of the feelings of the person he or she is with. Even the wish is not simply individual, as Freud thought, but is a reality *between:* "the wish in interpersonal relationships requires mutuality."

To open oneself to another in love means to be confronted with a vastly widened world including regions of which we never dreamed. This experience produces a vertigo in which we may genuinely wonder whether we are "capable of giving ourselves to our beloved and still preserving what center of autonomy we have." Sartre would answer no; for he has made real giving to the other and self-preservation opposites. May, using Tillich's language of the "centered self" which transcends itself, goes beyond Sartre. "Contrary to the usual assumption, we all begin life not as individuals, but as 'we.' " Only because this is so, can love push us toward a new dimension of consciousness in which we transcend our isolation.

What this does not tell us is whether there will be the resources in any particular situation "to meet others and hold our ground when we meet them." Still less can we say with confidence of ourselves what May says in a commentary on a traditional people, namely, that "the community gives a humanly trustworthy, interpersonal world in which one can struggle against the negative forces." On the contrary, it may be just the absence of this "humanly trustworthy, interpersonal world" that leads to that "crisis of confidence" which sets the stage for the modern split between libidinal passion and superego which Freud took to be human nature. "The unaffectedness of wishing is stifled by mistrust," writes Buber. "The divorce between spirit and instincts is here, as often, the consequence of the divorce between man and man."

The special form of the divorce between person and person in our day, says the psychoanalyst Leslie H. Farber, is the "disordered will," that willfulness that wants to handle both sides of the dialogue. If this willfulness expresses itself in the "life of suicide," it is found even more regularly in the contemporary approach to sex. Indeed, Farber goes so far as to state as his conviction "that over the last fifty years sex has, for the most part, lost its viability as a human experience." The emphasis here is on the word *human*. Sexual activity itself has not decreased, but the human possibilities of sex are becoming ever more elusive, and the couplings that take place are "poultices after the fact" which "further extend the degradation of sex that has resulted from its everincreasing bondage to the modern will." Sex has been emancipated, to be sure, but its "emancipation" is really an abstraction from all of life—except the will—and its exaltation as the very measure of existence. As a result, what sex once brought us—the possibility of that mutual knowing and being known within which we regain *our own* body through knowing the body of the loved one—is lost in favor of an empty *knowing about* in which both bodies again escape us. Farber traces this decline in a series of steps: viewing nature as a variety of energies to be harnessed and utilized, a machine to be kept healthy so it might lead to never-ending progress and prosperity; coming to regard the human body as just such a machine; the decision that the dominant energy of the human machine is sex; the claim of the erotic life as the exclusive province of sexology and psychoanalysis; and the abstraction and isolation of sex into the function of the sexual organs.[9]

The true *reductio ad absurdum* of this historical process is William H. Masters' study of the female orgasm in an actual laboratory situation, excluding all subjects that could not produce orgasms at will, relying principally on automanipulation, or masturbation, and recording the results with color movies. Whatever else may have been discovered in this way, Farber suggests, nothing could be discovered about the human relationship between persons in sexual love. We might go further and say that here the paradox has reached its point of greatest tension: the uttermost hiding and eclipse of the human image brought about by what claims to be the farthest outpost of the revelation of the human! Although many Women's Liberationists have lined up behind Masters and Johnson, as if the clitoral orgasm were the very bastion of feminine freedom, and have characterized Farber as a "male chauvinist," Germaine Greer has rejected this emphasis on the very same grounds as Farber: that it reduces human sexuality to something partial and mechanical rather than whole and personal. She sees in Masters and Johnson a basically authoritarian attempt to tame sex, "the blueprint for standard, low-agitation, cool-out monogamy. If women are to avoid this last reduction of their humanity, they must hold out not just for orgasm but for ecstasy." Only the domination of "the performance ethic" can explain women's

9. Leslie H. Farber, *lying, despair, jealousy, envy, sex, suicide, drugs, and the good life* (New York: Harper Colophon Books, 1978), Chapter 8, "I'm Sorry, Dear."

finding the clitoris "the only site of their pleasure" instead of its "acting as a kind of sexual overdrive in a more general response." This stress on the clitoral orgasm is but part of a larger picture in which "Sex for many has become a sorry business, a mechanical release involving neither discovery nor triumph, stressing human isolation more dishearteningly than ever before." Greer, like Rollo May, sees the modern ideal of sex as really being mechanized sex, "laboriously and inhumanly computerized," just as "the male sexual idea of virility without languor or amorousness" is a profoundly desolating illustration of how the expression of the release in mechanical terms leads to seeking it mechanically. "Sex becomes masturbation in the vagina." That is sex for the man. But the overstress on the man's massaging of clitoris to produce orgasm is no less masturbation for the woman.

Though we cannot return to the unawareness of the past, neither can we remain standing in the pseudoclinical situation of the present, in which frigidity is seen as something *in* the woman, impotence as something *in* the man. Both frigidity and impotence as well as male and female orgasms are essential aspects of an interhuman betweenness in which *both man and woman must work together on the sexual problems,* as on the financial and other problems, of the relationship. I do not mean that both should deal together with *her* problem of frigidity and/or *his* problem of impotence. I mean that the problems themselves do not belong to and cannot be simply located in one partner in the relationship; for they are a function of the relationship itself.

When and if the mutual trust that upholds the relationship is broken, especially if the separation is traumatic, it is inevitable in most cases that sexual "hang-ups" will be relegated by each partner to the other. One protects oneself from one's former closeness by turning the other into a caricature of a person—an object possessing such and such characteristics. Actually, one does not know what the other might be in another relationship. I am not denying that some relationships are too difficult to work out. But I am saying that precisely when we know exactly what is wrong with our former partner and wonder why we wasted ten years of our lives with such a person, precisely when we seem to have reached an objective and secure ground, is the point when we have ceased to

make him or her present to us as a person and are protecting ourselves from feeling any concern—from living in and with that person.

When I was thirteen, my young brother-in-law replaced my almost total ignorance of sex with the philosophy of the "man of
action"—a philosophy which I did not put into practice for many
years to come, if at all, but which left me, nonetheless, with the
idea that sex was a Good Thing, regardless of whom one made
love to or what one's relation was to one's partner. Later I came
to recognize this same relationship not only in the college-boy
boastings of "laying a girl" or "having a piece," but even in the
morality of a society that claimed all premarital or extramarital
sexuality to be wrong in abstraction from both the particular relationship and the concrete situation. When this morality was unmasked as the hypocritical double standard that it is, it was
replaced for a great many by a no less immoral approval of sex as
a "natural" act, again in abstraction from the actual relationship
and the actual situation. Sex has been sought in our society as an
"experience," as sensation somehow supposed to be of value in
itself. Only this power of abstraction could lead so many to spend
so much of their strength and effort trying to prove their "potency" with ever-fresh partners or trying to extend the variety
and scope of their experience by the exchange of partners.

The mark of success in our society, the distinguished American
psychiatrist Harry Stack Sullivan once said, is what you can do
with your genitals to someone else's genitals. I would go even further and say that most men and women in our society are ridden
by a deep anxiety concerning their sexual adequacy, that no
amount of actual sexual "conquest" or "experience" can ever really allay that anxiety, and that even those with the most self-
satisfying sexual prowess live with dread of that day when their
powers begin to fail. This day comes all the sooner, in fact, because of this anxiety, because of the compulsive need to allay it by
sexual activity, and because of the dread of its someday proving
the master. People are afraid of fumbling and faltering in sexual
relations; for they do not wish to appear un*master*-ly. Their harsh
self-judgment is, of course, accompanied by an equally harsh
judgment of others; for if things do not work out according to the
ideal of the sex books, then the blame must be placed on *his* "im-

potence" or *her* "frigidity." Some people manage to place all the
blame on their partners, some take all the blame to themselves,
and most go back and forth between blaming their partners and
blaming themselves. Few take seriously the extent to which "good
sexual functioning" is itself a function of good relationship or the
fact that even good relationship, including all the anxieties and
worries and fatigues of real life, is not on call to produce good sex
at stated periods!

We are flooded with false images—caricatures—of manliness
and femininity—from the John Wayne type of "he-man" to any
of a number of sexy, voluptuous, clinging, or dream-girl-soft
women. We fear in our sexual relationships themselves that
consideration—failure to press our case to the very verge of
exploitation—will be considered weakness or a lack of vitality. It
takes courage to falter, to hesitate, to show bewilderment, confusion, and self-doubt. Naturally, we are vulnerable here as in perhaps no other sphere of our lives, and our most personal
confirmation is at stake. "Love is being psychically wide-open to
another," says Shulamith Firestone.

> It is a situation of total emotional vulnerability. Therefore it must
> be not only the incorporation of the other, but an *exchange* of selves.
> Anything short of mutual exchange will hurt one or the other
> party.[10]

Without the mutual revelation of weakness, of humanness, of
hope and doubt, of faith and despair, of the very ground in which
each of us is rooted, and of the strengths and foibles of our unique
stances, there can be no revelation of the hidden human image in
sexual love. And when the human image remains hidden, it does
not flower in the darkness. It withers and atrophies and all the
masks and pretenses of our smiling faces cannot dispel the growing stink of putrefaction that arises from the depths. Only when
we cease to be concerned with our own images as masculine or
feminine and trust ourselve to the *between* itself—allowing ourselves to be changed by the other, by the relationship—will the
human image be revealed.

10. Shulamith Firestone, *The Dialectic of Sex: The Case for Feminist Revolution* (New
York: Bantam Books [paperback], 1971), pp. 128 f.

Chapter 17

Shame, Guilt, and Existential Trust

I N *On Shame and the Search for Identity,* Helen Lynd presents a phenomenology of shame especially valuable in that it traces shame to something irreducibly concrete and particular. Dmitri in Dostoievsky's *The Brothers Karamazov* is ashamed not because he has stolen money or bludgeoned his father and his old servant over the head; he is ashamed because he has to take his shoes off during the examination and let others see his big toe with its blunt toenail curving out to the right. By such examples Lynd captures the opaque, essentially unrationalizable immediacy of much experience of shame and, by the same token, the close relation between shame and one's sense of one's self, including bodily self—one's self in the fullest and most concrete sense. Shame is closely associated with anxiety, she writes, but it is not merely anxiety caused by fear of public exposure. "The public exposure of even a very private part of one's physical or mental character could not in itself have brought about shame unless one had already felt within oneself, not only dislike, but shame for these traits."

To understand shame, human goals and capacities cannot be too narrowly conceived, for "shame is an experience that affects and is affected by the whole self," and it is this that makes it a clue to identity. Shame is often associated with actions that are not only blameless but also trivial. Yet these incidents "have importance because in this moment of *self*-consciousness, the self stands revealed." Whether our gesture toward another was inappropriate or was simply not reciprocated, the experience of shame that it causes throws "a flooding light on what and who we are and what the world we live in is." This self-illumination, in fact, is the cause as well as the effect of the shame—the anxiety and sense of inadequacy—that becomes manifest in a situation in which we have totally involved ourselves: "One is overtaken by shame because one's whole life has been a preparation for putting one in this situation."

Shame, in Helen Lynd's understanding of it, is closely bound with the loss of trust. The loss of early trust may, of course, help determine in important ways a child's future sense of identity since for most people trust is not altogether lost so much as "it is transmuted into more mature and understanding confidence." But such loss of trust may go beyond the early shocks experienced by every child to a question of trust in existence itself. "Basic trust in one's world and especially in the persons who are its interpreters is crucial to one's sense of identity." If this is so, then shame as a function of a loss of trust surely points in the first instance to the relations between person and person as a dimension as basic as that "inner" realm that Lynd assigns to shame.

Lynd does not fail to make explicit the relation of shame to the problem of human resources and the tragic limitations imposed by "man's fate." "Failure to reach our own aspirations...leads to the question of how far disappointment and the failure of human effort lie in the unalterable nature of things." Disappointment and shame test the limits of one's faith in the possibilities of life and may even lead to the conviction that not only one's own life but that of all persons is empty, isolated, void of significance. "Experience of shame may call into question, not only one's own adequacy and the validity of codes of one's immediate society, but the meaning of the universe itself."

Experiences of shame are communicated only with the greatest difficulty, Lynd points out. Just because shame exposes the self— and beyond the self, the society to which one belongs—a person may respond to shame by "refusing to recognize the wound, covering the isolating effect of shame through depersonalization and adaptation to any approved codes." But another alternative is open to us—fully to face the experiences of shame and realize their import. If we do this, they may "become a revelation of one-self, of one's society, and of the human situation." One means of dealing with shame is an identification with other persons in situations that make them feel ashamed. This confrontation of the shame of others may be the beginning of the realization of shame as revelation *and* of the transcending of shame. Equally as important as the identification with the shame of others is the mutual love through which one risks the exposure of shame and enters into the mind and feeling of another person.

> If. . . one can sufficiently risk uncovering oneself and sufficiently trust another person, to seek means of communicating shame, the risking of exposure can be in itself an experience of release, expansion, self-revelation, a coming forward of belief in oneself, and entering into the mind and feeling of another person.[1]

Helen Lynd touches here on two profound paradoxes of shame—first, that unbearable as shame often seems, it perhaps can be endured if one taps deeper resources and becomes in so doing a wholer, greater person, by which she means a person more open to mutual, responsive, interhuman relations. Hence, the second paradox: The isolating quality of shame cannot be altogether removed. How could it, since shame puts its finger on us not as a part of some general category but as the unique, particular persons that we are? Yet mutual love can help us not only to risk exposure and communicate our shame but also to experience from the side of the other, the person whom we love, how she, too, lives in the recurrent shame of being the person that she is. When this takes place, our shame remains real, yet we are no longer so terrifyingly alone in it. It is no longer the shame of Dostoievsky's Underground Man—the shame at being the sole exception to the "happy breed" of humankind.

Through larger identifications—"with a group of other persons, a scientific investigation or an art form, a purpose or a belief"—one can, says Helen Lynd, transcend shame; for through them one attains an enlarged perspective, a Hegelian "comic frame of reference," a "sense of proportion that is the outcome of taking the individual self and the world in their widest

1. Helen Merrell Lynd, *On Shame and the Search for Identity* (New York: Harcourt Brace, Harbrace Books [paperback], 1969), p. 249.

reach of all that they can be." This confronting of shame makes "way for living beyond the conventions of a particular culture" and makes possible, by the same token, "the discovery of an integrity that is peculiarly one's own and of those characteristically human qualities that are at the same time most universal." Lynd comes very close to my use of the human image when she writes of "Amos, Socrates, Tycho Brahe, Galileo, Martin Luther, Freud, Cézanne, Rilke, Sephen Hero, Black Boy . . . whose sense of self is related to ideals that they conceive as widely human and at the same time peculiarly their own." Thus, she moves from shame as an irreducibly particular, cruelly isolating experience to universal ideals that transcend not only the isolated self but the limits of societies and cultures; and at the same time she retains the connection between these ideals and the individual person in his or her particularity and uniqueness.

By withdrawing shame and its overcoming from the "outer" social sphere and placing it in the "inner" personal sphere, on the one hand, and the universal, on the other, Helen Lynd is in danger of missing what, even from her own examples, is the real center and problematic of shame—the meeting point of the personal and the social. No sense of inner or universal values can ever quite remove the shame of exposure, of inappropriateness, of an unreciprocated gesture. Even Dostoievsky's Christlike Prince Myshkin is a figure of shame to himself as well as to others just *because* he acts in ways inappropriate to the social group in which he moves. One may question, therefore, whether Lynd has taken sufficiently seriously the problem she herself has set up—the relation between personal identity and social reality. Ludwig Binswanger in *Existence* makes a criticism of Erwin Straus's distinction between existential, or protecting, shame and purely concealing shame that might well be applied to Lynd's treatment of shame, even though her categories are different from Straus's. In concealing shame, according to Straus, "it is not a question of primal shame, originally intrinsic to being human (and not acquired in the course of the life history), but of the . . . public shame stemming from one's own reflection thrown upon the others." At bottom, however, writes Binswanger, existential and concealing shame belong together, just as being-oneself and being-with-others belong together. Existential shame, too, shows itself in blushing, thus revealing to the other precisely what it wants to hide.

The most serious question that *On Shame and the Search for Identity* raises concerns the contrast between shame and guilt that Lynd places at the center of the book. Following Gerhart Piers and Franz Alexander, Lynd sees guilt as the transgression of the taboos of society, shame as falling short of the self-ideal; guilt as related to the superego imposed or taught by others, shame as one's own line of direction discovered by oneself; guilt as connected with specific, detachable acts, shame as connected with the whole self and therefore as general and nondetachable. Guilt is connected with fear—the fear of mutilation; shame is connected with anxiety—the anxiety of abandonment. In guilt one lives in terms of conventions; shame leads beyond convention and one's immediate culture. In guilt one person can see another as merely external and instrumental, whereas in shame they can be a part of each other.

Out of all these contrasts Lynd forms a basic contrast between a "guilt axis" and a "shame axis." Guilt involves "an additive process," shame "a total response that includes insight"; guilt "competition, measurement on a scale, performing the acts prescribed as desirable," shame "pervasive qualitative demands of oneself, more rigorous than external codes." On the guilt axis is "being a good, loyal friend, husband, wife, parent"; on the shame axis, "having an overflowing feeling for friend, husband, wife, children which makes goodness and loyalty a part of the whole experience with no need for separate emphasis." Guilt entails "emphasis on decision-making: any decision is better than none," whereas shame entails "ability to live with some indecisiveness (multiple possibilities) even though it means living with some anxiety." "Surmounting of guilt," the last item states, "leads to righteousness," whereas "transcending of shame may lead to a sense of identity, freedom." The conclusion that Lynd draws is "that a sense of identity cannot be reached along the guilt axis alone."

Lynd expresses the belief that "in a society more directly and variously expressive of human desires" than our own, "the guilt axis and the shame axis, role fulfillment and personal fulfillment, might more nearly coincide." Even though role fulfillment and personal fulfillment may not coincide in our society, neither can they be separated in the way that Lynd seems to separate them. One's identity cannot be envisaged apart from one's interpersonal and interhuman relations, including, in some important measure, one's social role. One may question, too, her certainty that shame goes deeper than guilt because it leads us to question trust: "It is worse to be inferior and isolated than to be wrong." Unless we assume that the self is *not* centrally concerned with its relations with others, we can hardly relegate guilt to a subordinate position. If shame may help us see the world through the eyes of another, so that we become both "more separated from and more related to,others," it certainly does not follow that guilt means treating others merely as external and instrumental.

The greatest weakness in Lynd's approach is her assumption that guilt is merely a social product. Certainly there is purely social and even neurotic guilt derived from a set of mores and taboos imposed upon the individual by parents and society and incorporated into an internalized "superego." But there is also real guilt, guilt which has to do with one's actual stance in the world and the way in which one goes out to relate to other people from that stance. If there is such a thing as real or existential guilt, then it cannot be merely additive and atomistic, as Lynd has held, but, like shame, must be grounded in the whole self and never entirely detachable from it. What is more, since they are both involved in the problem of personal wholeness and direction, somewhere in the depths of the self existential guilt and existential shame must meet and interrelate.

One must also question, for those reasons, Lynd's assertion that guilt does not exclude communication, whereas shame is isolating. Certainly a completely objective, external, detachable guilt can be objectively communicated, but that is neither real guilt nor real communication. One is as alone with true guilt as with true shame, and it is no easier to confess the one than the other. Both Kierkegaard and Kafka have stressed the fact that personal gilt is incommunicable.

In Kafka's novel *The Trial,* Joseph K. can never even discover why he is arrested and what he is charged with. His guilt cannot be reduced to isolated, detachable, additive acts but concerns his existence as a whole. He himself, to be sure, wishes to reduce his responsibility to being answerable only for his external actions:

> He had often considered whether it would not be better to draw up a written defense and hand it in to the Court. In this defense he would give a short account of his life, and when he came to an event of any importance explain for what reasons he had acted as he did, intimate whether he approved or condemned his way of action in retrospect, and adduce ground for the condemnation or approval.[2]

K. wants to see himself as accountable only in his actions and not as a person. But, as I have shown in *Problematic Rebel*, everything in *The Trial* suggests that it is not his detached actions but precisely his existence which is on trial and that his insistence on regarding his life as no more than the sum of his actions is itself, perhaps, his chief guilt. This means that his guilt, so far as we can glimpse it, is neither legal nor social, but existential, that he is accountable, even in his social relationships, as a person and not just as someone who fulfills a social role.

When K. is taken to a vacant lot by two tenth-rate actors and a knife is plunged into his heart, he exclaims, "Like a dog!" to which the author adds, in the last words of the novel, "It was as if the shame of it must outlive him." In his "Letter to His Father," Kafka identifies these words with the 'boundless" sense of guilt inculcated in him since his childhood. If one takes seriously these last words of *The Trial*, one may question whether the deepest level of *The Trial* is not guilt but shame. Why, after all, do Kafka and his hero speak of a shame so great that it might outlive one if it were not that deeper than any sense of personal guilt, and certainly than any sense of guilt for a specific action, lay shame for his father and for himself? Following Helen Lynd, we should not find it difficult to interpret much of Kafka's attitude toward his parents and himself as an expression of that sort of irreducible, unrationalizable shame that is so closely associated with the body

2. Franz Kafka, *The Trial*, trans. Willa and Edwin Muir, revised, and with additional materials, trans. E. M. Butler (New York: Alfred A. Knopf, 1957), Chapter VII, p. 142.

and the sense of self, with the relation of the child to its parents and to itself.

This would not mean that we should have to chose shame *instead* of guilt, as Lynd does, unless we followed her in treating guilt as totally identifiable with the taboos and restrictions of a particular culture. If we think in terms of existential shame and existential guilt, then the ending of *The Trial*, as I suggest in *Problematic Rebel*, will point to the meeting and interfusion of these two responses rather than to a choice between them:

> A man may defend himself against specific accusations of guilt, but when he has a sense of "boundless guilt" rooted in a deep feeling of worthlessness, a shame for his very existence, he can only take all accusations on himself. Everything that happens to such a person confirms his essential shame at being himself, and no amount of external success or social confirmation will do more than enable him to forget it temporarily. The only "immortality" such a man may know is the very shame which may do him to death but will not die itself, so much is it the very air that he breathes, the all too narrow and constricting ground upon which he walks! This "boundless guilt" represents that area in the depths where existential shame and existential guilt meet and interfuse. Kafka and Joseph K. are ashamed for their very existences: being killed like a dog leads one to question not just the specific actions that lead one into this cul-de-sac but one's whole life. But by the same token, it means a recognition of personal existential guilt for what one's life has been. Since this guilt is not just a matter of specific acts, there is no point where one can accurately draw a line and say, "These acts were avoidable and these not; these acts are a subject for guilt and these for shame.[3]

Existential guilt is as closely tied to existential, or basic, trust, or the lack of it, as is existential shame and for the same reason: They are both rooted in basic, existential trust. A remarkably lucid example of how real guilt grows out of the presence and absence of existential trust is Hermann Hesse's novella, "A Child's Heart." In it the eleven-year-old boy goes up to his father's room in need of comfort. When he finds it empty, he is compelled by his

3. Maurice Friedman, *Problematic Rebel: Melville, Dostoievsky, Kafka, Camus,* 2nd rev., enlarged and radically reorganized ed. (Chicago: University of Chicago Press, Phoenix Books, 1970), pp. 475 f. See also Chapter 15, " 'The Trial': The Problematic of Guilt," pp. 346–373.

disappointment to steal some pen points and figs from his father's drawers. He spends the whole day in tormented anguish, longing for a punishment which does not arrive till the following day when he is already in another place emotionally.

He needs to penetrate his father's secrets, to find out something about him. But though he understands this unconsciously, there is no way he can bring it into words for his father, and instead the boy lets his fate carry him in solitary defiance into an ever worse position in which he "watched with pain and a strange gloating delight...how he suffered and was disappointed, how he appealed in vain to all my better instincts." He would do no more than nod when his father asked him whether he was sorry and marveled at how "this big intelligent man" could fail to see how the whole affair hurt him and twisted his heart. What he learns from all this is how utterly two well-intentioned human beings can torment each other, creating new tortures, wounds, and errors. Finally his father makes peace with him and he goes to bed with the certainty that "my father had completely forgiven me—more than I had forgiven him."[4] The basic trust of childhood is broken by a shame and guilt that try each partner in the relationship but that also in the end reestablish existential trust on a more mature, if less perfect, level.

Existential trust cannot be identified with the basic trust of childhood, even though it is originally grounded in it. Neither is it a secure possession of the "normal" adult. It is something that is shattered and renewed as long as we live, and shame and guilt, both neurotic and existential, are inextricably interwoven with its loss and its renewal. Existential trust is integrally related to the "partnership of existence," the life of dialogue. The beginning of dialogue is the acceptance of the reality of separation, of that ever-renewed distancing that is the prerequisite for all relationship. Dialogue begins with reality, with trust. I can go forth again to meet present reality, but I cannot control the form in which I shall meet it. We continue to care about and be responsible for the person who had been our partner even when we are not in actual dialogue with him or her. But we cannot *insist* that he or she remain a

4. Hermann Hesse, *Klingsor's Last Summer,* trans. Richard and Clara Winston (New York: Farrar, Straus & Giroux, Noonday Books, 1970), "A Child's Heart," pp. 3–42.

partner for us. This does not mean that every meeting must be brand new or that we do not look forward eagerly to seeing our friends and those we love. But when we insist that it has to be in a certain form, when we try to control it, then our friendship, love, or marriage will wither because we shall not allow it to be what it can become in the moment.

The existential trust that enables us to live from moment to moment and to go out to meet what the new moment brings is the trust that makes it possible that in new meeting we again become whole, alive, present. If I trust in a person, a relationship, this means that despite what may and will happen, I shall enter into relationship again and bring all the past moments of meeting into present meeting. The particular person who is my partner may die, become sick, disturbed; he or she may betray me, rupture the relationship, or simply turn away and fail to respond. Sooner or later something of this does happen for most of us. When it does, it is trust which enables us to remain open and to respond to the address of the new situation. If we lose our existential trust, conversely, we are no longer able to enter anew into real dialogue.

It is our existential trust that ultimately gives actuality and continuity to our discontinuous and often merely potential relationships to our human partners. And it is this trust, too, that gives continuity and reality to our own existence as persons; for in itself personality is neither continuous nor always actual. If it is the confirmation of others and our own self-confirmation that gets us over the gaps and breaks in the first instance, it is our existential trust that enables this individual course to become a personal direction rather than a meaningless flux.

Trusting persons accept the fact that a genuine relationship is two-sided and therefore beyond the control of their will. It is a readiness to go forth with such resources as you have and, if you do not receive any response, to be ready another time to go out to the meeting. Many people imagine that they are justified in a settled mistrust or even despair because one or twice they ventured forth and encountered a stone wall or a cold shoulder. After this they anticipate rejection and even bring it about, or they protect themselves from it by never risking themselves. Genuine trust recognizes as its corollary "existential grace," the grace which comes to us from the other who meets us but also from our own resources, which are not simply waiting for us to use them but come and go, only partially subject to our will. We cannot control our response by an act of will power or if we do we are falling into that willfulness that misuses and cuts back our potentialities, making spontaneity impossible. Thus, spontaneity and genuine responsibility are two sides of the same coin.

We need the courage to address and the courage to respond, a courage which recognizes that there are no formulae as to when and how to address and to respond and that includes the courage *not* to respond when we cannot do so in this situation as a whole person in a meaningful way. Our response should be to a true address to us; it ought not to be a mere reaction which is triggered off. If it is important not to allow ourselves to be "triggered off," it is equally essential not to withhold ourselves. One of the forms we have of withholding ourselves is that protective silence which makes us feel we never have to speak out, that we are merely observers in the group, that nothing is demanded of us. Another of the forms of withholding ourselves, however, is that anxious verbosity that overwhelms the situation so that we are not present and we do not allow anyone else to be present either. Still another form of withholding ourselves is substituting technique for trust.

Many encounter groups operate on the naive but widespread assumption that the mere expression of hostility is therapeutic under any circumstances. The operating principle of such groups is not that you should not withhold your *self* but that you should not withhold your surface feelings, especially the type of feelings that the group wants and expects, such as anger and hostility. When we reach the place where we are expecting and looking for a certain result, then we have traded in trust for arbitrariness and genuine will for willfulness. Among those whose whole life work is concerned with freeing others to their potentiality are some of the worst manipulators I have ever met, persons who cannot trust but have to be sure they get the result they want. All the members of "sensitivity awareness" groups can become amateur manipulators who tend to become more and more insensitive to the unique and concrete happenings *between* members of the group.

We address others not by conscious mind or will but by who we are. We address them with more than we know, and they respond—if they really respond—with more than they know. Address and response can never be identified merely with conscious intent or even with 'intentionality.'' Our resources have to do with what calls us and with the way in which we bring or do not bring ourselves into wholeness in response to this call. The courage to respond begins with openness and listening. Conversely, when we habitually fail to listen, we reach the place where we are not able to hear.

Even when we are still able to hear, the address is not always clear or even present nor can we always find the resources to respond when a voice does call. We live in an era of existential mistrust—a mistrust that arises from the loss of trust in our meeting with other persons in the interhuman, social, and political realms. We not only expect that the other is trying to put something over on us; we even suspect our own motivation as untrustworthy. (Abraham Heschel wrote that the modern golden rule is, "Suspect thy neighbor as thyself.") We no longer really believe that we can confirm others or they us; for we do not really mean them and they do not really mean us. In such a situation, only healing through meeting can restore our crippled capacity for existential trust.

PART FIVE

Conclusion

Chapter 18

Psychology and the Hidden Human Image

O N the basis of the "death instinct," which he ranges along-side the "love instinct" as equally primary in *Civilization and Its Discontents,* Sigmund Freud presents a devastating image of the human which no person living in the world today can afford to ignore:

> Not merely is the stranger on the whole not worthy of love, but, to be honest, I must confess he has more claim to my hostility, even to my hatred. He does not seem to have the least trace of love for me, does not show me the slightest consideration. If it will do him any good, he has no hesitation in injuring me, never even asking himself whether the amount of advantage he gains by it bears any proportion to the amount of wrong done to me. What is more, he does not even need to get an advantage from it; if he can merely get a little pleasure out of it, he thinks nothing of jeering at me, insulting me, slandering me, showing his power over me; and the more secure he feels himself, or the more helpless I am, with so much more certainty can I expect this behaviour from him towards me. . . .
>
> The bit of truth behind all this—one so eagerly denied—is that men are not gentle, friendly creatures wishing for love, who simply defend themselves if they are attacked, but that *a powerful measure of desire for aggression has to be reckoned as a part of their instinctual endowment.* The result is that their neighbor is to them not only a possible

helper or sexual object, but also a temptation to them to gratify their aggressiveness on him, to exploit his capacity for work without recompense, to use him sexually without his consent, to seize his possessions, to humiliate him, to cause him pain, to torture and to kill him.[1]

Homo homini lupus, Freud concludes: "Man is a wolf to man." "Who has the courage to dispute it in the face of all the evidence in his own life and in history?"

Who indeed? In the years since Freud's death in 1939 there has been as much new evidence of "man's inhumanity to man" as in the whole of recorded history up till that time: the Nazi extermination of six million Jews and a million gypsies, the Allied bombing of German cities, the atomic destruction of Hiroshima and Nagasaki by America, the slave-labor camps of the Soviet Union, the wars and uprisings and systematic exterminations. The view of the human being as an essentially good, rational creature who will gladly cooperate with others in his own self-interest is no longer a live option. Such evidence cannot be excluded from any serious contemporary image of the human.

It is evidence, nonetheless, of how the human being *acts* and not of what he or she *is*. Like the myths that Freud uses, it is a plausible, perhaps even a convincing, hypothesis—but one that can never be scientifically verified. Since we cannot know either instinct or human nature outside a historical context, we cannot categorically assert, as Freud has, that the desire for aggression is a part of the human being's instinctual nature. It would be equally possible to say with Erich Fromm that the destructiveness which human beings vent on one another is the product of an authoritarian character structure which is, in turn, the product of one or another type of authoritarian society. What is *not* possible is to ignore the enormous amount of hostility and destructiveness that human beings have displayed toward one another in history and in our own day. Rousseau held that the human being is by nature good and that it is only civilization that makes him bad. Freud, with much greater realism, recognizes that civilization is inseparable from Man. In this sense, it is meaningless to ask what Man is "by nature," since we only know Man as a social and civilized being.

1. Sigmund Freud, *Civilization and Its Discontents,* trans. Joan Riviere (New York: Doubleday, Anchor Books, 1958), pp. 59–61.

For the same reason, it is not necessary or even possible to accept Freud's view of "human nature" at face value. But it *is* necessary to confront his view of the human with utter seriousness and to take it into our own, (it is to be hoped) larger, human image.

Jung criticizes Freud for seeing the human being as basically evil, and he himself characterizes the "evil" side of the self as the "shadow," the complement of the good. If it is not suppressed, this "evil" can be brought as such into that very integration which Jung calls the "self," thus achieving a type of wholeness in which the individual knowingly succumbs to evil "in part." Good and evil are both relativized here to mere functions of wholeness. Human values are transcended by "the voice of Nature, the all-sustainer and all-destroyer." "If she appears inveterately evil to us," says Jung, "this is mainly due to the old truth that the good is always the enemy of the better." But what is this "better" of which he speaks? It is that "individuation," or wholeness in the unconscious, which has no reference, check, or court other than itself, no direction, guide, or criterion by which to distinguish one voice of the archetypal unconscious from another. If we still recognize apparent evil in the unconscious, then it is our task, for the sake of this "better," to succumb to it in part so that we may realize our destiny:

> The inner voice brings the evil before us in a very tempting and convincing way in order to make us succumb. If we do not partially succumb, nothing of this apparent evil enters into us, and no regeneration or healing can take place. (I say "apparent," though this may sound too optimistic.) If we succumb only in part, and if by self-assertion the ego can save itself from being completely swallowed, then it can assimilate the voice, and we realize that the evil was, after all, only a semblance of evil, but in reality a bringer of healing and illumination.[2]

What sort of "healing and illumination" does this "semblance of evil" bring? Jung's immediate answer is that "the inner voice is a 'Lucifer' in the strictest and most unequivocal sense of the word, and it faces people with ultimate moral decisions without which they can never achieve full consciousness and become per-

2. C. G. Jung, *Collected Works,* Vol. XVII, *The Development of the Personality,* trans. R. F. C. Hull (New York: Pantheon Books, Bollingen Series, 1954), p. 185.

sonalities." But Jung's concept of a "moral decision" is very different from the old distinctions between right and wrong, just as the court of conscience is replaced for him by the criterion of wholeness and the address of the inner voice.

If the healing that such "moral decision" leads to is not obvious, still less is the "illumination" it provides: "The highest and the lowest, the best and the vilest, the truest and the most deceptive things," reads the very next sentence, "are often blended together in the inner voice in the most baffling way, thus opening up in us an abyss of confusion, falsehood, and despair." What is the way out of this "confusion, falsehood, and despair"? It is succumbing in part to evil, or, as Jung puts it in a later writing, not succumbing to either good or evil, but rising above them, which means, once again to relativize them. Jung means by this, of course, that evil must be confronted in order to be integrated. The Carpocratian Gnostic teaching of going along with one's own body in its instinctive demands is cited favorably by Jung in *Psychology and Religion* and is freely read by him into Taoism as what *must*, according to his own insights, be the secret of Taoist detachment:

> Have we, perhaps, an inkling that a mental attitude which can direct the glance inward to that extent owes its detachment from the world to the fact that *those men have so completely fulfilled the instinctive demands of their natures* that little or nothing prevents them from perceiving the invisible essence of the world? Can it be, perhaps, that the condition of such knowledge is freedom from those desires, ambitions, and passions, which bind us to the visible world, and *must not this freedom result from the intelligent fulfillment of instinctive demands*, rather than from a premature repression, or one growing out of fear?[3]

In his critique of Jung in *Eclipse of God*, Buber confesses that he is particularly concerned by Jung's Modern Gnostic resumption, under the guise of psychotherapy, of the Carpocratian motif of mystically deifying the instincts instead of hallowing them in faith. "The soul which is integrated in the Self as the unification in an all-encompassing wholeness of the opposites, especially of

3. C. G. Jung, "European Commentary" in *T'ai-i, The Secret of the Golden Flower*, trans. and explained by Richard Wilhelm, trans. into English by Carl F. Baynes (London: Kegan Paul, Trench, Trubner & Co., Ltd., 1931), pp. 80 f.

the opposites good and evil, dispenses with the conscience as the court which distinguishes and decides between the right and the wrong. It itself arbitrates an adjustment between the "principles." This "narrow as a knife's edge" way leads Jung to the positive function of evil. Evil is integrated in the "bridal unification of opposite halves" in the soul, which is the goal of the process of individuation. The self which is indistinguishable in its totality from a divine image and the self-realization which Jung describes as "the incarnation of God" goes back, Buber points out, to "a Gnostic figure, which probably is to be traced back ultimately to the ancient Iranian divinity Zurvan (not mentioned, as far as I know, among Jung's numerous references to the history of religions) as that out of which the light god and his dark counterpart arise."[4]

In his distinguished book, *The Symbolic Quest,* the American Jungian analyst Edward Whitmont asserts that Buber has seriously misunderstood and misquoted Jung. What Whitmont actually offers is not evidence of misquoting or even necessarily of a misunderstanding but an alternate interpretation of Jung's statements, one which may, to be sure, see Jung more from within than Buber did, though modified at the same time by Whitmont's own personal extensions of Jung's theories:

> When he says that we have to experiment with evil—Martin Buber attacks him for this—he means that we must experiment with what may appear to be evil to our ego-identified attitude and to our collectivized value system, because it is still the primitive daimon. But we must struggle with, accept, follow it, not identify with it. This means paying attention to our own deepest conscience and guarding against falling in with that which this deepest conscience reveals to us as destructive.[5]

Whitmont's disclaimer on Jung's behalf is less effective than it might be because of the ambiguity of the distinction between ac-

4. Martin Buber, *Eclipse of God: Studies in the Relation Between Religion and Philosophy* (New York: Harper Torchbooks, 1957), "Religion and Modern Thinking" and "Supplement: Reply to C. G. Jung," trans. Maurice Friedman, pp. 86–90, 136 f.

5. Edward C. Whitmont, *The Symbolic Quest: Basic Concepts of Analytical Psychology* (New York: G. P. Putnam's Sons for the C. G. Jung Foundation for Analytical Psychology, 1969), p. 227.

cepting and following evil and identifying with it. But what makes
it still more problematic is the reference to "our own deepest conscience"; for, in Jungian terms, as we have seen, this may refer
not to conscience at all in the ordinary sense but the process of individuation. Similarly the force of the word "destructive" depends upon what is assumed to be "constructive"—one's
relations with others or the integration and individuation of the
self in the depths of the personal unconscious.

Perhaps the most important issue between Jung and Buber is
the question of what, in fact, happens to the drives toward evil,
what the Talmud and the Hasidim call the "evil urge." Jung says
we give in to them intelligently and in part. Buber calls this "mystically deifying the instincts instead of hallowing them in faith."
Whitmont, not at all in the context of the Buber-Jung interchange
but very much to the point for that interchange, insists that they
are constructively transformed:

> Transformation, however, postulates a change of the drives them-
> selves so that there is no longer any need for sublimation. As a
> result of the transformation the drives would cease to be threaten-
> ing and destructive and would become converted into helpful ele-
> ments. This goal is to be brought about by a widening of the ego's
> position and approach to the drives which opens new channels of
> expression.[6]

If this is an accurate interpretation of Jung and not a modifica-
tion, then Buber's, and my own, criticism of him on this point
may indeed need to be modified.

Erich Fromm criticizes Freud for seeing human beings as antisocial by nature and only secondarily in relationship. Fromm
holds, as does Harry Stack Sullivan, that one becomes destructive
only when one's neurosis turns one aside from a creative relationship with other people and with one's work. For Fromm, human
nature is potentially good or evil, with health on the side of good.
It is significant, however, that Fromm was not content with this
explanation of the evil of Naziism as the product of authoritarian
society and character structure in *Escape from Freedom* and went on
to ever deeper and more extensive analyses of human evil in *The*

6. Whitmont, *The Symbolic Quest*, p. 296.

Heart of Man and his voluminous study, *The Anatomy of Destructiveness.*

For the American psychologist Carl R. Rogers, in contrast to Freud, Jung, and Fromm, human nature is unqualifiedly good. Rogers' theory of the complete acceptance of the "client" by the therapist is based on the assumption that the client is "good" in his or her depths, that one is by nature social and constructive, that all one needs is to be accepted by the therapist so that one may accept oneself and one will make manifest the socially good person that one really is. Martin Buber's reply to Rogers on this point suggests that there is a third alternative to seeing the human being as "evil," to be controlled, or "good," to be trusted, and that is seeing the person as "polar" and in need of personal direction: "What you say may be trusted, I would say stands in polar relation to what can least be trusted in this man.... The poles are not good and evil, but rather yes and no, acceptance and refusal."[7]

"The aim of therapy is often that of helping the person to be better adjusted to existing circumstances," says Fromm in *Beyond the Chains of Illusion:*

> Mental health is often considered to be nothing but this adjustment, or to put in differently, a state of mind in which one's individual unhappiness is reduced to the level of the general unhappiness. The real problem...need not even be touched in this type of psychoanalysis.[8]

"Psychologists and psychoanalysts," writes Helen Lynd, "have given more encouragement to the adjustment of individuals to the realities of a given society than to personal differentiation and deviation from them."

> They frequently fail to give explicit recognition to the distinction between normal or healthy in terms of what are the generally accepted norms of the society and in terms of what is humanly desirable. If the psychoanalyst...does not rigorously examine his own

7. "Dialogue Between Carl Rogers and Martin Buber, Moderated by Maurice Friedman," in Martin Buber, *The Knowledge of Man: A Philosophy of the Interhuman* (New York: Harper Torchbooks, 1966), pp. 179 f.

8. Erich Fromm, *Beyond the Chains of Illusion: My Encounter with Marx and Freud* (New York: Simon & Schuster, "The Credo Series," 1962), pp. 139 f.

values in relation to those of society, he almost inevitably tends to accept tacitly the dominant values of the society as the norm of behavior, and to measure health and illness by these. Scientific objectivity, then, becomes indistinguishable from social determinants.[9]

Even if psychoanalysts do rigorously reexamine their values, as Lynd suggest, they are still likely to impose them under the mask of objectivity; for they are not going to lose their values through examining them. It is true, as Fromm says in *Man for Himself,* that it matters whether therapists encourage their patients to adapt or strengthen them in their unwillingness to compromise their integrity. It is also true, as other therapists would point out, that patients are sometimes so tied up in their neurotic rebellion against the culture that there is little else that they could do anyway. In either case, therapists cannot take the risk of encouraging patients to oppose society and to undergo privation unless they have a sure enough sense of those persons in their uniqueness. They must feel sure that their clients have a ground on which to stand as persons and that they stand there in some real and creative relationship to the society that they are going to oppose. Otherwise therapists cannot help encouraging patients to adjust to this particular society; for the therapists will see their patients' health and sickness in terms of that adjustment.

Frieda Fromm-Reichmann offers us a special insight into the problem of adjustment from her years of direct work with schizophrenics. Therapists who want to guide patients successfully toward discovering what degree of cultural adjustment is adequate to their personal needs must be persons with personal security and must have inner independence from the authoritarian values of the culture, including undue concern about their prestige as therapists.

> The recovery of many schizophrenics and schizoid personalities, for example, depends upon the psychotherapist's freedom from convention and prejudice. These patients cannot and should not be asked to accept guidance toward a conventional adjustment to the customary requirements of our culture, much less to what the individual therapist personally considers these requirements to be.[10]

9. Helen Merrell Lynd, *On Shame and the Search for Identity* (New York: Harcourt Brace, Harbrace Books [paperback], 1969), p. 203.

The image of the human has more to do with therapy itself than it does with our theories about therapy, important as the theories may be; for there is always the danger of the theory becoming a construct in which the therapist settles down. "Young therapists often regard the dreams of their patients as examinations," Fromm said to me. "They feel that they must be ready to give some theoretical interpretations, and as a result they do not really hear the dreams." When he was working with thirty of us in Washington, D.C., in a series of seminars on dreams and the unconscious, Martin Buber said that there are two kinds of relationships a therapist has to dreams—one in which he puts them into the categories of his school and the other in which he responds to them spontaneously and wholly in a "musical, floating relationship." "I am for the latter," Buber said.

This musical relationship in which the therapist really hears the unique person and experiences his or her side of the relationship is crucial for all therapy, regardless of the school or theory. No matter what schools therapists come from and no matter what knowledge and experience they have, the basic question is still *when* do their insights apply to these particular patients and when not. To answer this question, they must use the categories of their schools in a flexible, "musical" way in order again and again to try to arrive at the uniqueness of these persons. To do this therapists must practice what Buber calls the act of "inclusion," experiencing the patient's side of the relationship as well as their own. Rollo May stresses the centrality of such inclusion for therapy and love in terms of what might be called a "field theory" of the emotions:

> Our feelings, like the artist's paint and brush, are ways of communicating and sharing something meaningful from us to the world. Our feelings not only take into consideration the other person but are in a real sense partially *formed by the feelings of the other person present*. We *feel* in a magnetic field. A sensitive person learns, often without being conscious of doing so, to pick up the feelings of the person around him, as a violin string resonates to the vibration of every other musical string in the room.... Every successful lover

---

10. Frieda Fromm-Reichmann, *Principles of Intensive Psychotherapy* (Chicago: University of Chicago Press, 1950), pp. 32 f.

knows this by "instinct." It is an essential—if not *the* essential—
quality of the good therapist.[11]

Even the patients' "sickness" is part of their uniqueness; for
even their sickness tells of the road they have not gone and have to
go. If instead therapists make patients into objects to themselves,
as well as to the therapist, the therapists will have robbed the patients of part of their human potentiality and growth. This is not a
question of a choice between the scientific generalization and the
concrete individual, but of which direction is the primary one. Is
the individual regarded as a collection of symptoms to be enregis-
tered in the categories of a particular school or are the theories of
the school regarded as primarily a means of returning again and
again to the understanding of this unique person and his or her
relationship with his or her therapist?

An increasingly important trend in psychotherapy suggests that
the basic direction of movement should be toward concrete persons and their uniqueness and not toward subsuming the patient's symptoms under theoretical categories or adjusting them
to some socially derived view of the "ideal." This trend emphasizes the *image* of the human as opposed to the *construct* of the human. The image of the human retains the understanding of
human beings in their concrete uniqueness; it retains the wholeness of the person. Only a psychotherapy which begins with the
concrete existence of persons, with their wholeness and uniqueness, and with the healing that takes place through the meeting of
therapist and client will point us toward the image of the human.
In the last analysis the issue that faces all the schools of psychotherapy is whether the *starting point* of therapy is to be found in the
analytical category or the unique person—in the *construct* or the
image of the human.

The revelation of the human image—its coming forth from its
hiding—is a revelation that takes place *between* therapist and client
or *among* the members of a group. It cannot be equated with the
image of the human that each holds or comes to hold separately.
The coming into the light of the hidden human image is inseparable from the dialogue itself—a dialogue of mutual contact, trust,
and shared humanity. In this sense, "healing through meeting" is

11. Rollo May, *Love and Will* (New York: W. W. Norton, 1969), p. 91.

identical with the revelation of the hidden human image. This revelation is more than an individual finding an image of the human. It is a *becoming* of the human in relationship—becoming human with such resources as the relationship affords, including the possibility of tragedy when such resources are lacking. It is not the diploma on the wall which assures clients that they have the right therapist. The "rightness" of the relationship depends upon mutual existential trust—and upon an existential grace that is not *in* the therapist or *in* the client but moves *between* the two. When these are not present, or not sufficiently so, then the ground of tragedy has been reached—whether or not the relationship ends in suicide. This touching of the tragic itself unfolds the hidden possibilities of the human as well as showing the real limitations in which we stand.

Index

Absurd, dialogue with the, 143 f., 174

Adjustment, 213 f., 216

Age of Reason, The (Sartre), 180

Abraham, Karl, 134

Agee, James, 57

Ahab, Captain (Melville's *Moby Dick*), 145-148, 158

Aiming at the self, 57, 60 63

Aion (Jung), 50

Alienation of Modern Man, 139 f.

Anaximander, 85

Anima and animus, 44, 49, 55, 68

Answer to Job (Jung), 53 f.

Anxiety, x, 81 f., 95 f., 119 f., 134-144, 167 n.4, 173, 190, 192

Apfelbaum, Bernard and Constance, 69 f.

Archetypes, 44, 49, 52, 54, 135, 209

Aristotle, 57

Arvin, Newton, 158

Auden, W. H., 136

Basescu, Sabert, 96

Basic Forms and Knowledge of Human Existence (Binswanger), 102-104

Behaviorism, 29-35, 114

Being-in-the-world, 97, 106, 137

Berdyaev, Nicholas, 32, 107

Beyond Freedom and Dignity (Skinner), x, 29 f.

Binswanger, Ludwig, 83 f., 92 f., 97-108, 195

Boss, Medard, 57, 85, 92-95, 103, 105

Bowen, Murray, 127

Boszormenyi-Nagy, Ivan, 126-130

Brothers Karamazov, The (Dostoievsky), 158-163, 192

Buber, Martin, x, 3, 6, 9, 12 f., 15 f., 20, 22-26, 32, 36, 81 f., 89, 96, 99 f., 102-108, 112 f., 117 f., 125

f., 130, 138-140, 167-169, 178-184, 187, 210-213, 215

Camus, Albert, 6, 107, 135, 140, 143, 166 f.

"Case of Ellen West", 99-101

Castle, The (Kafka), 142

Clamence, Jean Baptiste (Camus' *The Fall*), 166 f.

Chein, Isidore, 36-38, 134

Civilization and Its Discontents (Freud), 43, 207-209

Clinicalist, the, 37 f.

Collective unconscious, 44, 47, 49

Communication, 89, 101 f., 118, 121-125, 197

Confirmation and disconfirmation, 121 f., 129, 142, 172-174, 181, 191, 199, 201

Confirmation of Otherness, The (Friedman), ix

Conscience, 40, 42, 48, 59 f., 95, 105, 157, 163, 174 f., 210-212

Construct of the human, 37, 40 f., 106, 134, 215 f.

Contemporary Psychology, Revealing and Obscuring the Human (Friedman), ix f., 9

Coulson, William R., 65, 72

Crime and Punishment (Dostoievsky), 135, 158

Daimon, 45-47, 211

Dasein (existence), 82 f., 93, 98, 102-105, 137

Death, 81, 100, 105, 137, 141, 185 f.

Death instinct, 40, 43, 81, 207 f.

Death of God, the, 139 f., 146

Decision, 24-26, 80 f., 102, 162 f., 196, 209 f.

Depression, 87 f., 128

Descartes, Rene, 13 f.
Devils, The (The Possessed)
   (Dostoievsky), 150-155, 158, 168
Dewey, John, 57
Dialogical Perspectives in Psychotherapy
   (Friedman), ix, xi, 80, 107
Dialogical view of the person, the, x,
   23-26
Dialogue, 3, 5, 9 f., 14-18, 21-26,
   36, 63, 66, 73, 103, 105-108, 110,
   117, 130, 139, 157, 181 f., 186 f.,
   200 f., 216
Dignity, 31 f., 35, 74
Dilthey, Wilhelm, 5, 14-16, 90
Direction, personal, 17-19, 21, 25,
   47, 58, 60 f., 138, 149, 157, 197,
   213
Distancing and relating, 13, 88 f.,
   118, 120, 200
Divided self, x, 135, 145, 147, 150
   f., 153, 155, 157-165
Divided Self, The (Laing), 108-112
Dolgoruky, Arkady (Dostoievsky's *A
   Raw Youth*), 155 f., 159, 163
Dostoievsky, Fyodor, 6, 38, 134 f.,
   141 f., 145, 148-156, 158-166,
   192, 194 f.
Dual mode, 101, 104 f.

Eclipse of God (Buber), 210 f.
Ego, the, 39 f., 43, 49 f., 52, 54,
   103, 209, 211 f.
Ego and the Id, The (Freud), 43
Eliot, T.S., 166, 176 f., 185
Elkin, Henry, 96
Encounter. See Meeting
Encounter groups, 57, 64-75, 202
Entering into relation, 13
Eros, 182
Evil, 207-213
Existence (May), 86 f., 195
Existential analysis, 90-106, 108, 115
Existential psychoanalysis, 91
Existential psychotherapy, 79-87, 107
Existentialism, 13-15, 17, 79, 83, 85
   f., 103-108, 179
Existentialists of dialogue, 83, 103,
   107 f.

Fairbairn, W. Ronald D., ix, 134,
   145
Fall, The (Camus), 143, 166 f.
Family psychiatry and family
   therapy, ix, 10, 69, 114-130
Farber, Leslie H., 7, 20, 107, 117,
   134 f., 187 f.
Fathers and sons, 157-164, 167
Faust (Goethe), 155
Feelings and emotions, 67-74, 104,
   186, 215 f.
Female Eunuch, The (Greer), 178
Feuerbach, Ludwig, 14-16, 113
Firestone, Shulamith, 191
Francesca and Paolo, 102
Francis of Assisi, Saint, 5, 41 f., 165
Frankl, Viktor, 61, 184
Freedom, 6, 9, 11 f., 16 f., 23-25,
   30, 35 f., 42, 48, 85, 91, 98, 100
   f., 111, 135, 139, 142 f., 145-158,
   166, 180, 182 f., 185 f., 188, 196,
   210, 214
Freud, Sigmund, ix f., 12 f., 25,
   39-43, 53 f., 60, 80 f., 83, 86, 90
   f., 97 f., 113, 134-136, 149 f.,
   157, 169, 178 f., 186 f., 195,
   207-209, 212 f.
Friedman, Maurice, x, 3-10
Fromm, Erich, ix, 15, 21, 57-60, 62
   f., 184, 208, 212-214
Fromm, Reichmann, Frieda, ix,
   108, 214

Gardner, Martin, 30
Gestalt Therapy, ix
Gestaltkreis, Der, 89, 91
Gibb, Jack, 65, 68
Giorgi, Amedeo, 5, 30 f., 37
God, 45-51, 53 f., 137 f., 140 f., 149
   n. 1, 151, 162, 210 f.
Goldstein, Kurt, 89 f.
Grace, existential, 201, 217
Grand Inquisitor, the (Dostoievsky's
   Brothers Karamazov), 164-166
Greening, Thomas, 67
Greer, Germaine, 178, 188 f.
Guilt, x, 6, 40, 81 f., 84 f., 95, 100
   f., 115 f., 120, 128-130, 134 f.,
   138 f., 141 f., 150, 158, 162 f.,

166-175, 185, 197-200
Guilt, existential, 81 f., 84 f., 95 f,
    167-175, 197-200
Guntrip, Harry, ix

Haigh, Gerald, 74
Hamlet (Shakespeare), 135
Harvard University, 138 f.
Healing through meeting, 80, 86,
    116, 203, 216 f.
Heart of Man, The (Fromm), 58 f.,
    212 f.
Heart-searching, 137 f.
Hegel, Friedrich, 14
Heidegger, Martin, 13, 15f., 57, 81,
    92-99, 101-103, 107 f., 137
Heschel, Abraham Joshua, 203
Hesse, Hermann, 199 f.
Hidden human image, x, 8 f., 19,
    22, 38 n. 15, 66, 74, 106, 115,
    176, 178, 188, 191, 216 f.
Hidden Human Image, The
    (Friedman), 4, 17, 19
Horney, Karen, 21, 57 f., 121
Huett, Richard, 63
Human nature, 9, 11-13, 16 f., 21,
    29, 40, 50, 92, 187, 208 f., 213
Human potential movement, 57, 64
    f., 74 f., 79
Human sciences, 30-32
Humanist psychology, 57-63, 79 f.,
    107
Husserl, Edmund, 5, 13-15, 90, 92
Hycner, Richard, x

I and Thou (Buber), 112
I-It relation, 15, 23, 25, 84, 108, 111
    f., 118, 124-126, 178, 181, 184
I-Thou relationship, 15 f., 23-26, 83
    f., 89, 96, 99-106, 108 f., 112,
    118, 124-126, 130, 178, 181-184,
    186
Id, ego, and superego, 39, 42, 54,
    109, 181
Identity, 21, 92, 112, 118, 192,
    195-197
Image of man. See Image of the
    Human

Image of the Human, ix f., 3-5, 8,
    10, 17-22, 33, 36-38, 40 f., 43, 47,
    57 f., 60 f., 63, 66, 75, 87, 91, 97,
    133, 138, 149 n. 1, 154 f., 157,
    160, 164, 174, 178 f., 191,
    207-209, 215-217
Imagining the real. See Inclusion
Immediary, sphere of, 89 f.
Inclusion, 25 f., 109, 182-184, 194,
    197, 215
Individuation, 44 f., 47 f., 120, 126,
    135, 209-212
Inferno (Dante), 102
Infection of meaning, 121-123
Inner man, 29, 33, 35
Inner-outer dualism, 35, 45, 48, 55
    f., 68
Interhuman, the, 96, 103, 105, 108,
    116, 157, 167, 194, 197, 203
Invisible Loyalties (Boszormenyi-
    Nagy), 127-130
Ishmael (Melville' *Moby Dick*), 140
    f., 146 f., 158
Ivanov, Vyacheslav, 149 n. 1

Jaspers, Karl, 107
Jesus, 61 f.
Jourard, Sidney, 107
Jung, Carl G., ix-xi, 13, 43-56, 114,
    134, 209-212

K., Joseph (Kafka's *Trial*), 168-175,
    197-199
Kafka, Franz, 6, 135, 142, 145, 158,
    166-175, 197-199
Kant, Immanuel, 13 f.
Karamazov, Alyosha (Dostoievsky's
    The Brothers Karamazov), 159-162
Karamazov, Dmitri (Dostoievsky's
    The Brothers Karamazov), 160-163,
    192
Karamazov, Fyodor (Dostoievsky's
    The Brothers Karamazov), 160-162
Karamazov, Ivan (Dostoievsky),
    151, 154, 158-164, 166
Kierkegaard, Soren, 14, 99, 106 f.,
    137, 140, 197
Kiesler, Sara, 70

Knowledge of Man, The (Buber), 89, 112, 169 n. 8
Koch, Sigmund, 73 f.
Kohut, Heinz, ix

Laing, Ronald D., 107-117
Love, 94-96, 100 f., 103-105, 110, 176 f., 180-188, 190 f., 194, 201, 207, 215
Love and Will (May), 80, 184-187
Lynd, Helen Merrell, 21 f., 82, 192-199, 213 f.

Man for Himself (Fromm), 58-60
Marcel, Gabriel, 83, 107
Marriage, 176, 183, 185, 201
Martin Buber: The Life of Dialogue (Friedman), 36
Marx, Karl, 14
Maslow, Abraham, 57, 62
Masters, William H., 188
May, Rollo, x, 4, 9, 21, 57, 80-87, 93, 95 f., 105, 107, 109, 184-187, 189, 215
Mead, George Herbert, 6, 15, 108
Meeting (*Begegnung*), 82-84, 86, 95, 101, 103-106, 112, 114, 118, 121, 177, 184, 187, 200f., 203
Melville, Herman, 6, 135, 140, 145-148, 158
Memories, Dreams, Reflections (Jung), 44-47
Merleau-Ponty, Maurice, 15, 108
Mind-body dualism, 12
Minkowski, Eugene, 87
Moby Dick (Melville), 135, 140, 145-148
Modern Exile, 5, 139, 141, 143, 145
Modern Job, 5, 143 f.
Modern Promenthean, 5, 141, 143, 146
Modern Promethean, 5, 141, 143, 146
Morality and ethics, 33-35, 59 f., 69, 209 f.
Motivation and the crisis of motives, x, 12, 33, 37, 43, 134, 139, 143, 145, 149, 164-167, 178, 203

Mutuality, 89, 104, f., 108, 112, 116, 118, 121, 123, 181 f., 185, 188, 191, 194

Natural science, 30-32
Nietzsche, Friedrich, 14, 165
No Exit (Sartre), 180

Oedipus complex, 135 f.
On Shame and the Search for Identity, 21 f., 192-197
Orgasm, 188 f.
Otherness, 24-26, 69, 180-183

Parentification, 127-129
Parsons, Talcot, 113
Pascal, Blaise, 141
Passion, 177, 179, 181, 185-187
Pfuetze, Paul, 15
Phenomenology, 13-15, 30, 87-93, 95, 98 f., 105 f., 108, 192
Philosophical anthropology, 4, 13-17, 20, 88 f., 99, 135
Philosophy, 11-17, 20, 133
Politics of dialogue, 108-116
Politic of Experience, The (Laing), 113-115
Polster, Erving and Miriam, 107
Potentialism, x, 4, 57-75
Presence and presentness, 83, 185, 201
Primary World of the Senses, The (Straus), 88 f.
Problematic of modern man, 139, 142 f., 145, 150, 168, 174
Problematic Rebel: Melville, Dostoievsky, Kafka, Camus (Friedman), 4-6, 11 f., 17, 19, 135, 139, 142, 158, 198 f.
Projection, 49, 54 f.
Proust, Marcel, 38, 134, 180
Prufrock (T. S. Eliot), 166, 176 f.
Pseudomutuality, 118-120, 129
Psyche, the, 7-9, 39, 44, 46, 50-54, 91
Psychiatry, 19 f.
Psychoanalysis, 4, 7, 11 f., 19-21, 25, 39, 42 f., 86, 90-92, 97, 146,

149, 165 f., 168, 188, 213
Psychological compulsion, 11 f., 42, 100, 135, 139, 142 f., 145-158, 166
Psychological Man, 16, 39, 43 52, 54
Psychologism, x, 8 f., 39-57, 60, 63
Psychology and literature, x, 133-135
Psychology and Religion: East and West (Jung), 53, 210
Psychology as a Human Science (Giorgi), 30 f.
Psychotherapy, 210, 213-217

Quaker Religious Thought, 8

Raw Youth, The (Dostoievsky), 154-156, 158-160
Reality principle, 42 f.
Repression, 86, 168, 181, 185, 210
Responding and response, 36, 55 f., 62 f., 128, 181, 202 f.
Rogers, Carl R. ix, 57, 66, 69, 72-75, 79 f., 82, 107, 213
Rousseau, Jean-Jacques, 208

Sartre, Jean-Paul, 12 f., 15 f., 57, 61, 85, 91 f., 107 f., 112, 116, 179-184, 186 f.
Schizophrenia, 87 f., 99-102, 106, 108-112, 114 f., 117, 119-124, 127 f., 153, 214
Schutz, Will, 71
Schweitzer, Albert, 61
Science of Behavior and the Image of Man, The (Chein), 36-38
Scientism, x, 15, 20, 29-38
Seeming, 118, 181
Self and Others (Laing), 112 f.
Self-actualization, 62, 79
Self-realization, 21, 43, 48, 57-63, 79, 103, 211
Sex and love, x, 16, 25, 41, 81, 128 f., 135, 176-191
Shadow, the, 44, 49 f., 53, 55, 137, 209
Shakespeare, William, 38, 134 f., 178

Shame, x, 82, 135, 192-200
Shame, existential, 196 f., 199 f.
Skinner, B. F., ix f., 29-38, 114
Smith, M. Brewster, 62
Spatiality, 87 f., 99
Spontaneity, 202
Spontaneity, planned, 72-74
Stanton, Richard, x
Stavrogin, Nikolai (Dostoievsky's *The Devils*), 150-156, 158 f., 168 f.
Straus, Erwin, 87-89, 195
Sublimation, 25, 41, 181
Suicide, 80 f., 100 f., 141 f., 187, 217
Sullivan, Harry Stack, ix, 7 n. 2, 15, 21, 81 f., 108, 134, 190, 212
Superego, the, 40, 42 f., 54, 59, 119, 181, 187, 197
Symbolic Quest, The (Whitmont), 211 f.

Temporality, 87 f., 99
Three forces of contemporary psychology, x, 4, 6
Tillich, Paul, 17, 31, 96, 107, 137 f.,169 n. 8, 187
Time, 87 f., 141, 172, 174, 185
To Deny Our Nothingness (Friedman), x, 4-7, 17, 19, 44, 85 n. 2, 107, 133
Touchstones of reality, 8 f., 55, 63
Touchstones of Reality (Friedman), 8
Tragedy, 217
Transference, 83, 94, 113, 117, 146
Trial, The (Kafka), 135, 143,167-175, 197-199
Trüb, Hans, 107
Trust, 189, 193 f., 216
Trust, basic, 193, 199
Trust, existential, x, 73, 199-201, 203, 217

Unconscious, the, 12 f., 32, 44, 46 f., 49-52, 91, 117, 135, 179, 209-212, 215
Underground Man, The (Dostoievsky), 141, 150, 153 f., 156, 166, 194

Unique, the and uniqueness, 6, 9,
14, 18, 23, 25, 32, 37, 47, 195,
214-216

Values, 135, 140, 168, 209
Versilov (Dostoievsky's *The Raw
Youth*), 154-156, 158 f., 163
Vocation, 45-47, 55

Walden Two, 29, 34
Waste Land, The (T.S. Eliot), 176 f.,
185
Way of Man, The (Buber), 63, 138 f.
Weizsäcker, Victor von, 89, 91 f.,
107
West, Ellen, 99-101, 106
Wholeness, personal, 12 f., 16 f.,
24,f., 40, 44, 46, 48 f., 56, 68,
106, 149, 154, 173, 181, 197, 216
Whitmont, Edward, 211 f.
Wilbur, Richard, 44
Will, 23-25, 46 f., 49, 80, 91 f., 141,
143, 147, 153, 186-188, 201 f.
Woolf, Virginia, 64
World design, 90, 93-97, 106
Wynne, Lyman, 117-126

Zossima, Father (Dostoievsky's
Brothers Karamazov), 159-161